Economic and Financial Developments in Latin America

Centre for the Study of Emerging Markets Series

Series Editor: **Dr Sima Motamen-Samadian**

The Centre for the Study of Emerging Markets (CSEM) Series provides a forum for assessing various aspects of emerging markets. The series includes the latest theoretical and empirical studies from both academics and practitioners in relation to the economies and financial markets of emerging markets. These cover a wide range of subjects, including stock markets and their efficiency in emerging markets, forecasting models and their level of accuracy in emerging markets, dynamic models and their application, exchange rate regimes and their merits, risk management in emerging markets, derivative markets and hedging decisions in emerging markets, and governance and risk in emerging markets.

The series is one of the main sources of reference on emerging markets, both within and outside those markets, for academics, national and international agencies, and financial institutions.

Titles include:

Sima Motamen-Samadian (*editor*)
DYNAMIC MODELS AND THEIR APPLICATIONS IN EMERGING MARKETS

CAPITAL FLOWS AND FOREIGN DIRECT INVESTMENTS IN EMERGING MARKETS

RISK MANAGEMENT IN EMERGING MARKETS

ECONOMIC TRANSITION IN CENTRAL AND EASTERN EUROPEAN COUNTRIES

GOVERNANCE AND RISK IN EMERGING AND GLOBAL MARKETS

GLOBAL STOCK MARKETS AND PORTFOLIO MANAGEMENT

ECONOMIC AND FINANCIAL DEVELOPMENTS IN LATIN AMERICA

Also by Sima Motamen-Samadian:

INTERNATIONAL DEBT AND CENTRAL BANKING IN THE 1980s (*edited with Z. Res*)

EMERGING MARKETS
Past and Present Experiences, and Future Prospects (*edited with C. Garido*)

Centre for the Study of Emerging Markets Series
Series Standing Order ISBN 1–4039–9521–4

You can receive future titles in this series as they are published by placing a standing order. Please contact your bookseller or, in case of difficulty, write to us at the address below with your name and address, the title of the series and the ISBN quoted above.

Customer Series Department, Macmillan Distribution Ltd, Houndmills, Basingstoke, Hampshire RG21 6XS, England

---

Economic and Financial Developments in Latin America

Edited by

Sima Motamen-Samadian

palgrave
macmillan

First published 2006 by
PALGRAVE MACMILLAN
Houndmills, Basingstoke, Hampshire RG21 6XS and
175 Fifth Avenue, New York, N.Y. 10010
Companies and representatives throughout the world.

PALGRAVE MACMILLAN is the global academic imprint of the Palgrave Macmillan division of St. Martin's Press, LLC and of Palgrave Macmillan Ltd. Macmillan® is a registered trademark in the United States, United Kingdom and other countries. Palgrave is a registered trademark in the European Union and other countries.

ISBN-13: 978–1–4039–9158–4
ISBN-10: 1–4039–9158–8

This book is printed on paper suitable for recycling and made from fully managed and sustained forest sources.

A catalogue record for this book is available from the British Library.

Library of Congress Cataloging-in-Publication Data
Economic and financial developments in Latin America / edited by Sima Motamen-Samadian.
p. cm.—(Centre for the Study of Emerging Markets Series)
Includes bibliographical references and index.
ISBN 1–4039–9158–8 (cloth)
1. Finance—Latin America—Case studies. 2. Monetary policy—Latin America—Case studies. 3. Latin America—Economic conditions—Case studies. I. Motamen-Samadian, Sima. II Series.
HG185.L3E26 2006
330.98—dc22 2005055336

10 9 8 7 6 5 4 3 2 1
15 14 13 12 11 10 09 08 07 06

Printed and bound in Great Britain by
Antony Rowe Ltd, Chippenham and Eastbourne

Contents

List of Figures and Tables

Figures

Tables

Preface

This volume is a collection of seven studies on Latin American countries, with a particular focus on Argentina, Mexico and Brazil. All the three countries implemented varieties of liberalization policies and have gone through substantial structural change during the last two decades. Despite the reform policies, they all continued to experience severe external debt and a financial crisis once again some years after the reforms. In an attempt to manage the crisis and improve economic conditions, the authorities in every case changed the exchange rate regime and adopted new monetary and exchange rate policies. The studies that are presented here assess the extent of success of the new policies that have been introduced in each country, as well as their shortcomings. In this respect Chapter 2 provides an analytical assessment of the role of the currency board in Argentina and highlights the role of government borrowing and fiscal mismanagement in the 2001 crisis. Chapter 3 examines the effectiveness of international prudential regulation in preventing a banking crisis in Latin America. Chapter 4 analyses the features of monetary policies that are usually adopted in emerging economies such as Mexico that have undergone structural reforms. The author highlights how the new policies might lead to accumulation of huge external debts, and adversely affect the export sector that is supposed to be the instigator of growth. Chapter 5 offers an empirical assessment of the role of inflation targeting in Mexico and Brazil, and explains the systemic risks that might emerge when such monetary policies are combined with a managed floating exchange rate regime. Chapter 6 discusses the importance of credibility and state capacity in a country's ability to attract foreign direct investment (FDI). Here the author argues that the recent fall in flow of FDI into Mexico has been mainly due to the fall in the state's credibility and ability fully to implement the reform policies that can reduce transaction costs for investors. Chapter 7 presents a model of bank disappearance, and finds out that in the case of Mexico bank specific variables appeared to have played a more important role in the fall in the number of banks than macroeconomic variables. Finally, Chapter 8 examines the relationship between foreign exchange rate regime and vulnerability of companies' foreign activity in Brazil.

Overall this volume provides a comprehensive assessment of the latest monetary and foreign exchange policies that have been adopted in

Latin American countries and factors that have affected the operation of these countries' banking sectors. The book is particularly useful for all those who are working on Latin America and emerging markets as a whole, and wish to find out more about the latest empirical studies on the area.

SIMA MOTAMEN-SAMADIAN

Acknowledgements

This volume is a collection of some of the papers that were presented at the International Conference on Emerging Markets and Global Risk Management in June 2004 in London. The conference was organized by the Centre for the Study of Emerging Markets (CSEM) at the Westminster Business School. In this respect my sincere thanks to Hanna Scobie at the European Economic and Financial Centre who inspired and supported me in organizing the conference.

My special thanks to all the contributors for their timely delivery of the chapters and to Jacky Kippenberger and Rebecca Pash at Palgrave Macmillan for their patience and support during the period of production of the book. I am also indebted to my family, and in particular my husband Vahab Samadian, for their continuous support through the period when I was working on the book.

Sima Motamen-Samadian

Notes on the Contributors

Albert A. Gonzalez is a graduate of the Communication, Culture and Technology MA and International Business Diplomacy programs at Georgetown University, USA.

Clemente Hernandez-Rodriguez is Professor of Economics and a Researcher at the EGADE (Graduate School of Management), CICADE (Centre for Research and Consulting in Business Administration), in ITESM (Tec de Monterrey), Guadalajara Campus, Mexico.

Guadalupe Mántey is Professor of Monetary Theory at the Department of Economics, National Autonomous University of Mexico, Acatlan Campus, Mexico.

Alexandre Minda is Associate Professor of Economics and Director of Postgraduate Studies at the Institut d'Etudes Politiques de Toulouse, and Researcher at LEREPS (Laboratoire d'Etude et de Recherche sur l'Economie, les Politiques et les Systèmes Sociaux, Université Toulouse 1 Sciences Sociales), France.

Sima Motamen-Samadian is the Director of the Centre for the Study of Emerging Markets and Principal Lecturer in Economics at the Westminster Business School, University of Westminster, United Kingdom.

Etelberto Ortiz is Distinguished Professor of Economics, at the Department of Producción Económica, Universidad Autónoma Metropolitana, Xochimilco Campus, Mexico.

Jose Luiz Rossi, Jr is a Researcher in Finance at Yale University, USA.

Stéphanie Truquin is a Researcher at the LEREPS (Laboratoire d'Etude et de Recherche sur l'Economie, les Politiques et les Systèmes Sociaux, Université Toulouse 1 Sciences Sociales), France.

1
Introduction

Sima Motamen-Samadian

During the last three decades, Latin American economies have gone through numerous upheavals. Most were badly hit at one point or another by problems of balance of payments and budget deficit, large external debt, currency and financial crisis, huge currency devaluation, a high level of inflation and, at the same time, a high level of unemployment. Three of the countries whose Latin American economies have been most severely affected by the problems of external debt are Argentina, Brazil and Mexico. In all those countries, various liberalization, privatization and structural reform policies were adopted at different stages to stabilize the value of the countries' currencies, reduce inflation and develop their financial system. Yet, in each case, despite the initial signs of improvement, the countries began to experience new problems and faced a different type of crisis.

The present volume provides an evaluation of the monetary and foreign exchange policies that have been adopted in various Latin American countries, and their limitations. The studies in particular focus on Argentina, Mexico and Brazil, and discuss the success and failure of the macroeconomic policies that have been adopted there and their ramification for financial sector and external accounts. As well as providing an in-depth analysis of the policies, the chapters also present some empirical studies to assess the extent of success of the policies and the role of other factors that affected the economies.

In Chapter 2, Sima Motamen-Samadian examines the role of convertibility law in Argentina and disputes the view that the 2001 financial crisis was caused by the overvaluation of the peso. In determining the main causes of the crisis, she looks at a number of other factors, such as government's excessive external borrowing and mismanagement of public finances, which were among the main factors responsible for the crisis. She also considers the mismatch between the currency of assets and liabilities of the bank borrowers, and the extent by which the government's external borrowing had adversely affected the ability of the currency board to survive. By examining the country's pattern of trade, and the price and income elasticity of demand for imports and exports, she argues that devaluation of the peso could not have increased the country's foreign exchange earnings sufficiently to cover the external debt. She also assesses the extent by which the change in exchange rate regime has made a difference in Argentina's economy. She argues that though the rise in exports in response to devaluation of the peso helped the current accounts (CA) of balance of payments, the more important factor responsible for the improvements in the CA has been the substantial fall in demand for imports, in turn caused by the drastic fall in income level following the crisis. Therefore, as the economy rebounds, the rise in demand for imports will increase import expenditure, and hence reduce the current account surplus, and push inflation up. Moreover, despite the abandonment of the currency board and devaluation of the peso, and some improvements in the current accounts, total debt has actually increased rather than fallen.

The effectiveness of international prudential regulation in preventing banking crises in Latin America is examined by Alexandre Minda and Stéphanie Truquin in Chapter 3. Here, the authors argue that despite the introduction of a wide range of reform policies in Latin America, their financial sectors remain fragile. Opening up of boundaries has made the subcontinent even more vulnerable to international capital movements and changes in economic conditions of large developed nations. The authors argue that financial development in Latin America has been uneven, and banks continue to be the only institutions capable of producing positive externalities. In this respect, while an efficient banking sector can produce positive externalities and support growth, an ailing banking sector can bring negative externalities to the rest of the economy. In their assessment of position of Latin American banks, the authors first analyze the causes of instability of the banking systems, and then examine the applicability of the Basel Accord to the banking systems and the extent by which it can limit their instability.

In Chapter 4, Etelberto Ortiz develops a theoretical model in which he shows how monetary policies that are designed to attract capital inflows into small open economies can create serious problems for the private sector. Ortiz points out that in most cases, the authorities, in order to attract foreign savings, have to implement severe structural reform policies in the form of trade and financial liberalization that help to develop their capital market. The model rests on the principles of zero inflation and zero public deficits, where the only active policy is monetary policy with fiscal policy adjusting passively.

The monetary policy works by targeting inflation and sending price signals that can attract foreign savings. Ortiz calls this a model of the 'tyrannical auctioneer', as the Central Bank in this model is only concerned about the public balances, the balance of payments and balances of commercial banks. In other words, it is not concerned about the disequilibria of the private agents, such as unemployment, over borrowing, excess capacity and so on. Ortiz applies the above model to Mexico and shows how the operation of the 'tyrannical auctioneer' has affected the proper development of both the Mexican capital market and the export sector. He argues that the problem in such cases arises because the structural transition is mostly financed by external borrowing that ends up strangling the capability of the country to adjust to changes. He argues that the monetary authorities can either pursue policies that attract capital inflow, or those that encourage export performance. They cannot pursue both. The economy might find a way to adjust temporarily through the accumulation of external debt but, in doing so, it jeopardizes the development of the export sector. The whole project then ends up resting on external debt, rather than export led growth strategy.

In Chapter 5, Guadalupe Mántey presents an empirical study of inflation targeting in emerging countries that have been subject to structural inflation. The author argues that monetary policies in the form of inflation targeting are inadequate to deal with inflationary pressures that arise from trade and technological dependence of the country. Such policies, in practice, disregard the asymmetries that might arise in the behaviour of the economy at different stages of development. Mántey analyzes the results of inflation targeting in Mexico and Brazil, where trade liberalization policies had been implemented, and concludes that inflation targeting supported by managed floating exchange rate regimes generates systemic risks. The author also shows that long-term stability in prices and trade accounts requires selective monetary and fiscal policies that are capable of influencing the income elasticities of imports and exports.

In Chapter 6, Albert Gonzalez examines the relevance of credible commitments and state capacity in attracting FDI in the case of Mexico. In particular, he argues that the commitments Mexico has made under the NAFTA theoretically should reduce the cost of transactions for investors and adds to the country's comparative advantage over other emerging markets. Yet, it appears that in recent years Mexico's ability to attract FDI has declined. Gonzalez argues that the effectiveness of Mexico's membership of the NAFTA as a determining factor in attracting FDI has weakened in recent years. This is mainly because the state has not been able to make credible commitments or preserve the country-specific advantages the NAFTA intended to enhance. In demonstrating the above, the author first reviews the political economy behind the state's ability to make credible commitments, and then examines the state's commitment in pushing forward the reform programmes in three different areas; namely, the electricity sector, the labour market and the taxation system. The three case studies reveal the state's limitation in making a credible commitment and reducing the transaction costs that are important to investors.

In Chapter 7, Clemente Hernandez-Rodriguez tries to assess the role of various factors that played a role in the significant fall in the number of Mexican banks in the 1990s. The author estimated a comprehensive model in which he examined the relationship between the probability of the disappearance of banks, and their characteristics and macroeconomic conditions. In his assessment, Hernandez-Rodriguez uses a framework that permits a bank to disappear either by government intervention and subsequent acquisition by another bank, or by a merger. He uses Cox's (1972, 1975) proportional hazards models with time varying covariates. The study shows that observable bank specific factors such as rate of return on equity, available funds to traditional deposits ratio, interest earnings to total loans ratio and overdue loans to total loans ratio can better explain the disappearance of banks in Mexico than macroeconomic factors. His study also shows that only three of the five elements of CAMEL: asset quality, earnings, and liquidity, were significant in the explanation of the disappearance of banks in the Mexican case. The macroeconomic factors such as high real interest rates, and depreciation of the exchange rate had a pivotal role.

Chapter 8 diverts the attentions to Brazil. Here Jose Luiz Rossi, Jr. carries out an empirical study of non-financial Brazilian companies between 1996 and 2002, and analyzes the relationship between the choice of the exchange rate regime, and companies' foreign vulnerability and their financial policies. His results indicate that the exchange rate regime plays an important role in the determination of companies' foreign vulnerability and induces changes in corporate financial policies. The author shows that the floating exchange rate regime reduces companies' foreign vulnerability by encouraging them to lower currency mismatches in their balance sheets. It also discourages the companies from borrowing in foreign currency and encourages them to engage more in hedging activities.

References

Cox, David R. (1972) 'Regression Models and Life-Tables', *Journal of the Royal Statistical Society Series*, B 34, 187–220.
Cox, David R. (1975) 'Partial Likelihood', *Biometrika*, 62 (2), 269–76.

2
Convertibility Law and its Role in Argentina's Economy

Sima Motamen-Samadian

Introduction

Following the introduction of the Convertibility Law in 1991, Argentina appeared to enjoy approximately ten years of low inflation, and a higher rate of gross domestic product (GDP) growth than had a number of other Latin American countries for some years. From 1999 onwards, however, the Argentine economy moved into a recession and, by the end of 2001, the country's financial crisis reached its peak. In 2001, in response to a number of announcements by the government, the public lost its confidence in the government's ability to manage its finances and suspected the possibility of peso devaluation. That, in turn, led to a bank run at the end of 2001 that pushed the banking sector to the brink of a liquidity crisis, and later forced the government to freeze bank deposits.

On 23 December 2001 president Saá announced Argentina's default on US$ 50 billion external debts. The news shocked the international community and moved the country into a state of chaos. In early January 2002, President Saá resigned and President Duhalde took over the government. The new president first abandoned the Convertibility Law, and few days later pesofied bank deposits and loans at the asymmetrical rate of 1.40 pesos per dollar for deposits and one-to-one for loans, and floated the peso for all transactions. The asymmetrical 'pesofication' totally undermined the property right of depositors and adversely affected the position of banks, who found themselves with a substantially higher level of peso denominated liabilities than assets. That was at the time when the peso had already depreciated to two pesos per dollar in the foreign exchange markets.[1] Within a short period of time the peso plunged to one quarter of its value against the dollar, the inflation based on the consumer price index (CPI) shot up to 41 per cent and unemployment rose to 23.6 per cent.

During the first two quarters of 2002, the Argentine economy continued to shrink[2] and inflation continued to rise.[3] Around August 2002, the economy began to stabilize and, from the third quarter, started to show some signs of recovery with exports and GDP rising again and the peso regaining some of its lost value. In the same year, Argentina experienced a considerable trade and current account surplus. The authorities attributed the improvement in the trade balance and current account to the devaluation of the peso, but the truth was that the new surplus was mainly caused by the dramatic fall in imports, which had dropped by 57 per cent compared to 2001 levels. That was indeed largely in response to the substantial fall in income, rather than devaluation of the peso. By the first quarter of 2003, the wholesale and consumer price indices began to fall, but again picked up throughout 2004 and 2005.

The question that is important to address here is what exactly caused the Argentine crisis and what has helped the recent apparent recovery? Was it the Convertibility Law that caused the so called 'overvaluation' of the peso and government's inability to deal with external shocks, or the government's fiscal policies and the measures that they adopted in dealing with external shocks that caused the crisis?

Some of the observers who subscribe to the first view are Roubini, (2001), Carrera (2002), Grandes and Reisen (2002) and Krugman (2002) Perry and Serven (2002), and Sachs (2002), Stiglitz (2002). Others, such as Calvo *et* (2002) and Torre and Schmukler (2002), blamed the government's fiscal mismanagement and excessive borrowing for causing the crisis. Hanke (2002a, 2002b, 2003) and Powell (2002), Schuler (2002, 2003), on the other hand, disputed the overvaluation of the peso and blamed the successive tax rises introduced by President de la Rúa's government for the continued economic recession of 2000–1. They also blamed the government for undermining the position of the Currency Board, and frightening the public about the future value of their peso deposits; a factor that caused the 'silent run on bank, as Schuler (2003) calls it, and the full blown crisis that occurred at the end of 2001. The subsequent 'pesofication' of banks' assets and liabilities was just the last blow to the growing crisis that pushed the economy into a depression. Pesofication not only completely ignored property rights, it acutely undermined public confidence in the financial system as a whole for years to come.

This chapter tries to shed some light on the role of the Convertibility Law in Argentina's economy and to analyze the effect of other factors in the build up to the crisis of 2002 and Subsequent. In this respect, section the next provides a brief overview of the role of the Currency Board in economic stability and growth of Argentina between 1991 and 1998. The subsequent section highlights some of the important external and internal factors that contributed to the economic recession of 1999–2001. The chapter then goes on to evaluate the role of the peso in Argentina's balance of payments, and then examines the role of the government's fiscal policies in the build up to the crisis. The performance of the economy after the abandonment of the Convertibility Law is examined in section six, and the conclusions drawn close the chapter.

The role of the Convertibility Law in the Argentine economy (1991–98)

Prior to the introduction of the Convertibility Law in 1991, Argentina suffered from chronic periods of hyperinflation, twin deficits and a high level of external debt. Between 1976 and 1991, successive Argentine governments introduced various stabilization programmes, three changes of currency denomination and eight changes of exchange rate regime. Yet, despite the pegged exchange rate regime that was in place between mid-1985 to 1989, inflation continued to remain very high.

In June 1989, the new administration of President Menem came into office, and initially floated the exchange rate. At the same time, they introduced a number of policies to control inflation and reduce the fiscal deficit. During 1990, inflation initially peaked to almost 5,000 per cent, but then gradually dropped to an average of over 1,300 per cent. In June 1991, the Convertibility Law was introduced and pegged the peso to the US dollar at the parity rate of one to one. Under the new arrangement, which referred to it as the 'Currency Board', the Central Bank was no longer able to print money to finance fiscal expenditure or act as the lender of last resort. Moreover, 80 per cent of M1 had to be backed by the international reserves. Hanke (2003) argued that Argentina did have a strict Currency Board. That is because contrary to the strict rules of a currency board, the BCRA was frequently engaged in sterilization, and its net domestic assets were not frozen.

Nevertheless, within a short period of time, inflation declined to 84 per cent in 1991, and later to as low as 0.2 per cent in 1996. See Figure 2.1.

However, soon after the abandonment of the Currency Board in December 2001, and the devaluation of the peso, inflation began to rise again and, by the end of December 2002, it peaked at 41 per cent, though the average for the year amounted to 25.9 per cent. Thus,

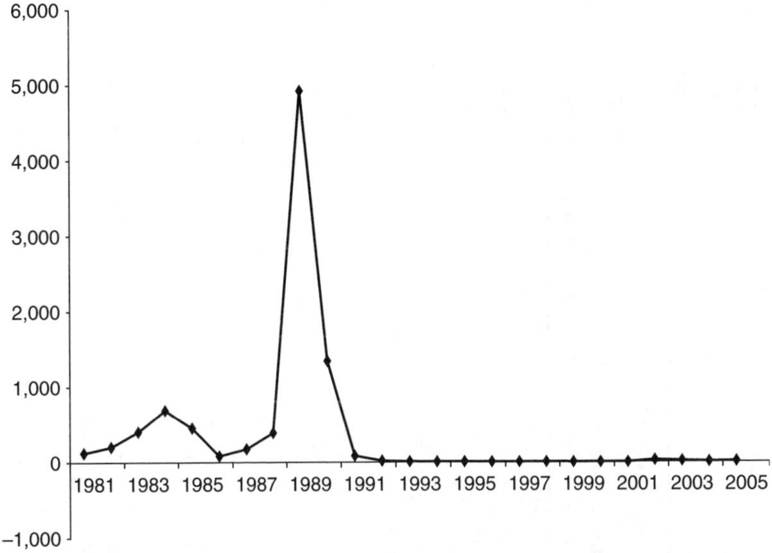

Figure 2.1 Average annual inflation based on consumer price index (CPI), 1981–July 2005

Sources: Compiled by the author based on data collected from *Latin Focus* 2003, EIU 2003; and Table A.4.2, Argentine Ministry of Economy and Production, September 2005.

between 1981 and 2002, every time the authorities adopted a floating exchange rate regime, inflation shot up and ultimately forced the government to abandon the floating exchange rate regime.

Along with the Convertibility Law, President Menem's government introduced a whole range of other economic reform programmes that included the privatization of 67 public enterprises and banks. The reform programmes, which were aimed at reducing public expenditure, were also used in the process of debt–equity swaps, and encouraged capital inflows.

At the same time, the pegging of the peso to the dollar helped to lower interest rates in line with international rates. As can be seen from Table 2.1, throughout the period between 1996–2000,[4] the difference between the peso and the dollar lending rates remained very low. Similarly, the spread between the peso deposit and loan rates were very similar to the spread between the dollar deposit and loan rates. All these circumstances were a clear reflection of investors' confidence in the country's economy and the low level of country risk premium. Consequently, foreign direct investment increased from US$1,836 million in 1990 to US$8,236 million in 1999.

Table 2.1 Average annual interest rates

Year	Deposits in pesos		Deposits in dollars			Lending (prime)		Spread[1]	
	Savings account	Time dep. 30–59 d.	Savings account	Time dep. 30–59 d.	Call up to 15 d.	Pesos 30 d.	US$30 d.	Pesos	Dollars
1996									
Av.	3.47	7.36	2.56	6.10	6.23	10.51	9.12	3.15	3.02
S.D.[2]	0.07	0.57	0.05	0.40	0.93	0.64	0.44	0.32	0.14
1997									
Av.	3.31	6.97	2.48	5.87	6.63	9.24	7.84	2.28	1.97
S.D.	0.08	0.79	0.11	0.28	1.13	2.12	0.70	1.34	0.49
1998									
Av.	3.01	7.56	2.37	6.40	6.81	10.64	8.59	3.07	2.55
S.D.	0.07	1.17	0.07	0.61	0.72	2.87	1.93	1.74	1.33
1999									
Av.	2.87	8.05	2.5	6.42	6.99	11.04	9.07	2.99	2.65
S.D.	0.11	1.32	1.16	0.18	0.55	2.00	1.20	0.87	0.69
2000									
Av.	2.81	8.34	2.74	7.03	8.14	11.08	9.87	2.75	2.64
S.D.	0.11	1.54	0.12	0.87	2.07	2.43	1.59	0.96	0.75
2001									
Av.	3.13	16.16[2]	3.37	9.81	22.58[3]	26.47	17.67	10.31	7.86
S.D.	0.82	8.10	1.17	2.65	22.73	12.64	6.28	4.84	4.36

2002									
Av.	6.36	39.25	2.03	4.44	41.35	**52.97**	20.55	67.88	5.84[4]
S.D.	4.94	25.88	0.51	1.70	25.77	**27.90**	1.12	27.36	8.81
2003									
Av.	1.34	10.16	0.95	0.86	3.74	**19.40**	–	9.24	–
S.D.	0.46	6.76	0.95	0.35	2.45	**7.69**	–	2.29	–
2004									
Av.	0.73	2.65	0.13	0.39	1.96	**6.78**	–	4.12	–
S.D.	0.08	0.33	0.02	0.12	0.56	**1.49**	–	1.64	–
2005[5]									
Av.	0.75	3.25	0.12	0.33	3.20	**5.84**	–	2.59	–
S.D.	0.04	0.53	0.01	0.04	1.18	**0.46**	–	0.10	–

Notes: [1] Spread is the difference between the 30 day lending rates of peso and dollar and 30–59 day deposits of the peso and the dollar respectively.
[2] Standard deviations are calculated using twelve-month data in each year.
[3] The sudden increase in the above figures is primarily due to changes in interest rate that occurred in March following Mr. Cavallo's announcement of possible change in the peg from the dollar to a basket of currencies comprizing half dollars and half Euros.
[4] From October 2002, the dollar 30-day spread was zero.
[5] Average and standard deviations for 2005 correspond to the first seven months including July 2005.

Source: Produced by the author based on data collected from Table A8.1, Argentine Ministry of Economy and Production, September 2005.

The low interest rates encouraged investments and as a result, gross domestic investment as a proportion of GDP increased from 14 per cent in 1990 to 17.9 per cent in 1999. As can be seen from Figure 2.2, with the exception of 1995, when the economy was temporarily hit by the 'tequila effect', all the components of GDP grew in every year between 1991–1998. Over the same period, Argentina was growing at an average annual rate of around 6.7 per cent in real terms distinctly higher than the rate experienced in most other Latin American countries, except for Chile.

The Currency Board also appeared to have helped Argentina to withstand some of the major external shocks of the 1990s. In 1995–96, following the Mexican 'tequila effect', despite the severe pressure experienced by the banking sector, the Argentine economy managed fairly quickly to resume its economic growth and once again attract capital inflows. Similarly, following the South-east Asian crisis of 1997, Argentina was among the first emerging markets to regain access to international capital markets. Nevertheless, by the end of 1998 the average annual rate of growth had dropped to 3.9 per cent compared with 10.9 per cent in the previous year.

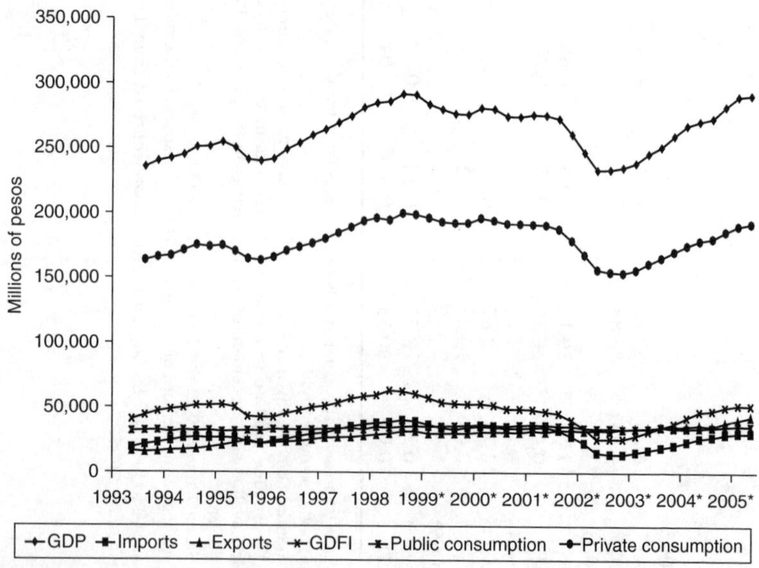

Figure 2.2 Real GDP and components (quarterly data based on 1993 prices) (1993–1st quarter 2005)

Note: * Preliminary figures.

Source: Produced by the author based on data collected from Table A1.9, Argentine Ministry of Economy and Production, September 2005.

1999–2001 economic recession

From 1999 onwards, Argentina was exposed to a whole series of new external shocks that pushed the economy into a recession and deflation. The first one was the Russian crisis of 1999, which adversely affected the flow of capital into all emerging markets. The next blow was the devaluation of the Brazilian real and appreciation of the dollar against other currencies, which adversely affected the export sector. The Brazilian devaluation, in fact, dealt a double blow to Argentina's export sector by; (a) reducing the Brazilian demand for Argentina's exports, and (b) by somewhat reducing Argentina's competitiveness with regard to Brazilian goods in international markets. In addition to these factors, Argentina's agricultural exports were hit by the foot and mouth disease in Europe, which adversely affected the demand for various meat products throughout international markets. Between 1999 and 2001, the economy went into recession and began to experience deflation.

The economic downturn of 1999, forced the federal government to increase its expenditure and run a higher budget deficit than in previous years. It was also at this time that, due to a presidential election, the government of President Menem had adopted a more relaxed approach towards provincial government expenditure. As the rules of the Convertibility Law prevented the government from financing its expenditure through money supply, the government primarily used foreign currency denominated bonds and loans from private creditors and multilateral agencies to achieve this. The rapid build up of public sector external debt, and the slow down in economic activity did not appear to alarm the lenders, as the presence of the Currency Board helped to maintain creditors' confidence in the ability of the government to restore economic recovery.

In 2000, despite devaluation of the Brazilian *real* and the claims of overvaluation of the peso, exports started to rise slightly and Argentina's trade balance and current accounts improved compared with 1999. Yet, the increasing budget deficit encouraged the new government of President de la Ruá, who had come to office in 2000, to raise taxes.

The tax increases adversely affected the economic activity and pushed the economy further into recession. By early 2001, the continued economic recession led to a change of economic minister and the appointment of Mr Cavallo,[5] who was contemplating the introducion of certain amendments to the Convertibility Law. In this respect, many analysts blame the government for pushing the economy further into recession and undermining the credibility of the Currency Board.

Soon after his appointment, Mr. Cavallo introduced a subsidy on exports, and tariffs on imports that in practice devalued the peso for the traded sector. The next blow came in March 2001, when it was announced that the government was planning to change the peg between the peso and the dollar to a peg between the peso and a basket of currencies that included half Euro and half dollars, once the Euro reached parity with the dollar. Later on, in May 2001, came the news of the resignation of the Central Bank governor, who was considered a hard liner and the guardian of the Currency Board by the investor community. His resignation reinforced the suspicion of a forthcoming peso devaluation, and further undermined the credibility and sustainability of the Currency Board.[6] Unfortunately, the above announcement further reaffirmed the public's suspicion of the possibility of collapse of the Currency Board and a forthcoming devaluation that could have eroded the value of their peso deposits.

A closer investigation of the data in Table 2.1 reveals that following the authorities' announcement of possible change of peg in March 2001, the spread between the peso and dollar lending rate distinctly increased. Table 2.1 also shows that while the volatility of peso loan rates, measured by standard deviation of twelve-month values, increased from 0.64 in 1996 to 2.12 in 1997 in response to the side effects of South-east Asia, they did not increase much afterwards until 2001, when market volatility suddenly jumped up from 2.43 (in 2000) to 12.64. Indeed, comparison of the SD of 1997 to 2001 shows that while, initially, the market had shown some signs of nervousness in response to South-east Asia in 1997, it managed to calm down by 1999, and remained fairly calm until March 2001 when government announcements totally undermined the position of the Currency Board.

Hence, in response to each piece of news, more and more people rushed to the banks to withdraw or convert their peso deposits to dollars. To discourage depositors from withdrawing their peso deposits, banks raised the interest rates on peso deposits. The dollar deposit and loan rates, however, remained unchanged for some time. Consequently, the 30- and 60-day peso time deposit rates jumped from 6.56 and 8.60 per cent in February to 10.81 and 13.37 per cent respectively in March, and the 30-day peso loan rates rose from 8.98 per cent in February to 11.25 per cent in March. The sharp rise in deposit rates was a clear indication of a rise in country risk premium and the inability of the banks to convince depositors to leave their funds in place, to the extent that in March 2001 the 30-day loan rates were below the 60 days deposit rates.

These increases in deposit rates continued throughout the year until November 2001, when the 30-day time deposit rates reached the height of 31.94 per cent, while the 60-day time deposit rates increased to 27.90 per cent. (See Figure 2.3.) The above difference between the 30- and 60-day time deposit rates clearly indicates the degree of liquidity shortage that was prevailing in the market. All these were happening at the time when some of the government's borrowings were approaching maturity, and the rapid increases in interest rates were making it more and more difficult to use new borrowing for repayment of maturing debt.

By the end of 2001, the government could no longer borrow from private lenders. Consequently, the public lost its confidence in government's ability to maintain the peso–dollar pegging, and rushed to withdraw their peso and dollar deposits. In response to public panic, bank deposits were frozen. Later, in December 2001, the government defaulted on its foreign debt and, by 6 January 2002, the government abandoned Convertibility Law.

It is important to note that while the economy was clearly suffering from a recession from 1999 onwards, the Currency Board did not allow

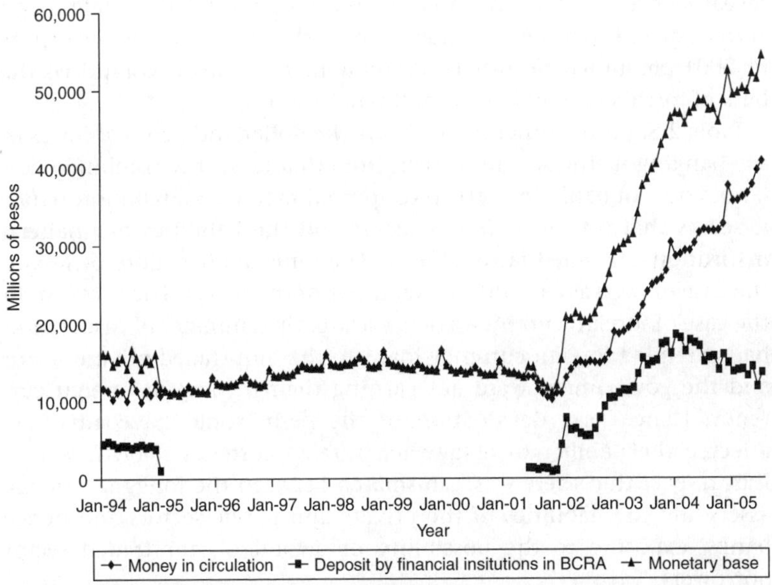

Figure 2.3 Money supply (millions of pesos), 1994–July 2005

Source: Produced by the author based on data collected from Table A8.2, Argentine Ministry of Economy and Production, September 2005.

the money supply to rise. Indeed, towards the end of 2001 the money supply was well below its 1999 level. This was despite the fact that contrary to rules of a strict currency board the Central Bank, in order to support the exchange rate, was buying domestic currency and selling foreign currency and thus running down the reserves. But, despite some level of sterilization, it was not allowing the money supply to move back to its original level. In other words, given that it was not observing the strict rules of a currency board, it should have provided more support to the economy at the time when it was most needed. Such discretionary expansionary monetary policy could not have had any inflationary implications at the time when the economy was operating well below capacity.

Therefore, if the authorities had reduced the ratio of international reserve to money supply at its most desperate time, they probably would have been able to prevent the crisis.

Another factor that played an important role in the financial crisis of Argentina was the mismatch between the currency of income and expenditure of bank borrowers. An examination of the currency of assets and liabilities of financial institutions might not immediately reveal such a mismatch. As can be seen from Table 2.2, the total foreign currency loans that were extended to both the private and public sectors in 2001 amounted to over US$51 billion. These loans comprised the bulk of foreign currency assets of financial sector.

Table 2.3, on the other hand shows the dollar and peso liabilities of the banking sector. As can be seen from that table, the combined dollar deposits of banks in 2001 were approximately US$50 billion. Thus, it seems that foreign currency assets and the liabilities of financial institutions matched fairly closely. The same applies more or less in the case of peso assets and the liabilities of the banks. The problem in the case of foreign currency assets was that in a number of cases banks had extended foreign currency loans to the non-traded private sector and the government were not earning their income in foreign currency. Hence, any devaluation of the peso would have adversely affected their ability to repay their foreign currency debt. It was in that respect that there was a mismatch between the foreign currency assets and the liabilities of the private and public sectors and hence banks' exposure to the possibility of default of non-traded sector borrowers.

The questions that have to be addressed here are: (a) Was there a sound spread of risks among banks' assets? and (b) was there any maturity mismatch between the foreign currency loans and assets of banks? The answer to the first question is a clear no, as nearly a quarter of banks' assets were concentrated in the form of loans to one borrower; namely, the public sector that was finding it increasingly difficult to repay its debt, in particular in 2000 and 2001. Such a poor spread of asset risks raises a question about the quality of risk assessment of banks, as they continued extending more and more loans to the public sector, and the logic or motivation behind their decision. With respect to the second question, a quick examination of maturity of assets and liabilities might suggest that there was not a serious maturity mismatch. As can be seen from Table 2.3, more than two thirds of banks' liabilities in 2001 were kept in the form of foreign currency deposits, of which more than 80 per cent were kept in time deposit accounts. The problem with time deposits, however, is that they can turn into instant demand deposits once expectations about the possibility of bank failure begin to rise. In other words, even when deposits are kept in the form of time deposits, depositors are ready to forgo the higher interest rate if they begin to doubt the ability of banks to repay their deposits. In such cases, the implicit risk premium of depositors rises well above the nominal interest rate that any bank can pay. Hence, a clear mismatch of maturity emerges between the assets and liabilities of banks, and a classic scenario of bank run develops.

In the case of Argentina, the banking sector was in some sense exposed to the risk of mismatch of maturity of its assets and liabilities. That is because most of the foreign currency assets of banks were in the form of foreign currency-short to medium-term loans to the public sector, which was increasingly demonstrating signs of inability to repay its debt. During 2001, the government was mostly relying on short-term borrowing from multilateral agencies to repay its debt service. That was at the time when external lenders were becoming increasingly reluctant to extend any further loans or aid for that matter. Once the multilateral agencies began to pull the plug, the government found itself unable to repay its debt service and loan to domestic banks, and once the public found out about it the panic began. Thus, it was not so much the mismatch in the size or maturity of foreign currency assets and liabilities of banks according to banks' books that put them in difficulty. It was mostly a combination of the composition of banks' assets, which included a high concentration of loans to a single borrower, and the mismatch between the income and expenditure of the borrowers that caused the problem.

Table 2.2 Lending by financial institutions,[1] balances at end of period (millions of pesos)

	To public sector			To non-financial private sector				To non-residents			Total lending	
End of	In pesos 1	In foreign currency 2	Total 3=1+2	In pesos 4	In foreign currency 5	Total 6=4+5	Total 7=6+3	In pesos 8	In foreign currency 9	Total 10=7+8+9	In pesos 1+4+8	In foreign currency 2+5+9
1994	1,721	3,429	5,150	19,743	27,382	47,125	52,275	4	333	52,612	21,468	31,144
1995[2,3]	2,088	3,544	5,632	18,233	28,523	46,756	52,388	0	305	52,693	20,321	32,371
1996	1,926	4,432	6,358	19,549	31,684	51,233	57,591	6	451	58,049	21,481	36,568
1997	1,766	5,244	7,010	22,032	37,893	59,925	66,935	1	236	67,173	23,799	43,373
1998	1,479	7,837	9,316	24,741	42,350	67,091	76,407	11	1,056	77,475	26,231	51,243
1999	1,676	10,316	11,992	24,385	40,856	65,241	77,233	14	434	77,681	26,075	51,606
2000	826	14,134	14,960	23,323	38,740	62,063	77,023	3	350	77,376	24,152	53,224
2001	1,006	20,837	21,843	14,046	36,116	50,162	72,005	0	381	72,385	15,051	57,333
2002[4]	29,886	263	30,149	28,475	2,875	31,350	61,499	n.a.	n.a.	61,499	58,361	3,138
2003	23,658	129	23,787	27,078	1,288	28,366	52,153	n.a.	n.a.	54,643	50,736	1,417
2004	20,410	186	20,596	34,212	1,579	35,791	56,387	–	–	59,504	54,622	1,765
2005[5]	17,558	161	17,719	39,321	2,306	41,627	59,346	–	–	63,642	56,879	2,467

Notes: [1] These figures do not include government bonds or private securities or financial trust for restructured banks.
[2] Beginning in August 1995, loans of customers rates as bad debts and totally covered by the relevant allowance are netted according to the BCRA's Communqué 'A' 2357.
[3] Loans granted to the non-financial private sector as of December 1995 include a tax moratorium.
[4] According to Decree No. 214/02, loans nominated in US dollars will be converted into pesos at the ratio $ 1 = US$ 1.
[5] The figures for 2005 correspond to July 2005.

Source: Compiled by the author based on data reported in Table A8.4, Argentine Ministry of Economy and Production, September 2005.

Table 2.3 Bimonetary aggregates[1] **(average of period in millions of pesos)**

	Peso current A/c 2	Dollar Current A/c 4	Savings A/cs in pesos 6	Pesos Time dep. 7	Dollar savings A/cs 9	Dollar time dep. 10	Deposits: Pesos 12=2+6+7	Deposits: Dollars 13=4+9+10	Deposits: Total[2] 14=12+13
Av. 94	7,849	875	5,245	9,698	3,842	16,583	22,792	21,300	44,093
Av. 95	7,082	1,069	4,616	7,335	3,546	17,347	19,032	21,962	40,994
Av. 96	8,981	1,188	5,466	8,953	4,055	21,304	23,400	26,547	49,947
Av. 97	11,237	1,659	7,177	11,665	4,791	26,215	30,078	32,665	62,743
Av. 98	12,304	1,535	8,314	13,991	5,203	33,092	34,608	39,830	74,438
Av. 99	11,995	1,723	8,209	13,549	5,572	38,334	33,752	45,629	79,381
Av. 00	12,070	1,764	8,140	13,108	5,534	42,606	33,317	49,903	83,221
Av. 01	10,140	2,401	6,354	9,999	6,600	41,257	26,493	50,258	76,751
Av.02[3]	16,418	2,717	11,211	27,377	1,508	1,538	55,005	5,764	60,769
Av.03	21,647	444	11,608	36,572	272	680	9,827	1,396	73,933
Av.04	30,637	426	19,882	39,540	1,358	1,411	90,059	3,194	99,494
Av.05[4]	34,371	496	23,393	47,153	1,525	1,787	104,917	3,809	115,985

Notes: [1] Includes deposits from non-residents. Deposits in current accounts are net of the use of FUCO (Unified Fund for Official Accounts) and include other deposits.

[2] The items related to the total for 2002 and 2003 are calculated in exactly the same manner as the remaining data. However, they do not appear to be exactly the sum of columns 12 + 13, even after allowing for conversion at the rate of 1.40 pesos per dollar.

[3] From 11 January 2002 the exchange regime rules (Decree No. 71/2002) set by Law No. 25561 established the ratio $ 1,40 = US$ 1. Thus, in order to express the total of deposits (column 14) in a single currency, balances of accounts in US dollars should be converted into pesos using this ratio.

[4] Average of the first seven months including July 2005.

Source: Calculated by author based on data provided in Table A8.3 Argentine Ministry of Economy and Production, September 2005.

It was ultimately Argentina' default in the debt to the World Bank in November that convinced the public of the forthcoming end of the Convertibility Law and pressed them to withdraw their peso and dollar deposits which pushed the banks to the brink of collapse. On 30 November, the overnight interest rate rose to 689 per cent and the government put a freeze on bank deposits. Later, in January 2002, the government introduced the asymmetric pesofication of stock of financial contracts and confiscated all dollar reserves of banks at the rate of 1.4 pesos per dollar. There is no doubt that the latter action, though might have helped debtors to some extent in reducing the value of their debt to domestic banks[7], had the most adverse impact on public confidence in financial institutions. By October 2002, the freeze on savings accounts came to an end, though they continued to remain on time deposits and, by March 2003, pesofication was announced to be illegal by the courts. Nevertheless, the huge losses experienced by banks as a result of symmetric pesofication exceeded the capital of the consolidated banking system.

As can be seen from Figure 2.4 , during 2001 the high interest rate pushed the number of bankruptcies to the highest level recorded since the 1980s. The numbers of bankruptcies continued to remain high after pesofication, and a number of utility companies and financial institutions (including Banco Galicia, the largest domestic private sector bank) went bankrupt.

The impact of the Currency Board on the balance of payments

A number of analysts blamed the overvaluation of the peso for Argentina's downfall. It was argued that the fall in capital inflow after the Russian crisis of 1999, the Brazilian currency devaluation and the pegging of the peso to the dollar contributed to overvaluation of the Argentine peso. Such pegging, it was argued, was not right when trade with the USA accounts for only about 11 per cent of Argentina's trade. Most of the above studies used the CPI in their assessment of peso overvaluation.

Schuler (2002), on the other hand, disputed the validity of their claim and argued that had the researchers used the producer prices and a different base year in their estimations, they would have found a different set of results. Based on March 1991 producer prices, Schuler (2002) found that while the overvaluation of the peso peaked at 15 per

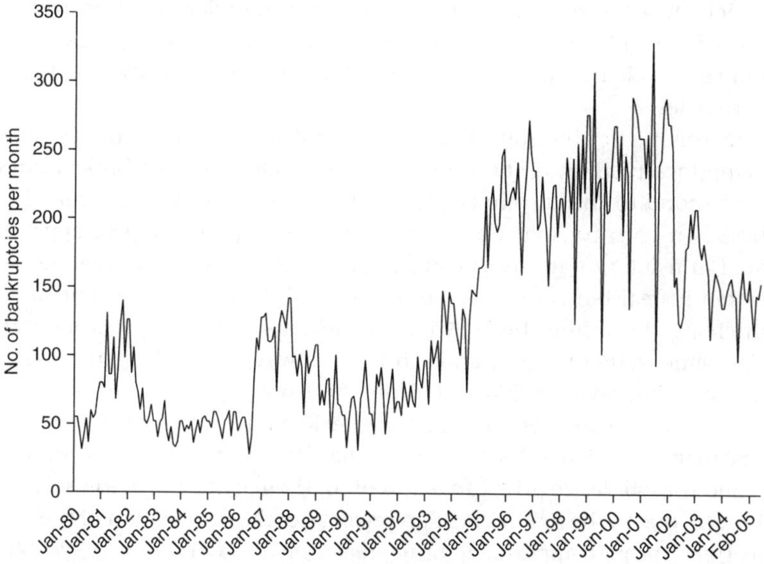

Figure 2.4 Preventive legal procedures and bankrupt companies, January 1980–June 2005

Source: Produced by the author based on data collected from Table A1.23, Argentine Ministry of Economy and Production, September 2005.

cent in mid-1996, it fell below 2 per cent by 1999, which was well below the figures reported by the others. Further, his estimations showed that between December 2000 to December 2001, the peso was in fact undervalued rather than overvalued.

Hanke (2003), too, argued that the use of CPI in assessment of the overvaluation of the peso is not acceptable as it includes a number of non-traded goods that are not subject to international commodity arbitrage, which affects exports. Moreover, his own calculations of the real exchange rate shows the wide divergence between the equilibrium rates based on the consumer and producer price index. Indeed, other reports, such as the survey of prices in 58 largest cities in the world, carried out by the Union Bank of Switzerland, showed that Buenos Aires was ranked 22, which was mid-way on the list in terms of expensiveness. Similarly, the *Economist's* Big Mac index showed that the peso was 2 per cent undervalued against the dollar in early 2001.

Here, to assess the extent of the peso's over-or under valuation against the US dollar (Brazilian), we use both consumer and whole sale price indices to calculate the real exchange rates[8] between the peso and those currencies.

In this figure, the solid lines correspond to the real exchange rates being measured using the whole sale price index, and the broken lines correspond to the consumer price index. As can be seen in Figure 2.5, based on both consumer and producer price indices, the peso appreciated in real terms against the Brazilian real in 1991–94, but then depreciated in real terms in 1994–96. Between 1996 and 1997, it remained unchanged and from 1997–99 it once more appreciated against the real. The same trend of appreciation in the real was observed again, though at a very low level, in 2000–01. From 2001 onwards, however, after the devaluation of the peso, the peso depreciated in real terms against the Brazilian real. Figure 2.5 also shows that the same trend was observed when the wholesale price index was used, though at a much lower level. Indeed, due to the rise in Brazilian prices after the devaluation of the real in 1999, the peso appeared to be depreciating in real terms in 1999–2000 but then, because of further deflation in Argentina, it began to appreciate in real terms against the real in 2000–01. That also explains the rise in exports to MERCOSUR over that period, which seemed somewhat strange in view of the earlier nominal devaluation of the real. With respect to the US dollar, the real exchange rate between 1992 and 1997 appeared to have appreciated only very slightly when the wholesale price index is used, rather than consumer price index. Indeed, when the producer price index is used, there appears to be some real depreciation from 1997 onwards. This depreciation substantially increased after the devaluation of the nominal peso at the beginning of 2002. Thus, comparison of the real exchange rates based on two different price indices shows that with the producer price index there was much less real appreciation than with the consumer price index. All these clearly show that the arguments about overvaluation of the peso should be considered with greater caution.

In the case of the Euro,[9] the peso appeared to have appreciated against the Euro in real terms throughout the period between 1998–2001. This was, of course, mainly due to the fact that during that period the Euro had been continuously depreciating against the dollar.

Clearly, to assess the extent of overvaluation of a currency it is much more appropriate to use the producer prices rather than consumer prices, which include all sorts of non-tradable goods. This point has

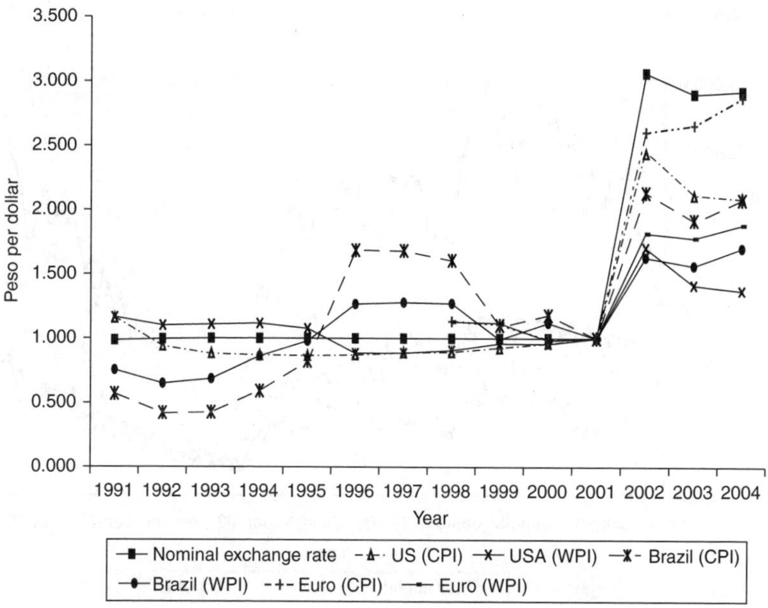

Figure 2.5 Real exchange rate with USA, Brazil and Eurozone Index, 1991–2004 (Base 2001 = 1)

Source: Produced by the author based on data collected from Table A8.1, Argentine Ministry of Economy and Production, August 2005.

also been emphatically discussed by Schuler (2003). Moreover, overvaluation of the peso is important only if both price elasticity of demand for exports and imports is high, and income elasticity of demand for imports is low. Otherwise, the devaluation of currency would not help the trade balance much. Therefore, it is important to first identify Argentina's main trade partners and examine the composition of her imports and exports, which give an indication of their elasticities.

An examination of Argentina's trade relation with her partners shows that Argentina's main trade partners are MERCOSUR, NAFTA and the EU. As can be seen from Figure 2.6, up to 2002 the combined levels of goods and services that Argentina has imported from the USA[10] and the EU has been consistently higher than that of her imports from MERCOSUR. The above trend, however, has changed since the devaluation of the peso in 2001. The more recent data, however, reveal the switching

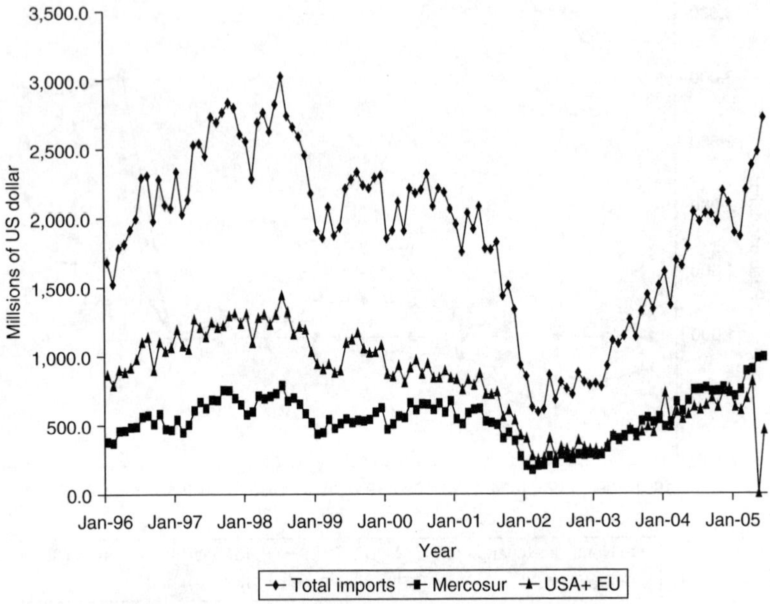

Figure 2.6 Imports by destination, January 1996–June 2005

Source: Produced by the author based on data collected from Tables A5.7–5.9, Argentine Ministry of Economy and Production, September 2005.

effect of peso devaluation and show that Argentina has shifted more in favour of imports from MERCOSUR rather than the EU and the USA.

Figure 2.7, on the other hand, which demonstrates the composition of Argentina's exports by destination, shows that throughout the period between 1996 and 2002, the combined level of goods and services that Argentina exported to the USA and the EU was higher than that of MERCOSUR, and the same trend has followed after the devaluation of the peso with a slight accentuation.

These differences in patterns of imports and exports are very important when one considers the type of goods that Argentina exports and imports. Throughout the years 1992 to 2002, between 60–70 per cent of Argentina's total imports were made of capital and intermediate goods, and parts and accessories. The majority of these goods tend to have a low price elasticity of demand. This is also confirmed by Catão and Falcetti (1999), who estimated the long run price and income elasticity of demand for Argentina's imports to be around 0.7 and 2–2.5 respectively.

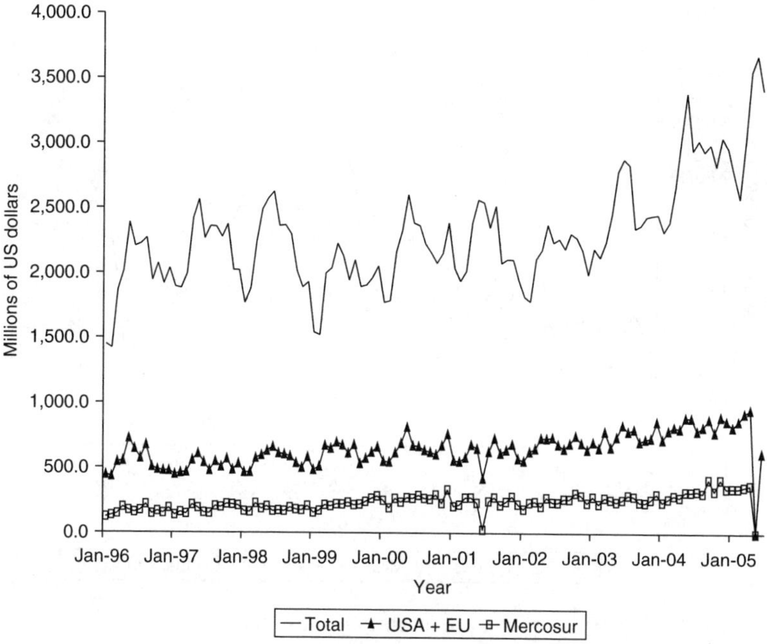

Figure 2.7 Exports by destination, January 1996–July 2005

Source: Produced by the author based on data collected from Table A5.8, Argentine Ministry of Economy and Production, September 2005.

On the other hand, as can be seen from Figure 2.8, the majority of over 70 per cent of Argentina's exports are usually made up of primary products, processed agricultural goods[11] and fuels and energy. These are mostly exported to the NAFTA and the EU, and have a low price elasticity of demand. The rest of Argentina's exports are made up of manufactured industrial products that tend to be exported to MERCOSUR. These tend to have a higher price elasticity of demand. These points are also somewhat confirmed by Catão and Falcetti (1999) who estimated the price and income elasticity of demand for exports to MERCOSUR and the rest of the world to be around 1.3 and 1 respectively. Their estimates also revealed the high income elasticity of demand for exports to MERCOSUR.

Therefore, it is apparent that, while devaluation of the peso could have helped her export earnings from MERCOSUR, it could not have increased her exports earnings from the EU and NAFTA or, for that matter, the USA who was Argentina's largest export destination among the NAFTA. What is even more interesting is that while throughout the

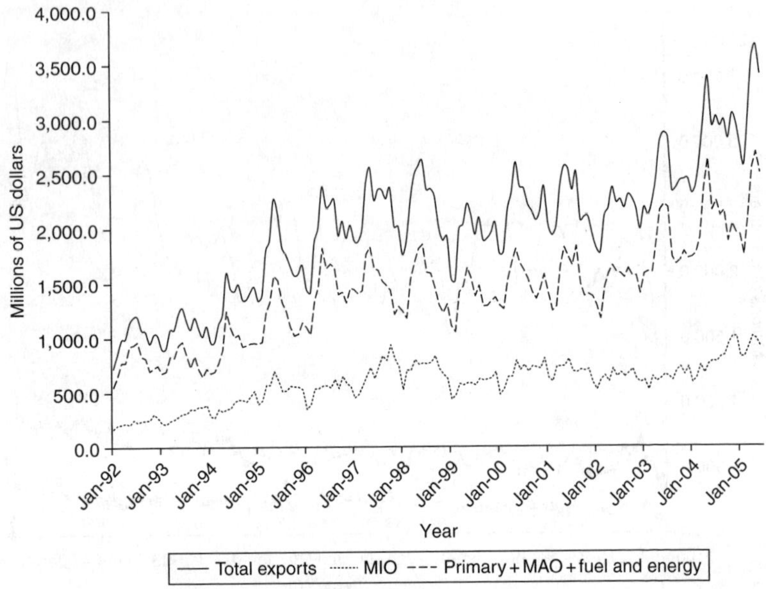

Figure 2.8 Exports by type of products, 1992–July 2005

Notes: MIO= Manufactured industrial output
MAO = Manufactured agricultural output

Source: Produced by the author based on data collected from Table A5.6, Argentine Ministry of Economy and Production, September 2005.

period between 1994 and 2003 Argentina was experiencing a trade surplus with MERCOSUR, she had always had a trade deficit with the NAFTA and the EU. This is evident from Figure 2.9, which shows Argentina's trade with the USA, the EU and MERCOSUR.

According to the data provided by the Argentine Ministry of the Economy and Production (2005), the size of the trade deficit with the NAFTA was at its highest level in 1997, when the peso was not yet considered to be overvalued, but improved from 1999 onwards, partly due to the fall in imports in response to lower income, and partly due to the rise in exports. This shows that overvaluation of the peso and a lack of competitiveness was not exactly the cause of Argentina's trade deficit with the NAFTA. It is also interesting to note that although Argentina's exports to MERCOSUR dropped during 1999, they began to rise again in 2000 to a level above that of 1996, when the peso appeared to be undervalued against the Brazilian real. Indeed, the overall trade balance with that region improved in the following years. That was, of course, to a large extent due to the fall in income, and hence imports which were highly responsive to income. Therefore, despite the claims of the overvaluation of the peso, Argentina's export sector did not appear to do badly.

Now, if we look at the composition of Argentina's imports we notice that Argentina's imports from the USA and the EU are made of capital goods. These items account for the highest proportions of the imported capital goods used by the manufacturing industry. Thus, it is clear that had the peso devalued earlier, the rise in the costs of imports would have dealt a severe blow to Argentina's industry. Indeed, a close examination of the data reported by the Argentine Ministry of the Economy and Production (2005) reveals that in most years between 1989 and 2002, over 30 per cent of capital goods were used by the manufacturing sector. These ratios indicate the extent of reliance of various sectors on imported capital goods, and hence the extent by which a devaluation of the peso would have affected the entire economy by raising the costs of imports. This is, in fact, what has happened since the devaluation of the peso in 2002, when inflation has been rising again.

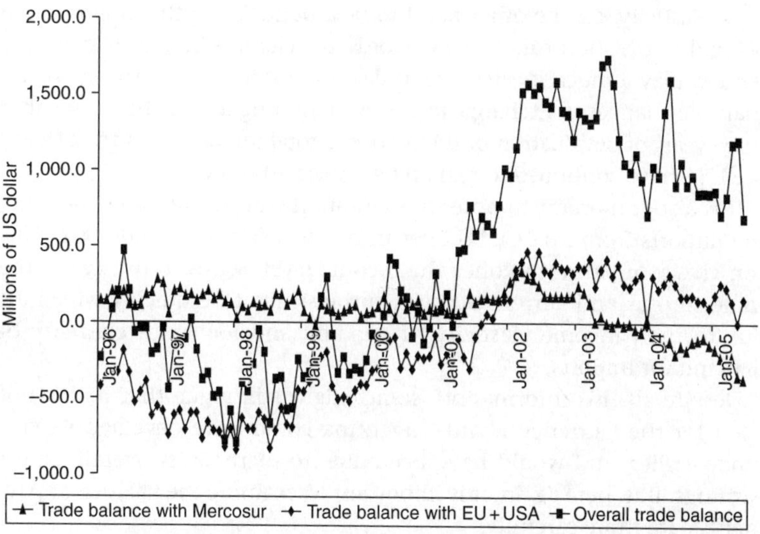

Figure 2.9 Trade balance by destination, 1996–July 2005 (millions of US dollar)
Source: Produced by the author using data provided in Tables A5.7–5.10, Argentine Ministry of Economy and Production, September 2005.

In 2002, imports of capital goods dropped by 69 per cent, and the level of import of intermediate goods fell by 40.5 per cent. The significant fall in these import items had a significant impact on both domestic production and the production of certain manufactured exports. But, on the other hand, the fall in the amounts of imports from the EU and the USA, helped the trade balance with those two regions to move into surplus from mid-2002 onwards.

Some argue that these changes are primarily attributable to the abandonment of the Currency Board and the depreciation of the peso in the open market. It is important to note, however, that despite the devaluation of the peso, total merchandise exports dropped by 3.1 per cent in 2002, and exports of services dropped by more than 33 per cent (see Table 2.4). In other words, the change in trade balance from a deficit to a surplus was primarily caused by the significant 50 per cent decline in total imports. No doubt, the sharp fall in imports was partly caused by the depreciation of the peso and the critical condition of the country, which made it difficult for importers to get credit from any bank. But it was also caused by the significant fall in income and the high responsiveness of demand for imports to income. This behaviour is consistent with the findings of Catão and Falcetti (1999), who found the long-run and short-run demand for imports to be elastic, and reported them to be 2.25 and 3 respectively. They found price elasticity, on the other hand to be around 1.5 in the long run and below 1 in the short run. In other words, the changes in domestic income tend to play a much greater role in demand for imports in the short run than the changes in exchange rate. It is interesting to note that even after three years of devaluation of the peso, the total imports from the EU and the USA have continued to remain below the 2001 level.

It is also important to note that despite the depreciation of the peso, the imports from MERCOSUR began to rise again from mid-2002. This can give some idea that once the income level begins to rise again, the trade surplus and current account surplus might be quickly wiped off due to high income elasticity of demand and low price elasticity of demand for imports.

Despite all this information, some might still argue that had it not been for the Currency Board, Argentina could have devalued its currency earlier, and would have been able to increase its overall export earnings. But, here again, it is important to examine the balance of payments data more carefully.

Table 2.4 shows that throughout the years of the Currency Board, Argentina experienced a current account deficit that was compensated for by a large surplus in the capital and financial accounts. Even during

1996 and 1997, when the economy was considered to be in good shape, Argentina experienced a trade and current account deficit. The deficit in those years was not entirely caused by Argentina's loss of competitiveness or overvaluation of the peso. Rather, it was partly caused by the rise in domestic demand for imports that was stimulated by the improved economic conditions, and partly due to the fall in exports of livestock due to foot and mouth disease among sheep in Argentina and 'Mad Cow' disease in Europe, which reduced the demand for both livestock and meat manufacture.

As it can be seen from Table 2.4, in 1998 Argentina's trade deficit was at its highest level. In the following years, however, the deficit began to decline due to an economic downturn and reduced demand for imports.

At this stage, it is useful to examine the components of the current account more carefully. As can be seen from Table 2.4, while in the earlier part of 1990s the trade balance accounted for around 70 per cent of the current account, by 2000 its share of current account dropped significantly to 20 per cent. That was mainly because of income transfer items, such as interest payments on debts, which became more and more important in determining the level of the current account balance. As it can be seen from Table 2.4, interest payments as a proportion of exports increased from 23 per cent in 1992 to 41 per cent in 1999 and 39 per cent in 2001. In other words, it was the interest payments on debts that were absorbing an increasing proportion of export earnings and raising the current account deficit. Clearly, if the peso had been devalued earlier, the burden of interest payments would have increased too, putting extra pressure on the economy. As can be seen from Table 2.4, while in 1992 the amount of interest paid was US$3,494 million, by 2000 it had gone up to a peak of US$12,352, which was an increase of 313 per cent. The decline that appears in the interest paid after 2001 is mainly because the government unilaterally defaulted on its external debts and entered into a moratorium and negotiations with the IMF and other domestic and international creditors.

It is also important to draw attention to the significant surplus in the capital and financial accounts of the balance of payments that was covering the current account deficits in the 1990s. The fact that Argentina managed to enjoy a high rate of growth in the early 1990s was to a large extent due to the growing capital inflows that entered the country. In this respect, the Currency Board and its ability to reduce the rate of inflation and stabilize the economy had clearly played an important role.

Once again, as can be seen from Table 2.4, the bulk of the capital and financial accounts was made up of financial surpluses that were coming

Table 2.4 Estimates for balance of payments[1] (millions of US$)

	1992	1993(1)	1994	1995	1996	1997	1998	1999	2000	2001	2002	2003	2004
Current account	−5,548	−8,206	−10,979	−5,118	−6,769	−12,137	−14,482	−11,944	−8,8981	−3,291	8,673	7,659	3,349
Merchandise	−1,396	−2,364	−4,139	2,357	1,760	−2,123	−3,097	−795	2,452	7,385	17,178	16,448	13,239
FOB exports	12,399	13,269	16,023	21,162	24,043	26,431	26,434	23,309	26,341	26,543	25,651	29,566	34,550
FOB imports	13,795	15,633	20,162	18,804	22,283	28,554	29,531	24,103	23,889	19,158	8,473	13,118	21,311
Services	−2,558	−3,326	−3,779	−3,436	−3,547	−4,385	−4,444	−4,111	−4,284	−3,863	−1,582	−1,390	−1,694
Exports	2,984	3,071	3,364	3,826	4,405	4,519	4,854	4,719	4,935	4,627	3,290	4,205	5,147
Imports	5,542	6,396	7,143	7,212	7,952	8,904	9,298	8,830	9,219	9,490	4,873	5,601	6,841
Trade balance*	−3,954	−5,689	−7,918	−1,079	−1,787	−6,508	−7,541	−4,906	−1,832	3,522	15,506	15,058	11,545
TB/CA* (%)[2]	71	69	72	21	26	53	52	41	20	−107	179	196	345
Incomes	−2,384	−3,069	−3,559	−4,636	−5,401	−6,144	−7,405	−7,491	−7,540	−7,237	−7,484	−7,970	−8,884
Invest. income	−2,395	−3,069	−3,569	−4,648	−5,474	−6,141	−7,400	−7,502	−7,556	−7,241	−7,466	−7,952	−8,858
Interest	−1,470	−1,578	−1,770	−2,555	−3,374	−4,221	−5,107	−5,887	−5,947	−6,983	−7,697	−7,319	−6,890
Earned	2,024	2,037	3,004	3,820	3,954	4,606	5,240	5,442	6,405	5,179	2,653	2,613	2,874
Paid	3,494	3,609	4,774	6,375	7,353	8,826	10,347	11,329	12,352	12,162	10,349	9,932	9,764
Interest paid/exports%*	23	22	25	26	26	29	33	41	40	39	36	29	24
Earnings and div.	−924	−1,501	−1,799	−2,094	−2,080	−1,920	−2,293	−1,616	−1,609	−258	230	−633	−1,968
Earned	335	489	460	525	461	857	869	598	978	635	350	451	599
Paid	1,259	1,990	2,358	2,619	2,541	2,777	3,162	2,213	2,588	893	120	1,084	2,567
Capital and financial a/c.	9,119	14,196	13,781	7,701	12,249	17,709	18,354	13,772	8,631	−5,439	−11,404	−3,176	1,908
Capital a/c.	16	16	18	14	51	66	73	149	106	157	406	70	45

Financial a/c	9,153	14,180	13,764	7,617	12,198	17,643	18,281	13,623	8,737	−5,595	−11,810	−3,246	1,864
Banking	1,305	−1,695	1,999	4,692	−197	−909	3,505	1,330	67	11,588	−253	−3,001	−3,097
BCRA(2)	288	−3,064	444	1,922	1,003	−586	−512	−1,033	762	10,743	−1,808	−868	1,990
Other financial institutes	1,017	1,369	1,555	2,770	−1,200	−323	4,017	2,363	−695	854	−765	2,133	−1,107
Non-financial public	796	7,014	3,994	5,855	9,024	8,163	9,361	10,886	8,258	−3,618	4,618	4,637	4,946
National govt	1,352	6,376	4,367	6,325	8,755	6,808	9,525	10,188	7,414	−2,923	3,683	4,785	5,072
Local govt	43	879	190	394	733	1,733	149	1,364	1,276	−59	237	167	191
Company and others	−599	−241	−563	−864	−464	−376	−313	−586	−433	−404	−302	−265	−317
Non-financial	7,053	8,861	7,771	−2,860	3,371	10,389	5,414	1,407	305	−13,798	−12,856	−4,882	15
Changes in international reserves	3,274	4,250	682	−102	3,882	3,273	3,438	1,201	−439	−12,083	−4,516	3,581	5,320
BCRA's reserve	3,105	4,480	561	−69	3782	3062	3,442	1,093	−424	−12,005	−4,437	3,643	5,527
Adjustments	−169	230	−121	33	−100	−211	4	−108	15	79	79	62	208

Notes: * Author's own calculation.
[1] Figures in 1993 include debt settled through debt refinancing under the 1992 Financial Plan. The corresponding issuance is recorded under Non-financial public sector (national government) together with the rest of the rescheduled debt.
[2] The negative sign in 2001 was due to the fact that the trade balance in that year turned into surplus while the current account was in deficit. In the following years, between 2002 and 2004, both the trade balance and current account moved into surplus with the trade surplus much larger than the current account surplus.

Sources: Data collected from Table A5.1, Argentine Ministry of Economy and Production, September 2005, based on the data produced by the National Bureau of International Accounts INDEC.

through financial institutions in the form of borrowing by banks and government borrowing in the form of foreign currency bonds and securities.

The question that might arise here is why did the Currency Board not prevent the government and banks from excessive external borrowing? Clearly, it should have been apparent that the large amounts of interest payments on borrowings could not have been maintained for long, and their growth was endangering the very existence of the Currency Board and the stability of the economy.

The large amount of external debt that had reached over US$145 billion in 2002 clearly had an asymmetrical impact on the ability of the Currency Board to maintain the value of currency. Indeed, the capital account surplus was drastically reversed later when a large number of depositors who suspected the collapse of the Currency Board tried to move their funds out of the country. Within a short period of time, financial accounts of balance of payments dropped from over US$8.6 billion surplus in 2000 to nearly US$12.6 billion deficit in 2002.

Government fiscal policies

At this stage it is important to examine the position of the government budget and its expenditures. As can be seen from Table 2.5, apart from in 1993 (when the government experienced a budget surplus) throughout the following years it was running a growing budget deficit. By 2001, the budget deficit had increased to the high level of 8.71 billion pesos. It is important to note that the 2.73 billion pesos surplus in 1993 was primarily built up due to the large number of privatization programmes that took place in the early 1990s. But the significant fall in the budget balances was a clear indication of the mismanagement of public funds.

Table 2.5 clearly shows that the budget moved into deficit even before the external shocks of 1999. The bulk of the budget deficit was financed through external borrowing. This is evident when we compare the amount of interest paid on external debt and domestic debt. That was particularly problematic in view of the fact that the government was not earning much foreign currency. Indeed, even in its best years Argentina's trade balance would not have been sufficient to cover the costs of interest payments. Table 2.5 also shows that only in one year between 1998 and 1999, during the presidential election campaign, the current

Table 2.5 Public sector finances non-financial public sector cash basis (millions of pesos)

	1993	1994	1995	1996	1997	1998	1999	2000	2001	2002	2003	2004
Current revenue	44,756	47,458	48,017	46,005	53,838	55,999	54,640	55,212	50,266	54,986	77,123	104,968
Taxes	29,007	31,614	31,035	33,176	38,352	40,363	38,626	40,671	37,165	40,034	60,737	83,584
Current expenditure	40,197	45,570	47,429	48,457	55,099	56,814	59,010	59,501	56,530	57,450	72,219	87,656
Interest on domestic debt	362	235	193	148	248	215	224	152	73	981	1,883	1,873
Interest on external debt	2,552	2,916	3,891	4,460	5,541	6445	8,000	9,504	10,102	5,828	5,000	3,830
Total income	45,423	48,265	49,273	46,506	54,574	56,508	57,418	55,613	50,455	55,083	77,215	105,106
Total expenses	42,693	48,349	50,646	52,021	58,894	60,581	62,187	62,405	59,174	59,633	75,409	93,448
Overall surplus	2,731	−842	−1,373	−5,514	−4,320	−4,074	−4,768	−6,792	−8,719	−4,549	1,805	11,658

Source: Data collected from Table A6.1, Argentine Ministry of Economy and Production, September 2005.

expenditures increased by nearly 3 billion pesos, which was clearly very difficult to finance through trade in goods and services.

At the end of 1999, when the government of President De la Rúa was elected to office, it was decided to raise taxes in order to reduce the budget deficit, and increase both income and Value Added Tax.[12] At a later stage, the government also increased fuel tax and introduced a financial transaction tax that charged private individuals and business for every financial transaction they made. These contractionary fiscal policies came at the worst possible time, with serious negative side effects. As can be seen from Table 2.5, although the new tax rules initially increased government revenue from 38.62 billion pesos in 1999 to 40.67 billion pesos in 2000, they soon began to backfire. The higher taxes not only adversely affected economic activities, but also encouraged the amount of tax evasion.[13] Accordingly in 2001, government tax revenue dropped to 37.1 billion pesos, even lower than the 1997 level.

Another side effect of the tax increases was that they alarmed the public over the government's deep financial difficulty, which raised the country risk premium. As a result, the government was faced with an increasing cost of borrowing, and became less and less able to repay its debt (see also Schuler, 2003).

It is interesting to note that public sector debt was mostly financed through borrowing in foreign currency either in the form of bond issues or short-term loans from multilateral agencies. They also borrowed from private banks and various official organizations (such the Paris club), though on a smaller scale. As can be seen from Table 2.6, while the size of public sector debt to official organizations dropped from 10,162 million pesos in 1996 to 4,477 million pesos in December 2001, its debt to multilateral agencies kept rising from 16,367 million pesos (or US$)[14] in December 1996 to 33,141 billion pesos/dollars in September 2001. In other words, within the span of five years Argentina nearly doubled its borrowing from the multilateral agencies.

Note also that the while share of debt to multilateral agencies of the total debt increased from 16.85 per cent in December 1996 to 22.40 per cent in December 2001, that of private creditors increased only from 0.29 per cent in 1996 to 1.10 per cent at the end of June 2001. This raises the link between the continuous lending by multilateral organizations and the issue of moral hazard. In other words, while private creditors were carefully restraining their lending to Argentina, multilateral agencies continued to lend irrespective of the growing size of Argentina's external debt. This clearly raised the issue of moral hazard.

Table 2.6 Total public sector debt by instrument and type of term[1] (millions of pesos)

End of	1992[2]	1993	1994	1995	1996	1997	1998	1999	2000	2001	2002	2003	2004	31-03-05
I-Total Debt (II + III	**63,250**	**71,112**	**81,820**	**88,711**	**99,046**	**103,718**	**114,134**	**123,366**	**129,750**	**144,222**	**152,974**	**178,768**	**191,242**	**189,754**
II- Medium and long-term transactions	54,018	71,112	81,820	88,7111	99,046	103,718	114,134	123,366	129,750	144,194	141,509	150,878	141,507	137433
Government bonds and securities[3]	**17,184**	**48,401**	**57,109**	**59,048**	**69,393**	**74,801**	**82,363**	**91,555**	**98,895**	**83,051**	**83,477**	**87,004**	**81,371**	**78,732**
(% of total debt)	**(27)**	**(68)**	**(70)**	**(67)**	**(70)**	**(72)**	**(72)**	**(74)**	**(76)**	**(58)**	**(55)**	**(49)**	**(43)**	**(41)**
Domestic currency	5,174	6,340	9,278	6,705	9,045	10,377	8,678	7,268	5,252	2,445	6,450	9,823	8,962	9,122
(% of Total Debt)	(8)	(9)	(11)	(8)	(9)	(10)	(8)	(6)	(4)	(2)	(4)	(5)	(5)	(5)
Foreign currency	12,010	42,061	47,831	52,343	60,348	64,424	73,685	84,287	93,643	80,605	77,027	77,181	72,408	69,610
(% of Total Debt)	(19)	(59)	(58)	(59)	(61)	(62)	(65)	(68)	(72)	(56)	(54)	(43)	(38)	(37)
Loans	**36,834**	**22,711**	**24,711**	**29,663**	**29,653**	**28,917**	**31,771**	**31,811**	**30,855**	**61,143**	**56,953**	**61,348**	**60,136**	**58,701**
Guaranteed loans	**0**	**0**	**0**	**0**	**0**	**0**	**0**	**0**	**0**	**21,284**	**11,636**	**14,124**	**14,612**	**15,269**
Official organizations	**7,380**	**9,698**	**10,8**	**11,904**	**10,063**	**8,311**	**7,634**	**6,258**	**5,017**	**5,876**	**4,935**	**4,428**	**3,382**	**3,139**
(% of total debt)	(12)	(14)	(13)	(13)	(10)	(8)	(7)	(5)	(4)	(4)	(3)	(2)	(2)	(2)
Multilateral organisations[4]	**7,279**	**10,944**	**11,6**	**14,86**	**16,2**	**16,79**	**19,16**	**20,31**	**21,75**	**32,35**	**31,37**	**32,11**	**30,59**	**28,98**
(% of total debt)	**(12)**	**(15)**	**(14)**	**(17)**	**(16)**	**(16)**	**(17)**	**(16)**	**(17)**	**(22)**	**(21)**	**(18)**	**(16)**	**(15)**
Guaranteed debt – Decree 1579/02 (BOGAR)	0	0	0	0	0	0	0	0	0	0	8,179	9,881	10,208	10,706
Commercial banks	21,736	1,564	1,702	1,908	2,280	2,366	3,585	3,655	2,168	715	563	527	397	358
(% of total debt)	(34)	(2)	(2)	(2)	(2)	(2)	(3)	(3)	(2)	(0.5)	(0.4)	(0.3)	(0.2)	(0.2)
Other creditors[5]	**439**	**505**	**512**	**989**	**1,053**	**1,445**	**1,385**	**1,587**	**1,913**	**911**	**264**	**273**	**940**	**243**
Transitory advances (Central Bank)	0	0	0	0	0	0	0	0	0	0	1,079	2,526	4,468	4,497
III Areas	**9,232**	**0**	**0**	**0**	**0**	**0**	**0**	**0**	**0**	**28**	**11,465**	**27,890**	**45,268**	**47,823**

Notes: [1] Domestic and external debt in the financial and non-financial public sector. The former includes the debt of BCRA and that taken by government-owned banks guaranteed by the nation, but excludes the debt destined to their own financing.

[2] Debt balances up to 31/12/92 were estimated to fit the registries according to the effect produced on those balances and its composition produced by the Brady Plan.

[3] Include Letes (Treasury bill).

[4] Include loans from the International Monetary Fund (IMF), International Bank for Reconstruction and Development (IBRD), InterAmerican Development Bank (IDB), Fund for the Financial Development of the River Plate Basin (FONPLATA), International Agricultural Development Fund (FIDA).

[5] Includes loans from suppliers and credit lines opened for provinces, according to Decree No. 1,023/95.

Source: Data collected by the author from Table A6.11, Argentine Ministry of Economy and Production, September 2005.

In the case of debt to private banks, though it increased fourfold from 1,452 million pesos in 1996 to 5,029 pesos in 1999, it began to fall from 1999 onwards when the government tried to use short-term borrowing from the multilateral agencies and long-term borrowing through bond issues to repay its debt to private banks.

By mid-2001, the government debt to private banks had dropped to 2.78 billion pesos, which was only about 2.11 per cent of its total debt. Nevertheless, as the government was the largest single borrower from banks, its failure to repay its debt to domestic banks was the most important factor in the bank liquidity crisis and the ensuing inability to repay depositors when the public began to panic.

As mentioned earlier, the government's main method of borrowing in the late 1990s was through bonds and other securities denominated in foreign currency. Between December 1996 and September 2001, the government borrowed over US$30 billion directly from the domestic and foreign institutions by issuing domestic and foreign currency bonds and securities. The level of domestic currency bonds, however, was very small compared with foreign currency bonds. As can be seen from Table 2.6, between 1996 and 2001, while the amount of foreign currency bonds issued increased from US$60.6 billion in 1996 to US$93.5 billion in 2001, the level of domestic currency bonds kept falling from US$8.1 billion in 1996 to US$1.5 billion in 2001.

This trend also clearly demonstrates the mismatch of currency liability and government assets, the government being the biggest borrower in the country. In other words, while government revenue was mostly in pesos, a very large proportion of its liabilities were in dollars. That is why the slightest hint of the possibility of government default had enormous implications for the lenders and, in that respect, for banks that had lent to the government, even though the size of domestic bank lending to the government was much smaller than that of other lenders. The fall in the amount of bonds issued in domestic currency also suggests the reluctance of domestic lenders to lend to the government. This, in turn, raises some questions about the strength of risk assessment by the multilateral agencies, who seem to have clearly misjudged the ability of the Argentine government to repay its debt.

The significant increase in external public debt is a clear indication of the asymmetry between the objectives of the Currency Board and the behaviour of the government. Currency boards, in principle, are responsible for protecting the value of a country's currency and enhancing its economic stability. Therefore, in order to prevent the possibility of currency devaluation, they should be able to have a say in the level of external borrowing by the public sector. Yet, in the case of Argentina the Currency Board did not seem to have been able to restrict government's external borrowing. This is particularly apparent from Table 2.7, which shows the growth of public debt service as a proportion of GDP. This ratio rose from 1.85 per cent in 1993 to 5.33 per cent in 2001. By 2001, the ratio of public sector debt service to GDP was 5.31 per cent, which was nearly half that of the export sector of GDP.[15] In other words, nearly half of the foreign exchanges that were earned through exports were absorbed by the public sector debt services.

The next question that has to be addressed is why did public sector debt grow so much? No doubt, the economic recession that had started in 1998 forced the government to take certain measures to help the economy to cope with external shocks. Consequently, public expenditure rose from over 55 billion pesos in 1997 to over 61 billion pesos in 1999. It is also true that under a currency board the only policy tool that remains available to a government is fiscal policy. It is equally important for the government not to undermine the ability of the currency board to protect the value of the currency, and hence refrain from exposure to external debt and excessive borrowing in general. This was clearly not observed in the case of Argentina, where government external debt increased by over 14 billion dollars between the end of 1999 and the third quarter of 2001. It might be argued that in 1999 the government was considering it more important to pull the economy out of recession than to be concerned with the long-term effects of borrowing. Moreover, the government was hoping to be able to raise more tax revenue once the economy was out of recession. But, by spending well beyond its means, the government merely postponed the emergence of the crisis.

The rise in public expenditure was not only due to government efforts to deal with external shocks, but also due to the relaxed spending at the end of President Menem's administration, when he was campaigning for a third term of office in 1998.[16] This is evident from the rise in expenditure on the operation of the state, which sharply increased by over three billion pesos between 1997 to 1999, and in particular in 1998. Both public expenditure and expenditure on the operation of the state dropped in 2000 once the presidential election was over. The combination of this spending cost the country nearly three billion pesos in the form of interest payments over three years, and much greater public debt which continues to burden the economy.

Table 2.7 Consolidated public expenditure by purpose (millions of pesos, of 2001) 1993–2002

	Operation of the state		Public expenditure		Economic services		Public debt services		Total	
Year		% GDP		% GDP		% GDP		% GDP		% GDP
1993	15,457	6.15	50,892	20.26	8,557	3.41	4,645	1.85	79,55	31.66
1994	16,833	6.30	55,986	20.97	7,346	2.75	4,680	1.75	84,845	31.77
1995	15,859	6.25	53,696	21.17	7,198	2.84	5,679	2.24	82,431	32.50
1996	15,414	5.87	52,681	20.06	6,335	2.41	5,800	2.21	80,230	30.56
1997	15,976	5.67	55,669	19.76	6,323	2.24	7,529	2.67	85,497	30.35
1998	17,409	5.98	58,049	19.95	6,857	2.36	7,833	2.69	90,147	30.99
1999*	19,510	6.90	61,230	21.64	6,067	2.14	10,087	3.56	96,894	34.24
2000*	18,083	6.47	59,273	21.21	5,186	1.86	11,916	4.26	94,458	33.80
2001*	17,833	6.64	58,112	22.00	4,944	1.84	14,264	5.31	96,153	35.78
2002*	11,567	5.62	40,110	19.47	2,863	1.39	5,407	2.63	59,947	29,11

Notes: * Preliminary figures.

Source: Collected from Table A6.4 Argentine Ministry of Economy and Production, September 2005

Economic performance after Convertibility Law

As mentioned earlier, from August 2002 the economy appeared to be stabilizing, and economic activities started gradually to resume some degree of normality. The relaxation of the freeze on chequing accounts in October 2002 also helped to reignite the economy, though deposit accounts continued to remain frozen until 2003. The government also seized the dollar reserves of banks, which cost them around 1.6 billion dollars, and imposed exchange control.

In November 2002, Argentine defaulted on its loan to the World Bank. But domestically they gradually relaxed some of the controls by first relaxing the '*corralito*' and unfreezing chequing and savings accounts, and later by removing the foreign exchange controls. Foreign exchange controls were further relaxed in January 2003, when the IMF agreed to renew Argentina's outstanding loans. On March 2003, the Argentine Supreme Court nullified the pesofication of certain deposits.

The last phase of unfreezing deposits began in April 2003, when depositors were able to recover 80–85 per cent of their original dollar deposits. According to Schuler (2003), at the above rate of recovery the depositors still lost US$9 billion. It is also important to note that the depositors received no compensation for inflation when interest rates were frozen.

A careful examination of monthly balances of lending by financial institutions to the public sector in Table 2.2 (p.18) clearly shows that from early 2002, while the balances of foreign currency lending to the public sector kept falling, the balances of peso lending to the public sector increased dramatically. This was largely due to both pesofication, which substantially reduced the balances of public sector debt to financial institutions, and partly due to the fact that no more new loans in foreign currency were forthcoming. More or less the same thing happened in the case of the private sector.

It is also important to point out that a large proportion of the loans in foreign currency were denominated in US dollars. According to anecdotal reports, on many occasions banks, in order to recover some of the dollar loans that they had extended to businesses, had to agree to write off a very large proportion of the debt on the condition that the borrowers repaid the remaining portion in dollars. In some cases, the amount of the write-off was as high as 75 per cent of the loan.

During 2002, despite the devaluation of peso, exports dropped by 4 per cent due to a shortage of credit which affected the entire economy, including the producers of exports. The sharp fall in lending in foreign currency also explains the dramatic fall in imports that was experienced during 2002.

The continuing difficulty in earning foreign currency income, also forced the government to default on its debt to the World Bank on 14 November 2002.

From 2003 onwards, however, there were more signs of a recovery, with inflation falling, the peso stabilizing and both the trade balance and the current account moving into surplus. According to the latest data reported by the Argentine Ministry of Economy and Production (September 2005), in June 2005, in real terms, based on 1993 prices, the Argentine economy grew by 11.73 per cent in 2003, and by 9.09 per cent in 2004.

Clearly, the initial rise in inflation, has been mainly due to devaluation of the peso and a high level of uncertainty about the future value of the peso, the state of the economy and the length of time during which deposits were to remain frozen. All those factors instantly created a substantial excess demand for goods as a store of value and a substitute for the currency and money whose value had become very unpredictable. The substantial fall in aggregate demand and economic depression of 2002, and later the stabilization of the economy, however, forced producers and retailers to restrain their price increases during 2003. Bearing in mind also that average annual real GDP had dropped to 235.2 billion pesos in 2002, which was well below previous years. Indeed, this level was well below the 256.6 billion pesos that had prevailed in 1996, when the economy was operating more or less at full employment with nearly zero inflation. That clearly indicates the extent by which the economy was operating below full capacity. Hence, it is easy to see why, despite the devaluation of the peso, inflation was falling in 2002–03. The more recent data, however, shows that since the first quarter of 2004, inflation measured by the consumer price index (CPI) has been rising again and, despite the growth in the productive sectors, it has considerably exceeded the 1994 levels when the Currency Board was in place (see Figure 2.10).

The questions that remains to be answered is the extent by which the present growth rate is likely to continue, and the extent by which the devaluation of the peso is likely to help the exports sector.

No doubt the economy is likely to exhibit a more impressive rate of growth when it is recovering from a very low level. But the extent to which the trend will follow is questionable. This is, indeed, evident from Figure 2.9, where we can see that the trade surplus that was experienced in 2003 is declining again.

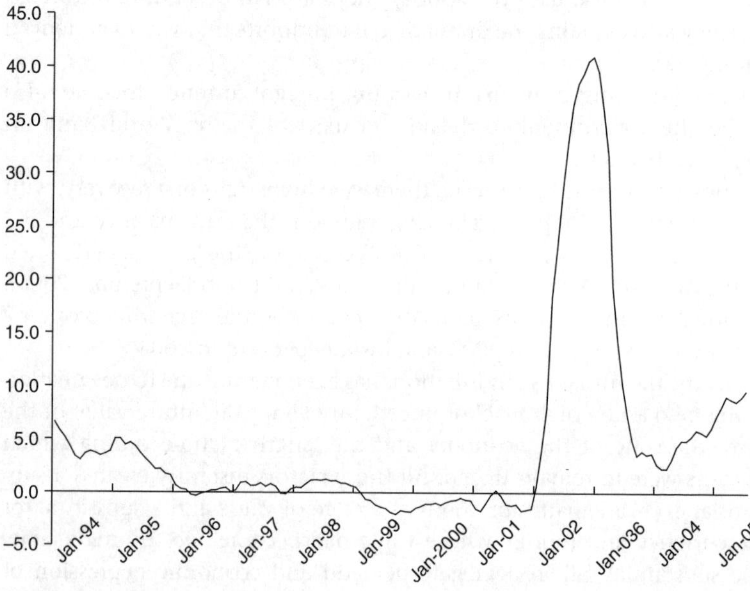

Figure 2.10 Annual inflation rate, based on monthly consumer price index (CPI), 1994–July 2005

Source: Produced by author using data provided in Table A4.2, Argentine Ministry of Economy and Production, September 2005.

It should also be pointed out that while imports in total fell by 50 per cent in 2002, imports of consumer goods fell by nearly 72 per cent, well below the 1991 level. It is obvious that such a dramatic fall in the import of consumer goods should have diverted demand away from imports and in favour of domestic goods; an important factor which has helped the increase in domestic production and the recovery of the economy in 2003. The gradual rise in imports since 2003 clearly has been in response to the recovery of economic activity. But it is also worth noting that in 2005, after nearly 3 years of devaluation, the overall level of imports is still below its peak in 1998, when the economy had started to experience recession. It is also interesting to note that although overall exports have increased since 2002, the increase in exports to MERCOSUR, the USA and the EU has not been very impressive, given the high level of devaluation of the peso against the US dollar. Indeed, the trend in Figure 2.8 confirms that exports of primary products and manufactured agricultural goods usually destined to the EU and the USA have not increased dramatically. The products whose exports have increased more are the manufactured industrial goods, which appear to have been exported to destinations other than the EU, the USA and MERCOSUR.

Moreover, there appears to be a distinct switch in favour of imports from MERCOSUR rather than the USA and the EU that tend to be the origin of imports of capital and intermediate goods (see Figure 2.6).

It is important to point out also that part of the current recovery is due to the fact that many businesses that had previously borrowed in foreign currency managed to receive a substantial discount on their debts to banks, which clearly reduced their cost. But that was clearly a one-off event and unlikely to reoccur.

It is also important to point out that, as is evident from Tables 2.4 and 2.6, despite the improvement in Argentina's trade surplus, the current account surplus is still well below the country's total debt, clearly indicating that devaluation of the peso cannot generate sufficient foreign exchange revenue to cover the external debt. Indeed, as can be seen from Table 2.6, Argentina's total debt has increased from 144.2 billion pesos in 2001 to 189.7 billion pesos in 2005, with the arrears increasing from 28 million pesos in 2001 to 47.8 billions in 2005. This is a clear indication that despite the abandonment of the Currency Board and devaluation of the peso, the improved trade balances have not been sufficient to reduce the total debt. Instead, the overall debt has continued to grow well above the earlier levels, with rising arrears.

Conclusion

The present study has shown that, contrary to the common view that overvaluation of the peso was responsible for Argentina's loss of competitiveness and the 2002 crisis, the overvaluation of the peso could not have been solely responsible for the crisis. Moreover, those who claim that the peso was overvalued appear to have used the consumer price index in calculation of the real value of the peso rather than the producer price index. Indeed, if one uses producer price index in an assessment of the real value of the peso in the 1990s, it becomes clear that there was much less overvaluation than was suggested by many authors, and in some years the peso was in fact undervalued rather than overvalued. A careful examination of the external accounts also revealed that despite the claims of overvaluation, Argentina had a trade surplus with MERCOSUR throughout the period of the Currency Board, and a deficit with the EU and the USA, a trend that is almost reversing since the devaluation of the peso, partly due to the substantial fall in imports from the EU and the USA and the switch in favour of imports from MERCOSUR.

It has also been highlighted that even though exports have increased in response to devaluation of the peso, the dramatic fall in imports has been the main factor responsible for the improvement of the trade balance and current accounts of the balance of payments. No doubt, devaluation of the peso was influential in the fall in imports but it was the economic recession that hit the country after the crisis that was the prime cause of the fall in imports, a trend that is very likely to be reversed once the economy fully rebounds, and demand for imports increases again. The study also found that despite the significant devaluation of the peso and some improvements in the current account, the country is still suffering from growing public debt and rising arrears.

The study showed that while the export sector continued to account for around 11 per cent of the GDP throughout the 1990s, the external debt continued to rise and peaked at 51 per cent of GDP in 2000, when the economy had moved into a recession. Following the devaluation of the peso, the increase in exports raised its share of GDP to 25.5 per cent, but despite the rise in GDP, the overall debt accounted for 42.7 per cent of GDP, which was still well above the share of exports. Thus, the study clearly shows that devaluation of the peso on its own cannot generate sufficient income to repay the debt.

The chapter has also highlighted the underlying asymmetries between the economic impact of fiscal policies and the Currency Board, and the need for greater flexibility in times of external shocks. Finally, it is important for currency boards to have greater control over the level of foreign currency lending by banks, external borrowing by the government and supervision of banks.

Notes

1. According to Schuler (2003) the cost of conversion for depositors was estimated to be equivalent to US$23 billion. Also, as loans were converted at the rate of one peso to one dollar, compared to 1.40 pesos per dollar, the cost to banks was estimated to be around 12 billion US dollars.
2. During 2002, the average annual real GDP based on 1993 prices fell by 10.9 per cent below the 2001 values and, at some point, dropped even below the 1993 level.
3. By the end of 2002 CPI inflation reached the peak of 41 per cent.
4. Following the Mexican financial crisis of 1994, the Argentine economy was initially hit by the so-called 'tequila effect', and its interest rate exhibited a considerable degree of volatility, but this soon stabilized and the spread between the dollar and peso rates declined to a low level.
5. Mr Cavallo was also the economy minister in 1991 during President Menem's office when the Convertibility Law was introduced.
6. The resignation of the Central Bank governor was in opposition to Mr Cavallo's intention to introduce certain amendments to the rules of the Convertibility Law to allow some use of the monetary policy to stimulate economic growth.
7. In a number of cases, the banks that had lent to the government were branches of foreign banks operating in Argentina.
8. The real exchange rate here is measured as follows:

$$RER = [NER(Arg\ \$/FC)/CPI\ (Arg)) \times CPI\ (FC)]$$

where RER is real exchange rate, NER is nominal exchange rate, FC is foreign currency, and CPI(Arg) is Argentine the consumer price index, and CRI(FC) is the consumer price index of the country of foreign currency.
9. These could have been calculated only from 1998 onwards when Euro had been officially launched.
10. Among NAFTA members, the USA is the largest market in terms of both destination of Argentina's exports and origin of imports.
11. The most important of Argentina's exports to the NAFTA, the EU and other non-neighbouring countries are items such as crude oil, soya, wheat, vegetable oils, leather and meat.
12. As reported by Schuler (2003), the combined rate of federal income tax paid by employers and employees went up to 32.9 per cent, with the top rate reaching as high as 35 per cent and VAT amounting to 21 per cent.
13. As reported by Schuler (2003), between 30–50 per cent of all transactions evade taxes, and around 23 per cent of payments are under the table payments to avoid tax
14. Based on the one to one exchange rate between the peso and the dollar, the amounts stated in the peso were the same as the amounts stated in the dollars.
15. According to the data provided in Table A1.4 of the Argentine Ministry of Economy and Production (2005), in 2001 exports accounted for about 10.5 per cent of GDP.

16. The constitution laws allow a president to run only for two terms of office. To be able to run for a third term of office, there was a need for an amendment to the constitution. Therefore, to win such an amendment, President Menem was trying hard to win the approval of provincial local authorities.

References

Calvo, A.G., Izquierdo, A. and Talvi, E. (2002) 'Sudden Stops, the Real Exchange Rate and Fiscal Sustainability: Argentina's Lessons', Inter-American Development Research Department, *www.iadb.org/res/pdf/Macro_Crisis.pd*

Carrera, J. (2002) 'Hard Peg and Monetary Unions. Main Lessons from the Argentine Experience', *150.108.69.10/public/m-union/ abstracts/Carrerapaper.pdf*

Catão, L. and Falcetti, E. (1999) 'Determinants of Argentina's External Trade', IMF Working Paper, September, WP/99/121, *www.imf.org/external/pubs/ft/wp/1999/wp99121.pdf*

Cuevas, A. (2003) 'Reforming Intergovernmental Fiscal Relations in Argentina', IMF Working Paper, WP/03/90, *www.imf.org/external/pubs/ft/wp/2003/ wp0390.pdf*

Grandes, M. and Reisen, H. (2002) 'Hard Peg versus Soft Float, A Tale of Two Latin American Countries', February, *www.oecd.org/pdf/M00029000/M00029269.*

Hanke, S.H. (2003) 'The Argentine Straw Man: A Response to Currency Board Critics', *Cato* 23, 1 (Spring/Summer).

Hanke, S.H. (2002a) 'International Economic and Exchange Rate Policy Hearings', May, *http://www.cato.org/testimony/ct-hanke050102.html*

Hanke, S.H. (2002b) 'Argentina: Caveat Lector', presented at the Cato Institute's 20th Annual Monetary Conference, October.

Krugman, P. (2002) 'Crying with Argentina', *New York Times*, 1 January, *http://www.pkarchive.org/column/010102.html*

Perry, G. and Serven, L. (2002) 'The Anatomy of a Multiple Crisis: Why Was Argentina Special and What Can We Learn From It', World Bank, *www.nber.org/crisis/argentina_bg.html*

Powell, A. (2003)'The Argentine Crisis: Bad Luck, Bad Management, Bad Advice', in S.M. Collins and D. Rodrik (eds), *Brookings Trade Forum 2002*, 1–59 (Washington, DC: Brookings Institution).

Roubini, N. (2001) 'Should Argentina Dollarize or Float? The Pros and Cons of Alternative Exchange Rate Regimes and Their Implications for Domestic and Foreign Debt Restructuring/Reduction', *www.bradynet.com/bbs/argentina/ 100122–0.html*

Sachs, J.D., (2002) 'Argentina's Monetary Mess', Project Syndicate, 29/01/2002, *www.project-syndicate.org/commentary/sac42/English*

Schuler, K. (2003) 'Argentina's Economic Crisis: Causes and Cures', Report to Joint Economic Committee, United States Congress, www.house.gov/jec/imf/06–13–03long.pdf

Schuler, K. (2002) 'Fixing Argentina', http:/www.dollarization.org

Stiglitz, J. (2002) 'Lessons from Argentina's Debacle', Global Policy Forum, 10 January, http://www.globalpolicy.org/socecon/bwi-wto/imf/202/0110stiglitz.htm

Torre, A. and Schmukler, S.L. (2002) 'Argentina's Financial Crisis: Floating Money, Sinking Banking', Latin American and the Caribbean Region, and the Development Research Group, World Bank, www.nber.org/~confer/2002/argentina02/schmukler.pdf

Union Bank of Switzerland (2000) 'Prices and Earnings Around the Globe: An International Comparison of Purchasing Power' (Zurich: Union Bank of Switzerland).

Official publications

Argentine Ministry of Economy and Production (September 2005), http://www.mecon.gov.ar/peconomica/basehome/infoeco_ing.html

Argentine Ministry of Economy and Production (August 2005), http://www.mecon.gov.ar/peconomica/basehome/infoeco_ing.html

Argentina Economic Indicators (January 2004), Ministerio de Economia República Argentin, www.mecon.gov.ar/default_english.htm

Argentina Stabilization Process (April 2003), *Secretariat of Finance Ministry of Economy*, www.mecon.gov.ar/default_english.htm

'Argentina at a Glance', 13 September 2001, www.worldbank.org/data/countrydata/aag/arg_aag.pdf

'Argentine Economic Program', Ministry of Economy (July 2002) www.mecon.gov.ar/basehome/comunicados_prensa/ economic_program.pdf

'Argentine Request for Stand-By Arrangement and Request for Extension of Repurchase Expectations', Staff Report, IMF Country Report 03/392 (December 2000), www.imf.org/external/pubs/ft/scr/2003/cr03392.pdf

Latin Focus (2003), http://www.latin-focus.com/latinfocus/countries/argentina/argentina.htm

World Economic Outlook (WEO) Database (December 2001) http://www.imf.org/external/pubs/ft/weo/2001/03/data/index.htm

3

International Prudential Regulation and the Prevention of Banking Crises in Latin America

Alexandre Minda and Stéphanie Truquin

Introduction

The assessment of Latin America's insertion into the process of globalization is a very delicate question. The Economic Commission for Latin America and the Caribbean (ECLAC) described the 1980s as the 'lost decade for development'. In spite of the wave of political democratization, the deployment of models of industrialization based on import substitution and the debt crisis caused a drop in per capita income. During the 1990s, the move towards a more extraverted strategy of industrialization and the adjustment programmes brought about economic progress, such as disinflation, productivity gains, the diversification of national production capacities and the growth of per capita income. However, because of the recurrence of financial crises and the absence of significant social progress we cannot say that it was a 'victorious decade'.

Despite the introduction of wide reforms, financial stability in Latin America remains fragile. The opening up of boundaries has made the subcontinent more vulnerable to international financial movements and to changes in the economic conditions of large developed nations. The Mexican, Brazilian and the recent Argentinean crises are examples of the financial instability of the region. Like foreign exchange and financial crises, banking crises are outward signs of this instability. The study of the banking sector is therefore fundamental because of the specific and particular role of this sector in the economy of a country. The banking sector plays an essential role in raising and allocating capital in emerging economies, where it intervenes more in financial intermediation than it does in developed countries.

Intermediating funds, transforming short term to long term, easing the flow of payments, managing liquidity, allocating credit, maintaining financial discipline among borrowers, all are banking functions that are essential for ensuring the smooth running of the real economy in the world. In Latin America, where financial markets are unevenly developed, banks are the one and only institutions capable of giving enough information to produce positive externalities.

However, banks evolve in an asymmetric information environment and are particularly prone to the imperfections of the market. They are intrinsically fragile. The fact that banking assets are less liquid than money balances makes their financial terms more burdensome and dependent on the confidence that savers have in the system. The slightest sign of trouble can lead to panic and push savers into withdrawing their funds from institutions. Banking crises have repercussions in the real sector likely to hinder economic growth Considerably. Thus, if an efficient banking sector can produce positive externalities and generate, or at least support, growth, an ailing banking sector can bring negative externalities to the rest of the economy.

The fragility of the banking sector can hinder the proper implementation of monetary policy by making its intermediate objectives less clear and by rendering the mechanisms through which monetary policy operates ineffective. Furthermore, public authorities bear a large part of the cost of financial crises, which raises public expenditure and increases the burden of national debt.

Nearly all of the crises that happened during the last decade came from emerging countries. One of the possible solutions to limit banking instability, widely discussed today, is to improve the regulation of the banking sector in developing countries. Is this normative regulation, supported by a group of measures concerning supervision and control (as in the Basel Accord, for example) appropriate to deal with the mechanisms of crises? Is it adapted to the economic and financial structures of emerging countries?

In order to answer these questions, we will first of all analyze the causes of the instability of the banking systems in Latin America. We will then examine the framework of the Basel Accord to see if it could be applied to the Latin American banking systems to limit their instability.

In Latin American banking systems

Banking crises are complex and are different from one another. There is a lot of literature on this subject that tends to make distinctions between macroeconomic and microeconomic causes. A great number of researchers have worked on this distinction in order to find 'predicative' indicators of crises; Caprio (1998), Demirguc-Kunt and Detragiache (1998), Evans *et al.* (2000), Hardy and Pazarbasioglu (1999). The study of factors that give rise to crises allows us to determine the typical behaviour of certain variables during the period preceding the beginning of banking failure.

In this chapter, we will present a non-exhaustive account of the different determining factors of the banking crises in Latin America in order to highlight the role of the 'bank actor' in the outgrowth of crises.[1] We will start by looking at the macroeconomic causes over which banks do not really have a hold and, in this sense we can consider them as being, in a certain way, the 'victims'. Then, we will expound the microeconomic factors where banks' involvement is much higher and where they become role-players in the fragility of the banking system.

Macroeconomic instability and banking fragility

The majority of banking crises are often preceded by the deterioration of macroeconomic conditions. Among the macroeconomic factors that contribute, directly or indirectly, to the instability of the banking systems in Latin America, we can mention monetary variables volatility, the exchange rate system, financial deregulation, the structure of deposits and economic policy.

Monetary variables' volatility

Latin American countries are often subject to large variations in the terms of trade; the first source of external volatility. This diminishes the borrowers' ability to repay their debts (i.e. Brazil, Figure 3.2). Gavin and Hausmann (1996) show that shocks effecting the terms of trade played an important role in the outbreak of the banking crises in Argentina, Chile, Columbia and Uruguay. Kaminsky and Reinhart (1996) identify the deterioration in the terms of trade as one of the stylized facts that precede banking crises, especially in mono-exporting countries or in countries where exports are concentrated in a few products (Venezuela or Ecuador) or in small economies that are not much diversified.

The volatility of international interest rates is another important external factor insofar as it can produce an induced effect on the flow of private capital. This volatility affects not only the cost of borrowing for emerging countries, it also calls into question the attractiveness of these countries for international investors. After a rise in rates, if banks were to find themselves in a situation where their money balances were too high, they could be tempted to grant more credit and would do this, at the price of poor quality.

A third source of external volatility is the evolution of real exchange rates which directly affects the banks' balance sheets (by causing a mismatch between assets and liabilities) and also the banks' clients. As with the variation in the terms of trade, Kaminsky and Reinhart (1996) consider the evolution of exchange rates as a factor announcing a banking crisis. This factor is particularly found in Latin American countries (see Figures 3.1–3.4) inclined to large fluctuations of their monetary variables. Furthermore, the volatility of these variables leads to 'blurring' information or, at least, to reducing its quality, and this could exacerbate the behaviour of moral hazard and adverse selection inherent in bank loans and reduce the horizon for investments.

As for the volatility of domestic variables, it is difficult for banks to evaluate credit risk when growth and inflation rates are very unstable: see the inflation curves of Argentina (Figure 3.1) and Brazil (Figure 3.2). In general, research on this subject shows that countries that have an unstable macroeconomic environment are also the countries that have the highest banking disorders. Fluctuations in the real sector, especially in the business sector, have repercussions on the strength of the banking sector through the quality of portfolio loans. Losses arising from bad debts, indeed, reduce the level of reserves and banks' capital.

Exchange rates system and banks' vulnerability

The exchange market is one of the channels in which credit risk and market risk, normally separated, become interdependent. It is also a favoured circuit of propagation towards neighbouring countries. Taking the example of Latin America, Gavin and Hausmann (1996) highlight the fact that exchange rate differences, considered to be untenable, have contributed to the outbreak of banking crises more so than strong variations in growth rates. It is true that the system of pegged or half-pegged exchange rates makes currencies more vulnerable to external shocks and this can cause a rise in interest rates or a balance of payments deficit. The Asian and Russian crises reinforced external constraints (world demand and raw material price shocks, redeployment of private capital, 'flight to quality'). Unable to devaluate, Latin American governments were forced to proceed to internal adjustments which brought their economies into recession and caused a deterioration of the solvency of the banks clients. If the move to a system of floating exchange rates, in certain cases, brought to a halt, the deterioration of solvency, the high level of external debt of Latin American countries

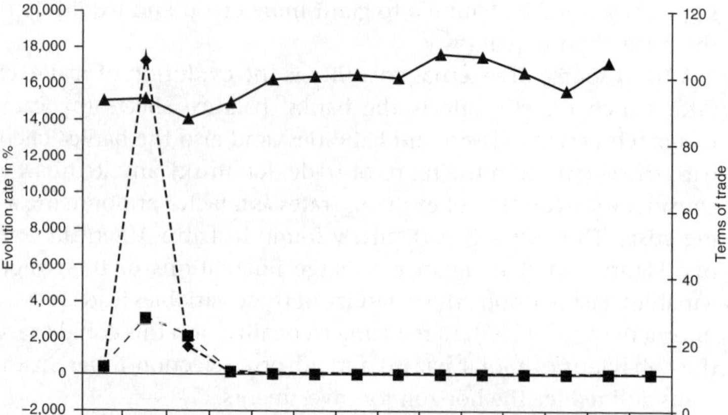

	1988	1989	1990	1991	1992	1993	1994	1995	1996	1997	1998	1999	2000	2001
Interest rate	371.9	17.235	1.517	61.7	16.8	11.3	8.1	11.9	7.4	7.0	7.6	8.1	8.3	16.2
Inflation	388.5	3.057	2.076	133.0	11.9	−1.5	2.9	3.2	−0.1	−0.5	−1.7	−1.9	0.8	−1.9
Terms of trade	93.1	93.6	87.7	92.5	99.4	100.4	100.9	100.0	107.1	106.3	101.6	96.1	104.5	

Years

Figure 3.1 Monetary variables' movements in Argentina
Source: World Bank Data Query (2002).

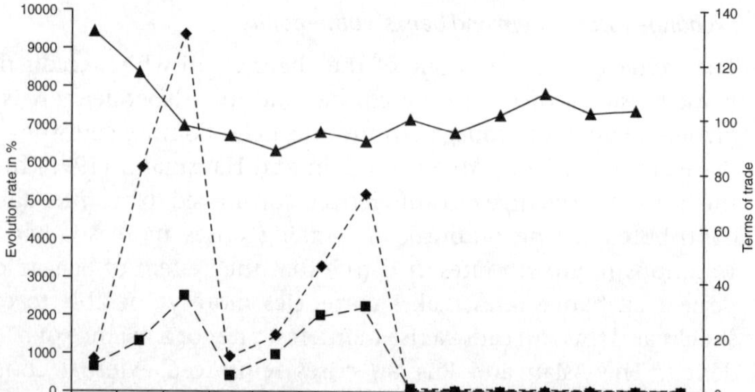

	1988	1989	1990	1991	1992	1993	1994	1995	1996	1997	1998	1999	2000	2001
Interest rate	859.4	5845.0	9394.3	913.5	1560.2	3293.5	5175.2	52.3	26.5	24.4	28.0	26.0	17.2	17.9
Inflation	651.1	1322.5	2509.5	415.3	968.5	1996.6	2239.1	77.6	17.4	8.3	4.7	4.3	8.2	7.4
Terms of trade	132.0	117.0	97.6	93.8	88.3	95.3	91.9	100.0	95.1	101.7	109.7	102.5	103.5	

Years

Figure 3.2 Monetary variables' movements in Brazil
Source: World Bank Data Query (2002).

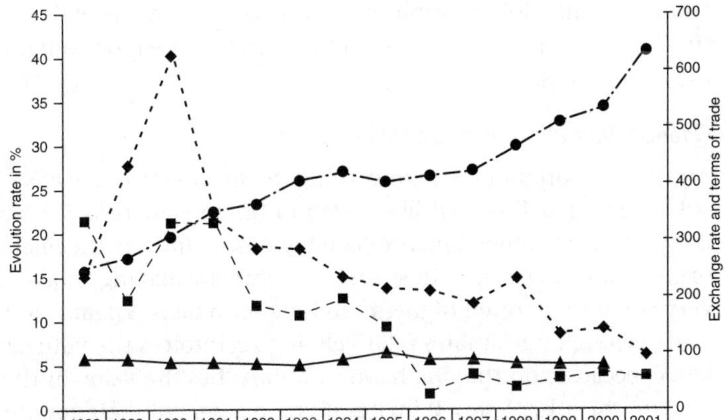

	1988	1989	1990	1991	1992	1993	1994	1995	1996	1997	1998	1999	2000	2001
Interest rate	15.1	27.7	40.3	22.3	18.3	18.2	15.1	13.7	13.5	12.0	14.9	8.6	9.2	6.2
Inflation	21.5	12.4	21.2	21.2	11.8	10.6	12.6	9.3	1.7	4.0	2.5	3.5	4.1	3.8
Exchange rate	245.0	267.0	304.9	349.2	362.6	404.2	420.2	396.8	412.3	419.3	460.3	508.8	535.5	634.0
Terms of trade	90.1	89.0	83.3	83.0	80.3	77.7	87.4	100.0	87.5	88.5	81.1	80.1	80.1	

Years

Figure 3.3 Monetary variables' movements in Chile
Source: World Bank Data Query (2002).

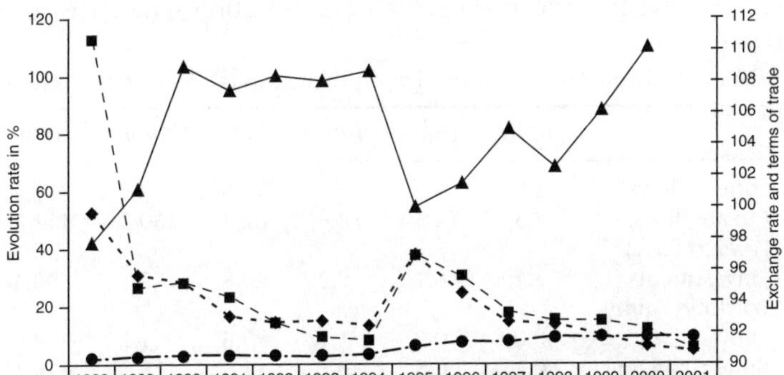

	1988	1989	1990	1991	1992	1993	1994	1995	1996	1997	1998	1999	2000	2001
Interest rate	52.7	30.9	27.9	16.6	14.5	15.1	13.3	38.1	24.7	14.7	13.8	9.6	6.3	4.7
Inflation	112.7	26.5	28.1	23.3	14.4	9.5	8.3	37.9	30.7	17.7	15.4	15.0	12.0	5.6
Exchange rate	2.3	2.5	2.8	3.0	3.1	3.1	3.4	6.4	7.6	7.9	9.1	9.6	9.5	9.3
Terms of trade	97.7	101.2	109.0	107.4	108.4	108.0	108.7	100.0	101.5	105.0	102.5	106.2	110.2	

Years

Figure 3.4 Monetary variables' movements in Mexico
Source: World Bank Data Query (2002).

and the partial dollarization of their financial systems make the use of the depreciation of exchange rates a dangerous weapon to fight against external shocks.

Financial liberalization and banking crises

Another important factor concerning the macroeconomic environment is the idea that financial liberalization brings new risks for banks and increases their vulnerability to banking crises.[2] Indeed, the liberalization of interest rates has modified their structure by making short-term rates very volatile and often higher than long-term rates. Salama (2001) states that keeping interest rates relatively high reinforces the vulnerability of banks because, on the one hand, it diminishes the value of their assets and, on the other hand, it incites them to augment their doubtful debts.

The fall in required reserves and, in particular, in the flow of foreign capital, often attracted to recently liberalized economies, highly increases money balances in a short period of time. In 1970, capital flows increased greatly, going from US$ 4.2 billion to US$ 142.6 billion in 1998, the year when capital flows reached their highest level (see Table 3.1). During the same period, official flows dropped (from 23 per cent of total flows in 1970 to 0.4 per cent in 2000), while private flows increased (from 76.4 per cent of total flows in 1970 to 99.6 per cent in 2000), principally in the form of foreign direct investments (representing 74.4 per cent of the total in 2000) and portfolio investments (20.3 per cent of the total in 2000). Liberalization allows new competitors

Table 3.1 Latin America: official and private capital flows (billions of dollars)

	1970	1980	1990	1995	1998	1999	2000
Official flows*	1,0	5,3	9,2	12,6	12,3	5,2	0,4
Private flows:	3,3	24,6	12,6	62,8	130,2	111,3	102,0
Foreign direct investments	1,1	6,1	8,2	29,8	72,1	90,4	76,2
Portfolio equity flows	0,0	0,0	1,1	7,6	1,7	3,9	9,9
Bond financing	0,1	0,8	0,1	11,5	18,3	19,1	11,0
Commercial banking and other loans	0,1	0,8	0,1	11,5	18,3	19,1	11,0
Total	4.3	29,9	21,8	75,4	142.57	116,5	102,4

Note: * Foreign aid plus debt financing from official sources.

Source: World Bank, *Global Development Finance*, 2001.

(foreign and domestic) to enter the domestic market and puts banks under great pressure to engage in more risky activities. All these factors, in conjunction with the inadequate preparation for financial liberalization, have promoted the emergence of banking crises, especially in Brazil, Chile and Mexico. Kaminsky and Reinhart (1996), have observed that out of the twenty-five banking crises that have affected emerging countries, the financial sector had been liberalized five years preceding the crisis in eighteen cases.

Credit expansion, the drop in assets price and capital flow

Gavin and Hausmann (1996) point out to the fact that the financial crises that hit Argentina (1981), Chile (1981–82), Uruguay (1982), Columbia (1982–83) and Mexico (1995), in nearly all cases had been preceded by a strong growth of bank credit. For Mexico, De Luna Martínez (2002) observes that between 1991 and 1994, bank loans grew eight times faster than the growth of real GDP. During this period, portfolio investments, attracted by high returns, brought important resources to credit institutions. Weak banking supervisory powers, opaque structures of governance, or sometimes the incompetence and corruption of local bank managers have encouraged financing speculative investment on real estate and stock markets (Minda, 1999). The emerging countries that have received the largest flow of private capital are also the countries where the expansion of the banking sector has been the fastest. This rapid expansion, however, has made it difficult for banks to distinguish between good and bad borrowers because, in periods of strong economic growth, many borrowers seem to represent a profitable and liquid investment but these characteristics are only temporary.

Changes in the structure of deposits

Goldstein and Turner (1996) have shown that advances in information technology combined with financial liberalization have facilitated the changes in the composition of bank deposits in foreign currencies of residents of emerging countries. The restructuring of these deposits has often widened the gap between assets in foreign currencies and international reserves, rendering banks highly fragile in the event of a 'deposit run' or a liquidity crisis. Furthermore, policies, and especially policies introduced to rescue the banking system, will be less effective in this situation of high exposure to foreign currencies. The structure of Latin American and Asian banks before the 1997 crises exemplifies this problem. These institutions were highly dependent on foreign funds and their debts were therefore denominated in foreign currencies (particularly in dollars). Moreover, these loans were issued with short maturities and the ratio of short-term debt to international reserves rose considerably during the years preceding the crisis, which is an important factor of illiquidity.

Banks as economic policy instruments

As far as economic policy is concerned, banks are often used as a policy instrument by authorities insofar as they can provide the means to implement monetary and fiscal policy or policies in support of certain industries. In Latin America, the high rate of required reserves combined with the possibilities of the refinancing of the central bank, have put banks at the mercy of the policy of monetary authorities. If government involvement is too strong, particularly in controlling loans (generally at a rate below the market rate) which could be channelled to low yield investments, its involvement can harm the profitability and efficiency of banks. Although, privatization was part of the financial liberalization programme that many Latin American countries followed, in certain countries a large part of bank assets remained in the public sector during the banking crises of the 1990s. Thus, the loans of these banks are channelled to certain sectors of the economy without doing a thorough analysis of the solvency of clients because they benefit from state support. Furthermore, state controlled banks are also protected by the state and they sometimes operate in a low competitive environment. This encourages the use of rigid practices and it also limits the incentive to innovate and to identify doubtful debts quickly or to control costs. For example, in 1994, one third of the debts of state banks in Argentina were doubtful debts whereas the rate of doubtful debts of private banks was 10 per cent (Goldstein and Turner, 1996).

More and more risky banking strategies

From a microeconomic point of view, banks have been directly implicated in the excessive risk taking that has led to banking crises. Prudent strategies will be encouraged if those who benefit from risk taking, that is to say the bank's stockholders, absorb the biggest share of the costs in the event of a bad investment. If stockholders see their banks' profitability drop, they will be tempted to 'play' with their profits to restore the situation. The Anglo-Saxon expression, 'gambling for resurrection' gives a faithful picture of this strategy. In a more and more competitive environment (competition from other banks and national non-banking institutions, international institutions and also domestic and international financial markets), owners and managers of banks take large risks in lending money to agents who may have unsound projects. Banks expose themselves to the insolvency of their clients and hold portfolios in which the share of doubtful debts is on the increase. When a bank is in a delicate position and is desperately looking for liquidity whatever the costs and risks may be, it tends to be less responsive to interest rates and other market signals or gives false information to the market. Such behaviour has important effects on other agents, especially other banks and can make fragility systemic.

The technique of 'ever-greening' (giving a new loan to a borrower who is already late in the repayment of another loan) tends to raise the concentration of risk. Furthermore, the bank manager may be tempted to commit fraud to restore profitability. Granting loans to stockholders and managers or to entities directly affiliated to them is a relatively common practice in Latin America, even in countries where these procedures are regulated. Thus, if a bank is part of a larger financial group, it can expose itself to the risks taken by the group, even though the bank, considered independently, may be a source of potential profit.

The quality and quantity of information that clients have on their banks limits the amount of control clients could have on financial intermediaries. Clients are often too small, too dispersed and insufficiently aware of banking practices to be able to provide adequate discipline. At the same time, the potential intervention of public authorities diminishes the client's incentive to take action (the phenomenon of moral hazard). Moreover, the existence of initial margins can push banks into adopting risky strategies, the potential losses incurred by such investments being more or less mutualized. For Caprio (1998), the main cause of banking crises arises from the insufficient amount of financial liberalization. The excessive risk taking by banks has been encouraged by public authority guarantees (lender of last resort, recapitalization programmes) which can give rise to a moral hazard, and this prevents market discipline from working. This type of behaviour has been brought to the fore by Miotti and Plihon (2001) in their analysis of the 1995 Argentine banking crisis. According to them, the defaulting banks were those that had a greater amount of speculative market operations capable of realizing stock market capital gains.

Weaknesses in the regulating framework

Latin American banking systems also suffer from the weaknesses of the legal environment and the inadequacy of accounting laws and norms of information disclosure. In many countries, accounting rules that allow classification of assets as bad debts are not precise enough to stop banks from overvaluing these assets by giving a supplementary loan to this 'bad' borrower (who will repay his first loan with the second loan). If bad debts are systematically minimized, provisions will be inadequate, and net banking revenue and the bank capital will be overvalued. These distortions explain why these variables are not highly predictable regarding the identification of banking bankruptcies. Imperfections in regulation structures will be particularly harmful in countries where market discipline is weak. Furthermore, market discipline will even be weaker if there are flaws in the accounting, legal and informational environment.

Authorities in charge of applying regulations should not only be independent from the banks they oversee, but also independent from political power. Regulators, however, are sometimes under pressure from bank owners who are politically well placed; in Latin America, power being frequently concentrated in only a few hands, regulators should have corrective powers to be able to punish fraudulent behaviour.

More generally, throughout the 1990s the supervision of bank aggregates, either at the level of each bank taken separately or at the level of the entire banking sector, was deficient. The bad supervision of liquidity ratios, bad debt rates or the structure of bank liabilities (in terms of maturity, currency of denomination, concentration of risk) by private and public authorities led to an under evaluation of risk, which was highly harmful to the viability of the banking sector.

International regulation and supervision: a solution to bank failure in Latin America?

It would be vain to try to find one unique cause of crisis and, as said before, bank failures often arise from a combination of many factors. However, we believe that, in addition to monitoring certain macroeconomic variables (which is already the case in many countries), setting up a banking regulation system would make it possible to bypass a certain number of these crisis mechanisms.[3] There is already an international framework of prudential standards – the Basel Accord – which Latin American countries have endorsed. However, this Accord was set up by and for developed countries where financial markets (stock, bond, monetary and inter-bank) are widespread and efficient, and where the banking sector has been restructured and integrated into an already liberalized economy. Are these standards adapted to the banking sectors of emerging countries? In order to answer these questions, we will study the international framework that the Basel Accord represents. We will then see to what extent it can be applied to Latin American countries to limit the instability of their banking system.

An international framework in operation: the new Basel Accord

For decades authorities have tried to limit the sphere of activity of banks, which allows these authorities to control credit. Authorities have also intervened in the composition of stock ownership and control foreign participation or limit the amount of private equity stake in banks. The form of regulation that we will study here is quite different. It seems to be that a consensus has emerged on the need not only to strengthen prudential banking regulation, and particularly standards concerning capital, but also on the need to promote the transparency and supervision of financial institutions.[4] These ideas are not new: in 1975 the Basel Committee on banking supervision was established by the governors of the central banks of the Group of Ten countries (G10), bringing together the national banking supervisory authorities.[5] The Concordat of September 1975 (the Committee's first agreement) was put in place for delineating the distribution of supervisory responsibilities of foreign banks between the authorities of the countries of origin and the host countries' authorities and the share of information between them.

This first agreement was modified and enhanced many times (in 1982, 1983 and 1986) but it was in 1988 that a major agreement on solvency ratios was approved. After a continuous period of erosion caused by the intensification of competition, the amount of capital held by large international banks started to become dangerously low. In order to keep these banks' capital at an adequate level to cover losses and to encourage their managers to act prudently, the governors of the G10 central banks imposed an 8 per cent solvency ratio (capital/assets weighted by their risk). The agreement weights risk according to the category of the debtor (states, banks, companies). These ratio advantages have been recognized internationally and at the beginning the 1990s, the 8 per cent standard was adopted by about a hundred countries, including the majority of Latin American countries. It has allowed significant reduction in the illiquidity and insolvency risks of large international banks, as well as the cost of banking bankruptcies supported by creditors. However, the relatively simple method of measurement of this capital ratio (the same method applied to all banks) has lacked efficiency in a world where the internal measures of economic capital have become increasingly complex. Banks have been tempted to take good assets off their balance sheets, thereby reducing the average quality of their portfolio. Furthermore, this agreement did not pay enough attention to the mitigation credit risk techniques such as guarantees.

The financial events that have occurred in recent years have brought to the fore the weakness of this agreement. This pushed the Basel Committee into proposing a new flexible framework in 1999, which would take greater account of risks. The aim of this new agreement, which will be implemented in 2007, is to improve the security and soundness of the financial system by providing greater importance to minimum capital requirements, internal control, the setting up of a supervisory process and market discipline. Although this agreement focuses on large internationally operating banks, its principles are designed to be applicable also to banks of varying degrees of sophistication and complexity. The new agreement offers a number of differentiating measures, going from a simple approach to a sophisticated approach of measuring credit risk and operational risk. It lays down a flexible framework within which a bank may apply an approach that best suits its complexity and risk profile. This agreement contains three chapters or 'pillars': the first concerns capital ratio reform, the second studies the process of prudential supervision and the third covers market discipline.

The definition of minimum capital requirements and the required 8 per cent level is maintained in the first pillar. The revised accord will be extended on a consolidated basis to bank holding companies to ensure that risks within the entire banking group are considered. The changes essentially concern the measurement of risk; that is to say, the denominator for the capital ratio which has weighted elements according to three types of risk: credit risk, market risk and operational risk, whereas the 1988 agreement only used credit risk. Three different approaches to measuring credit risk are proposed. On the one hand, a standardized approach uses the definition of the 1988 agreement but is more risk-sensitive. The weights used will be based on assessments made by external credit evaluation organizations (such as rating agencies) that meet very strict standards. On the other hand, two internal ratings based approaches allow banks to use their own assessments for the components of risks. The bank can calculate with internal rating only the borrowers' solvency or all the risk components[6] in a more complex approach. These approaches allow a greater risk differentiation. The Committee also proposes three approaches, with an increasing technicality, for the capital requirements compared to the operational risk (basic indicator, standardized and advanced measurement).

The second pillar defines the duties of supervisors who have to ensure that banks have set up sound internal risk assessment processes to assess the adequacy of their capital. The new agreement emphasizes the importance of banks' internal processes to make them aware of the risks they face. The Committee has established four key principles regarding prudential supervision (BCBS, 2003): (i) banks should have a process to assess the level of their overall capital with relation to their risk profile and a strategy to maintain this level; (ii) supervisors should examine and assess the banks' internal capital adequacy assessments and the strategies used to comply with the ratio requirements; (iii) supervisors should require banks to hold capital in excess of the minimum regulatory capital ratios; (iv) authorities should intervene quickly to prevent capital from going below the minimum levels needed to support the risk characteristics of a specific bank. They can apply prompt corrective action if the level of capital is not maintained or restored.

The third pillar aims to reinforce market discipline through enhanced information disclosure by banks. Efficient disclosure is essential to ensure that market participants can better understand the bank's risk profile and the adequacy of its investment decisions. The accord stipulates that banks must show how they calculate their solvency ratio and the methodology of risk models employed. The Committee defined four areas in which banks are asked to give specific qualitative and quantitative information: scope of the new capital requirements' application, composition of capital, risk exposure assessment and management process as well as capital adequacy. Thus, information such as the financial results, the financial situation (solvency, liquidity) or the accounting policies must be disclosed to the public. Any failure to disclose such financial information will entail the application of corrective measures going from 'moral suasion' through dialogue with the banks to reprimands or financial penalties.

From a technical point of view, a certain number of limitations apply to the structure of bank assets and strengthen this regulatory framework. In order to avoid interest conflicts or portfolio concentration, supervisors in a number of countries impose restrictions to loans given to a single borrower (generally limited to 25 per cent of the bank's capital), to loans granted to individuals close to the bank or working in the bank. There is also regulation on exposure of portfolios to exchange rates. In general, open positions on each currency taken individually are limited to 15 per cent of the bank's capital and the aggregated positions must not rise above 25 per cent of the bank's capital. However, each country is free to implement the regulation it deems desirable in these areas.

The significance and limits of the new Basel Accord for Latin American countries

The improvement of transparency (pillar 3) increases the access to information and this should lead to better financial choices. For some analysts, the latest crises in Latin America are linked to the opacity of financial systems, which hinders the production of reliable risk assessments and makes supervising financial actors a difficult task. This need for transparency applies to banks, but is applied less rigorously to other types of actors who have become preponderant in financial markets (such as pension funds or hedge funds). Transparency is desirable but it will not be enough to prevent banking crises. It is useless to disclose information if it is of poor quality and if it induces market actors into error. One of the first things to be done in emerging countries, and especially in Latin American countries, is to improve the quality of information by adopting clear accounting rules and legal dispositions concerning stockholders, creditors and other actors' rights. Once these reforms have been adopted, market participants have to be able to decipher the information given by banks, and therefore banks must not increase asymmetric information and market opacity ('too much information kills information'). The information disclosure about a bank having temporary difficulties but which has the capacity to recover must not become a source of panic over the bank which, in this case, could run it into permanent bankruptcy.

Banking intermediation depends on information that is private, abundant and secret as well as having bilateral relations with clients. Although it is necessary to market finance, transparency is thus incompatible with banking finance. The system of supervision must give banks the right not to disclose private information, which is the backbone of their business. As Plihon (2000) explains 'it is essential to carefully distinguish "reporting," that is to say, the legitimate obligation of transparency that banks have towards supervisory authorities, who have to respect the confidentiality duty, from "disclosure," that is to say the obligation of transparency towards public which can only be applied in a limited way'. Thus, if regulators – who have more information – are efficient and market operators have confidence in them, operators will anticipate that only viable and relatively healthy banks will be in the market. Panics and irrational capital movements will thus be theoretically restrained. Table 3.2 shows that the disclosure of bank balance sheets to supervisors is quite high (10 countries out of 10 in 2003) but is low to the public (6 countries out of 10). Concerning risk management procedures, much progress remains to be achieved.

Table 3.2 Banking information disclosure (Inquiries 2001 and 2003)[a]

	Argentina	Bolivia	Brazil	Chile	El Salvador	Guatemala	Honduras	Mexico	Peru	Venezuela
Are off-balance sheet items disclosed to supervisors?	yes (yes)	yes (yes)	yes (yes)	yes (yes)	yes (yes)	yes (no)	yes (yes)	yes (yes)	yes (yes)	yes (yes)
Are off-balance sheet items disclosed to public?	yes (no)	yes (yes)	yes (yes)	yes (yes)	no (yes)	yes (no)	no (yes)	no (no)	yes (yes)	no (no)
Must banks disclose risk management procedures to public?	no (yes)	no (yes)	no (no)	no (no)	no (no)	no (no)	no (no)	yes (no)	no (no)	no (no)
Are directors legally liable for erroneous or misleading information?	yes (yes)	yes (yes)	yes (yes)	yes (yes)	yes (yes)	yes (yes)	yes (yes)	yes (yes)	yes (yes)	yes (yes)

Note: [a] Data between parentheses correspond to the 2003 inquiry, whereas other data are from the 2001 inquiry.

Source: World Bank, *Bank Regulation and Supervision*.

Regulation, however, does have its limits. In Latin American countries, supervision is relatively ineffective against fraud especially when regulators themselves are implicated in fraud. Supervisors need incentives to perform their tasks correctly. In emerging countries, supervisory institutions are rarely independent from political power, the supervisors' wages are much lower than those of the supervised institutions, and they are subject to stringent penalties because they are legally responsible when acting in their official capacity. Table 3.3 shows that supervisors were responsible for their actions in 9 out of 10 countries in 2003. It is interesting to note that in countries such as the United States, the United Kingdom, Germany or Canada, supervisors are not held legally responsible for their actions (whereas they are in France) and, in general, it is the supervisory institutions (and not the employed supervisors themselves) that are held responsible. Before making prudential regulation more complex, one must assure that the existing regulation in a country is being applied appropriately. The increasing sophistication of instruments held by banks and the rapid growth of their value, limits the significance of inspections and occasional reports. More importantly, the establishment of an independent regulatory system needs political will to carry it out. In general, this implies that government authorities can no longer use the banking sector as a fiscal resource.

The level of minimum capital requirements (pillar 1) set by regulators from industrialized countries is scaled on the capacities of developed economies, which are generally less vulnerable to exogenous shocks than emerging countries. The imposition of more stringent obligations may seem to be costly and may present a possible obstacle to financial development but it seems difficult to avoid such obligations, if we want to give the supervisory authorities in emerging countries a real chance to support a bank failure before its capital is irremediably deteriorated. The establishment of capital ratios that are appropriate to the environment of Latin American countries must be done on a case by case basis. Regarding the risk weight in the calculation of solvency ratios, giving a 0 per cent weight factor (the least risky assets) to Treasury bills issued by emerging countries can be called into question because examples of public arrears are numerous.

Banks can attain the required capital ratio in two ways, either by raising their capital (the numerator) or by decreasing their risk-weighted assets (the denominator). In Latin American countries, raising capital has a cost that can be prohibitive and banks often chose the second solution. Thus, imposing a minimum amount of capital can create a credit crunch, which can hinder growth. Banks can also make trade-offs

Table 3.3 Banking supervision (inquiries 2001 and 2003)[a]

	Argentina	Bolivia	Brazil	Chile	El Salvador	Guatemala	Honduras	Mexico	Peru	Venezuela
Total number of professional bank supervisors	664 (285)	115 (80)	834 (819)	108 (150)	73 (60)	130 (109)	60 (46)	na. (600)	120 (89)	115 (98)
Number of professional supervisors per institution 2001*	2.44	6	4	1 to 5	1	2 to 3	12	11.5	3.6	1
Must infraction of any prudential regulation found by a supervisor be reported?	yes (yes)	yes (yes)	yes (yes)	yes (yes)	yes (yes)	yes (yes)	yes (yes)	yes (yes)	yes (yes)	yes (yes)
Any mandatory actions in these cases?	yes (no)	yes (yes)	yes (yes)	yes (yes)	yes (yes)	yes (yes)	yes (yes)	yes (yes)	yes (yes)	yes (yes)
Are supervisors legally liable for their actions?	yes (yes)	yes (yes)	yes (yes)	yes (yes)	yes (yes)	yes (yes)	no (no)	yes (yes)	yes (yes)	yes (no)

Notes: [a] data between parentheses correspond to the 2003 inquiry whereas the other ones are from 2001 inquiry.
* The question exists only in 2001 inquiry.

Source: World Bank, *Bank Regulation and Supervision*.

between the economic capital that they must hold to secure loans and the statutory capital, which is imposed. The introduction of numerous technological innovations has given banks a range of arbitrage techniques, such as securitization. A trade-off can also be made between substituting a sound asset for a more risky asset and this can lead to an increase in the average risk of a bank's portfolio. Minimum capital ratios can thus have perverse effects that contravene the positive effects of financial stability that the ratios can bring.

The adoption of a minimum solvency ratio is not sufficient to ensure the quality of assets. A close supervision of the rate and structure of bad debt is necessary, even if this measure is highly linked to capital ratios. It would even be a good idea to adjust solvency ratios to the level of bad debts. Many emerging countries have minimum capital requirements that comply with the standards of the Basel Accords. Table 3.4 shows that the majority of Latin American countries have a capital ratio well above the statutory ratio requirements. If this state of affairs seems to present a healthy situation, how can we consider the conditions in Venezuela in 2003 or in Peru in 2001 as being good when the non-performing loans ratio represents 26.64 per cent of total assets for the former and 33.6 per cent for the latter?

In order to ensure the solvency of their banking system, it may be a good idea for Latin American countries to raise their capital ratios to levels that are compatible with levels of their bad debt. Before doing this, however, one would need to conduct a thorough analysis and study each bank individually by differentiating their case. Thus, a bank that has accumulated risky debt to the point that it has doubts about its repayment should be obliged to increase its provisions. This implies that bank managers are able to produce an accurate diagnosis and assessment of their assets without underestimating the level of non-performing loans, as is currently the case in a number of Latin American countries. To implement this policy, time is needed to assimilate and adapt the assessment methods used by large international banks. The time schedule for the implementation of new regulation has to take these problems into account.

International cooperation, which promotes the mobility of experts of large international institutions (big banks or experts from institutions such as the Bank of International Settlements), would allow reduction of the amount of time needed to train bank managers and also the potential costs linked to new disturbances in the banking system. Raising the number of supervisors will not be enough to ensure the effectiveness of monitoring and supervision. Table 3.4 shows that Mexico, a country

Table 3.4 Capital adequacy ratio and non-performing loans (inquiries 2001 and 2003)[a]

	Argentina	Bolivia	Brazil	Chile	El Salvador	Guatemala	Honduras	Mexico	Peru	Venezuela
Minimum capital–asset ratio requirement (%)	11.5 (11.5)	10 (10)	11 (11)	8 (8)	11 (9.6)	10 (8)	10 (10)	8 (8)	9.1 (9.1)	12 (10)
Is it risk-weighted in line with Basle guidelines?	yes (yes)	yes (yes)	yes (yes)	yes (yes)	yes (yes)	yes (yes)	yes (yes)	yes (yes)	yes (yes)	yes (yes)
Does the ratio vary with a bank's credit risk?	yes (yes)	no (no)	no (no)	no (no)	yes (no)	no (no)	no (no)	yes (yes)	no (no)	no (yes)
Does the ratio vary with the market risk?	yes (yes)	no (no)	yes (yes)	no (no)	no (no)	no (no)	no (no)	yes (yes)	no (no)	no (no)
Actual risk adjusted capital ratio (%)	14.7 (16.4)	14.6 (11.4)	10.1 (15.8)	7.25 (12.8)	8.6 (na.)	7 (13.3)	12.5 (12.3)	14.7 (13)	9.7 (12.7)	14 (14)
Ratio of non-performing loans to total assets (%)	12.3 (9.4)	9.4 (5.7)	7.9 (3.14)	1.62 (1.42)	4.2 (2.9)	na. (7.14)	7.3 (na.)	5.74 (17.5)	5.3 (33.6)	26.64 (1.62)

Notes: na: not available.
[a] data between parentheses correspond to the 2003 inquiry, whereas other data are from 2001 inquiry.
Source: World Bank, *Bank Regulation and Supervision.*

that has a high rate of bad debt, has more than 10 supervisors per institution. In comparison, the number of supervisors per institution in developed countries is relatively low: 1 in Germany, 0.66 in the United Kingdom and 0.07 in the United States. One way to increase the quality of supervision in emerging countries would be to set up training programmes for supervisors.

The implementation of a system of regulation and supervision has a cost that many Latin American countries cannot afford. If it is easy to evaluate the cost of implementing such a system, we do not precisely know the benefits that it will bring. Its cost has, therefore, to be compared to the cost of banking crises. The nature of modern crises being rather systemic, public or private international aid (financial and technical) could help to implement regulation in the most fragile countries.

Recommendations and perspectives

The purpose of regulation, of course, is not to put an end to all banking crises – which would be impossible – but the implementation of prudential regulation in the banking sector can be an important way to prevent banking crises. Thus, this type of regulation seeks to put a better control on the causes of crises, particularly the exposure to risk that banks face. On the one hand, regulation seeks to reduce the shocks created by certain macroeconomic factors. For example, banks have to reduce their exposure to exchange rate and interest rate variations. On the other hand, microeconomic factors are directly taken into account by prudential supervision and monitoring because each bank has to comply with precise quantitative and qualitative criteria and non-compliance can lead to legal sanctions. Thus, financial instability caused by the erroneous comprehension of bank balance sheets leading to non-viable bad debt rates could be reduced. Furthermore, microeconomic supervision of this kind, may push banks into acting more rationally when faced with macroeconomic shocks.

In Latin America, the principles set out in the Basel Accords need not only to be adapted to the financial and economic situation of each country, but would not, in themselves, be enough to re-establish relative financial stability. The regulation of the banking sector must be part of a set of measures aimed at bringing stability to the entire economy. Thus, macroeconomic policies aimed at disciplining price volatility, reinforcing the bond and inter-bank market, making the calendar of financial liberalization more flexible or even temporarily controlling capital flows[7], can be an appendage to banking regulation.

Besides taking into consideration the financial and economic environment of countries, the particularities of the domestic banking sector have to be examined in detail. Thus, a number of points could be emphasized:

- The required capital ratio level could be adjusted according to the quality of debt and the level of bad debt. This ratio should be left to the discretion of the national monetary authorities, on the condition that it does not go below 8 per cent.
- International cooperation in the training and instruction of supervisors would not only be of great benefit to Latin American supervisory authorities but also to international supervisors, who would acquire a better understanding of national banking systems. This could increase the joint use of different regulation and supervisory methods.
- The cost of implementing banking regulation often goes beyond the financial capacities of Latin American countries. This cost should be mutualized in part through the use of public and private international funds.
- Finally, the calendar for the implementation of the Accords should be flexible, taking into account the work that remains to be done. Western countries that signed the new Basel Accords have already obtained a two-year delay for its implementation. The deadline is 2007. If the new regulations are to be effective, emerging countries that decide to adopt these Accords must give their banking systems enough time to adapt to the new conditions.

In the fight against crises, these recommendations could well improve the effectiveness of banking regulations, however, they are difficult to implement. International cooperation, and the consideration of specific national characteristics are necessary and this will need the involvement of many parties. Taking on this formidable task could be essential for the stability of the banking system in Latin American countries.

Notes

1. For a review of the different causes of banking crises, see Goldstein and Turner (1996). This article also has plenty of references and a relatively thorough survey of studies on the subject dating before 1996.

2. Among the empirical studies examining the role of financial liberalization in banking crises, see Kaminsky and Reinhart (1996), Demirgurc-Kunt and Detragiache (1998) and Gonzales-Hermosillo *et al.* (1997).
3. On this question, see Cornford (2000), Barth *et al.* (2001) and Cartapanis (2003).
4. All these questions are also discussed in international financial institutions such as the IMF (for example, in the discussions on an eventual 'new international financial architecture').
5. It is composed of high officials from the banking supervisory authorities and central banks of the following countries: Germany, Belgium, Canada, the United States, France, Italy, Japan, Luxembourg, Netherlands, the United Kingdom, Sweden and Switzerland.
6. Borrowers' probability of default, losses given default, exposure of default and effective maturity.
7. See Minda (2001) for the results of the experience in the selective control of capital inflows in Chile.

References

Bank of International Settlements (2003) 'Consultative Paper 3', Basel Committee on Banking Supervision Working Papers.

Barth, J.R., Caprio, G.J., and Levine, R. (2001) 'The Regulation and Supervision of Banks around the World: A New Database', in R.E. Litan and R. Herring (eds), 'Integrating Emerging Market Countries into the Global Financial System', Brookings-Wharton Papers on Financial Services (Washington, DC: Brookings Institution Press).

Basel Committee on Banking Supervision (BCBS) (2001) 'Overview of the New Basel Capital Accord', Consultative Document, Basel Committee on Banking Supervision (Basel: BIS) January.

Basel Committee on Banking Supervision (BCBS) (2003) *The New Basel Capital Accord*, Consultative Document, Basel Committee on Banking Supervision, (Basel: BIS), April 2003.

Caprio, G.J. (1998) 'Banking on Crises: Expensive Lessons from Recent Financial Crises', Development Research Group (Washington, DC: World Bank) June.

Cartapanis, A. (2003) 'Vers une Prévention Macro-Prudentielle des Crises Financières Internationales', *Revue d'Economie Financière*, 70: 89–100.

Cornford, A. (2000) 'The Basle Committee's Proposals for Revised Capital Standards: Rationale, Design and Possible Incidence', G-24 Discussion Paper, 3, May.

Demirguc-Kunt, A. and Detragiache, E. (1998) 'The Determinant of Banking Crises in Developing and Developed Countries', IMF Staff Papers, 45, 1: 81–109 (Washington, DC: IMF) March.

Evans, O., Leone, A.M., Gill, M. and Hilbers, P. (2000) 'Macroprudential Indicators of Financial System Soundness', Occasional Paper, 192 (Washington DC: IMF) April.

Gavin, M. and Hausmann, R. (1996) 'The Roots of Banking Crises: The Macroeconomic Context', in R. Hausmann and L. Rojas-Suarez, *Banking Crises in Latin America* (Baltimore Johns Hopkins University) 27–63.

Goldstein, M. and Turner, P. (1996) 'Banking Crises in Emerging Economies: Origins and Policy Options', BIS Economic Papers, 46, BIS (Monetary and Economic Department) October.

Gonzales-Hermosillo, B., Pazarbasioglu, C. and Billings, R. (1997) 'Determinants of Banking System Fragility: a Case Study of Mexico', IMF Staff Paper, 44: 295–314, September.

Hardy, D.C. and Pazarbasioglu, C. (1999) 'Determinants and Leading Indicators of Banking Crises: Further Evidence', IMF Staff Papers, 46: 247–58, September/December.

Kaminsky, G. and Reinhart, C.N. (1996) 'The Twin Crises: the Causes of Banking and Balance of Payments Problems', International Finance Discussion Paper, 455 (Washington, DC: Board of Governors of the Federal Reserve System) March.

Luna Martínez, J. De (2002) 'Las Crisis Bancarias de México y Corea del Sur', *Foro Internacional*, XLII: 99–153, Enero–Marzo.

Minda, A. (2001) 'Le Contrôle Sélectif des Entrées de Capitaux: les Leçons de l'Expérience Chilienne', *Revue d'Economie du Développement*, 4: 91–124.

Minda, A. (1999) 'Urgence et Gestion des Crises Financières: les Leçons des Crises Mexicaine et Thaïlandaise', *Techniques Financières et Développement*, 53/54: 28–39.

Miotti, L. and Plihon, D. (2001) 'Libéralisation Financière, Spéculation et Crises Bancaires', *Economie Internationale*, 85: 3–36.

Plihon, D. (2000) 'Quelle Surveillance Prudentielle pour l'Industrie des Services Financiers?', *Revue d'Economie Financière*, 60: 17–32, Décembre.

Salama, P. (2001) 'Les Nouveaux Paradoxes de la Libéralisation en Amérique latine', *Problèmes d'Amérique latine*, 41: 71–111, Avril/Juin.

World Bank Data Query (2002), WDI, The World Group, *http://devdata.worldbank.org/data_query*

World Bank (2001, 2003) *Bank Regulation and Supervision, http://www.worldbank.org/research/projects/bank_regulation.htm*

World Bank, *Global Development Finance (2001)*, Washington, DC: World Bank.

4

From Financial Repression to Financial Regression: The Limits of the 'Tyrannical Auctioneer' and Monetary Policy

Etelberto Ortiz

The issues

Financial reforms are usually aimed at 'freeing the capital markets' in order to create a world of possibilities for growth. A greater efficiency in the allocation of resources should lead to higher growth rates and growing savings rates. An additional very important purpose is that, in a world of efficient capital markets, there would be more room for a freer monetary policy. The only difficulty foreseen was the transition to such a state, if it were affected by the difficulties of structural reform (McKinnon 1973). Otherwise, the sole condition for reform to be viable was to be already in a state of basic financial order with a null fiscal deficit and very low inflation. Evidently, the trouble is in the process of transition, and it is right there that problems arose. Current literature has recognized that almost every financial reform has gone into some form of financial crisis or at least of strong volatility (Caprio *et al.* 2001). That literature has been attentive to a number of conditions and the sequencing that should be observed during the reform, but it has hardly discussed the monetary policy framework, particularly because the actual role of monetary policy as developed under the present model has not been understood. The presumption was that macroeconomic fundamentals could be achieved through fiscal austerity and nil inflation under any condition (Caprio *et al.* 2001). In such a framework, financial reform would improve the fundamentals of resource allocation.

Nevertheless, orthodox notions about monetary policy lead to a contradictory proposition: the transmission channel from the monetary to the real sectors still seems to rest on the notion that there is no incidence of monetary policy on the real side, while inflation and related phenomena are considered through the relationship between the rate of interests and the rate of inflation. The link between the real and monetary sides would work through expectations if, and only if, ex-hypothesis general equilibrium conditions prevail on the real side.[1] Consequently, whichever policy comes from the monetary side, ex-hypothesis the presumption is, it would always be neutral. Nevertheless, the problem of formation of prices and expectations may not necessarily go through a process that is necessarily in equilibrium. If price expectations are 'rational', then any solution for a single representative agent is always of equilibrium.[2] The image of financial reform, characterized as a condition of lower interest rates and a more abundant supply of savings, would seem extremely appealing. The sole difficulty is that the transition to a new model is the core of the policy issue, which is not considered at all.

That is why the situation for a small open economy poses a threefold difficulty:

- Recent models place the emphasis between price expectations and the rate of interest (Taylor 1993, 2001), but neglecting completely the particular characteristics of a small open economy, because it is assumed that an open economy is isomorphic to a closed system, and the price equations do not consider any incidence of an external price link, as in Clarida *et al.* (2001). Such characteristics are postulated ex-hypothesis and not demonstrated as the relevant case.
- Nothing can be said about the transition from one state of equilibrium to another. Furthermore, standard comparative statics models do not afford us much information (Fisher 1999). Unfortunately, this is the actual ground for economic policy; that is, on the actual effects of moving the economy from one state to another.
- The open economy case poses one interesting question once the rate of exchange is introduced. According to Ball (2001), targeting inflation through the rate of interest is inefficient, in the sense of Pareto, because it rests on the restrictive incidence on income. But targeting inflation through both (E, i) in an open economy, can be efficient if instead of targeting the short-run rate of inflation it targets the long-run rate of inflation. Then, the relationship between the rate of interest and the exchange rate is not simple nor linear.

Nevertheless, it is striking that the argument for structural and financial reform is built as a case in which transition matters because it rests on the presumption that there will be winners and losers (Balassa 1985). But in the case for transformation, it is unambiguously clear that the corner stone of the process is the build up of new productive capabilities oriented to manufacturing exports and the creation of a capital market. The orthodox view emphasizes that all it needs is price stability. How it is possible for both to engage in the transformation is not evident.

Conventional wisdom in monetary theory seems to be at odds with the common practice of the day-to-day conduct of monetary policy. Blinder (1998) expressed it very well: central banks do not operate by targeting the necessary amount of money every day. Even worse, it seems to be impossible and useless to pretend to control the quantity of money at any given time. What central banks do is target certain fundamental prices for the economy. Blinder finds that the US economy seems to work on targeting the rate of interest. Such a target rate is not rigid. It is set with the intention of putting a restraint on inflation, and/or to bring capital to the economy or in response to whatever other purpose is considered relevant (Bernanke and Mishkin 1997; Alvarez *et al.* 2001). The actual direction of monetary policy, then, comes from the fundamental prices for the economy; for a closed economy, the rate of interest; and for an open economy, we also have the exchange rate. The quantity of money then adjusts consequently.

However, the case of the open economy is considerably more complex, because it has to give way to two restrictions:

- The basic price vector must consider that there is a very complex interaction between the rate of interest and the exchange rate, that generally is not considered at all in macro and micro fundamental models.
- Those two prices, the rate of interest and the rate of exchange, are crucial for the actual profitability of investment, and the overall stability of the system, particularly for the real and financial sectors.

Ignoring these conditions is the source of the fact that financial reforms generally turned into significant financial crisis.

Consequently, the theoretical construction necessary to analyze the impact of monetary policy has to be a price structure where it is possible to consider the different impacts of both, the rate of interest and the exchange rate, on a price structure that is not necessarily homogeneous. Pricing in an economy like that is always in the world of actual monetary transactions: rephrasing Clower (1967), *commodities buy money, money buy commodities*, therefore the price vector is open for adjustment to the vector of basic prices agents receive, the exchange rate E, and the rate of interest, i. That vector (E, i), even if it is open to the interplay of different markets, has a strong interaction through the capital market, but always with the immediate price vector the central bank is sending to the economy. The role of the central bank, is to help to find the right price vector for the economy. In a small open economy such as Mexico, it is certain that the role of the central bank goes even further, actually also fixing the minimum wage w.[3]

Even if the real side of the economy were neutral to changes in the quantity of money in the long run, the actual operation of monetary policy is the other way round, through prices. This is not to deny that daily central banks intervene in the classical model of open market operations buying and selling bonds, money and strong currencies, but always in response to a stand for a certain target price vector (E', i', w'). The essential proposition is that actual monetary policy can best be understood through a model that builds up the relationship between the real and monetary sides based on the structure of prices, through the link between pricing and investment. Therefore, the link between the real and monetary sectors is the form in which concerned agents, firms, decide the amount of investment to advance given a certain basic price vector (E, i, w), and then form a particular demand of credit. Monetary policy, then, is essential to form the magnitudes of effective demand and the basic framework for firms to decide their price and quantity vector. The coherence of the price vector is to be realized at the end of the process if firms are able to pay their debts and/or recover the capital advanced for production. Within this context, the neutrality of money is meaningless.

Literature on targeting the rate of interest,[4] transmits the idea that the monetary authority is concerned with targeting only one price, the rate of interest. To a large extent this is to be attributed to two characteristics in that literature: (i) their framework is for a large economy, somehow as if it were a closed economy, where the exchange rate is observed as not important for the pricing process in the economy; (ii) the presumption is that once one of them has been targeted (i.e. the rate of interest) the other adjusts consequently. The first condition is entirely unrealistic for a small open economy, whose price structure is likely to be highly entangled with the exchange rate; it omits important characteristics of targeting in an economy whose financial system is open to financial flows that might threaten the aims of targeting the inflation rate. One such characteristic is a high burden of debt service (amortization or renewal of debts) particularly for private debt liabilities denominated in dollars, which may turn their balances to bankruptcy with a small devaluation, even if the rate interest is not too high. The other is that an economy in this state is open to speculative attacks due to diverging spreads between the rate of interest and the rate of exchange, given a particular rate of inflation target. Some open models, as in Ball (1997, 2001), consider an ad hoc IS construct and some form of Phillips curve where the impact of the exchange rate is considered. It is interesting that this literature considers that inflation targeting in an open economy is inefficient, because the channel of incidence is through the level of output. Ball considers that long-run targeting improves the efficiency of monetary policy on curbing the rate of inflation. In practice, the monetary authority has, in fact, to consider additional forms to anchor the inflation target, including the wage rate and direct intervention on the amount of credit. Wage control is a heritage from the old-time income policies, where ratcheted price and wage indexation lead to accelerated inflation. Nowadays, in Mexico, the wage rate constitutes an important anchor on the rate of inflation (according to the Bank of Mexico) because it considers it has an inflationary impact. Inflation targeting experience in Mexico can be observed in Figures 4.1–4.4.

The essential observation from these graphs is that the distance between the rate targeted and the inflation rate is smaller in the wage rate graph, while the worst performance is found in the exchange rate. It is also important to observe that variance in the rate of growth of M1 is far greater than the variance through price targets. The inflation gap through the interest rate shows a lag in high or accelerating inflation periods, while it presents a forward gap in periods with a reducing inflation rate. The exchange rate also shows some degree of overshooting.

The working of a basic price vector (*E, i, w*) may have a strong resemblance to the standard model of the Walrasian auctioneer. Let us remember that the image of the Walrasian auctioneer is a figurative construct about the manner in which pricing forms a general equilibrium price vector. A price vector is sent by the auctioneer, and the excess demand and supply equations (one for every economic agent in the economy) provide him with a disequilibria signal who kindly adjust the price vector observing the sign of those excess demand equations. The adjustment process continues until every agent is in equilibrium because he can sell and buy as much as he wants, given a certain budgetary constraint. It is only then that exchange can take place.[5]

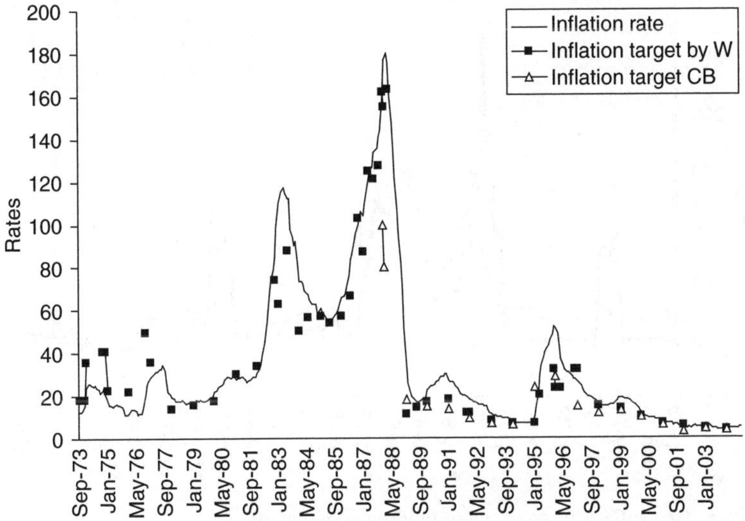

Figure 4.1 Inflation target given by minimum wage target*

* Inflation rates are monthly figures measured by the National Consumer Price Index, and inflation targets are the targets that El Banco de México declares to Congress at the beginning of every year. The wage rates are the rates of adjustment to the minimum wage rate, reported in the Comisión Nacional del Salario Mínimo.

Sources: Produced by the author based on data reported in the Economic Indicators, Bank of Mexico, 1970–2004, and Statistical Series, 1950–2004, of the Comisión Nacional del Salario.

The operation of the basic price vector sent by the tyrannical auctioneer (namely, the central bank) differs in three different fundamental ways:

- There is one institution that works as a real auctioneer (namely, the central bank) not through the auction of dollars or debt instruments, but through the basic price vector targeted by monetary policy: (E, i, w).
- The central bank has a figuration of equilibrium from a set of balances that can actually be observed, and are the bank's own concern; namely, the current account deficit, the balance between the banking system, and the balance of the public sector. In some cases, the central bank might consider another balance essential for society, though not for the equations of the economy, which is the rate of unemployment. Nevertheless, this is not necessarily the standard.

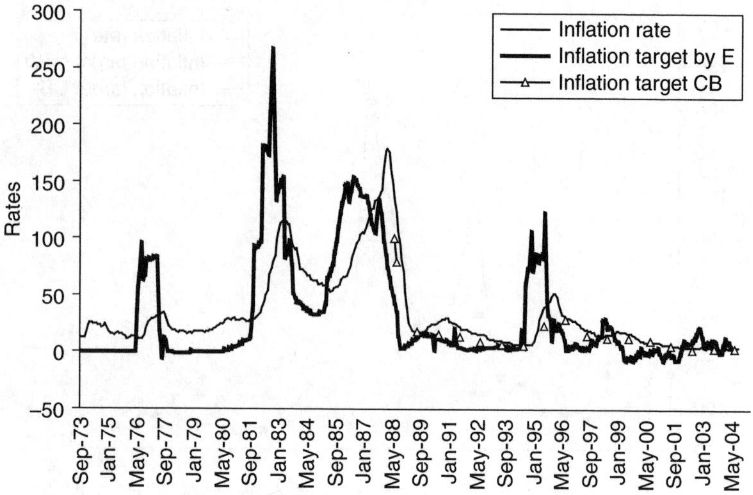

Figure 4.2 Inflation target given by the exchange rate *E**

* Inflation (measured by the National Consumer Price Index) and exchange rates are monthly figures. Inflation targets are the targets that El Banco de México declares to Congress at the beginning of every year.

Source: Produced by the author based on data reported in *Economic Indicators*, Bank of Mexico, 1970–2004.

- The central bank seems not to be interested in the actual balance of the main economic agents in the economy; that is, firms and workers. Therefore, the accumulation of unused production capacity, unemployment and debts is overseen.

The last two characteristics caused me to name that model of monetary policy as the Tyrannical Auctioneer (TA) because the sender of the basic price vector does not in any way consider its impact on economic agents. This is not to be characterized as a rigidity. The TA actually adjusts, even daily, but not necessarily in response to the disequilibrium perceived by firms. Therefore, it is possible that the TA considers it is doing its job very well in terms of its own balances. It can even think adjustments are made following a flexible model, but nevertheless the TA might take the real economy and the banks to bankruptcy.

The next section of this chapter incorporates the frame of the pricing model, including the impact of the rate of exchange and the rate of interest. The pricing decision is framed into the investment decision.

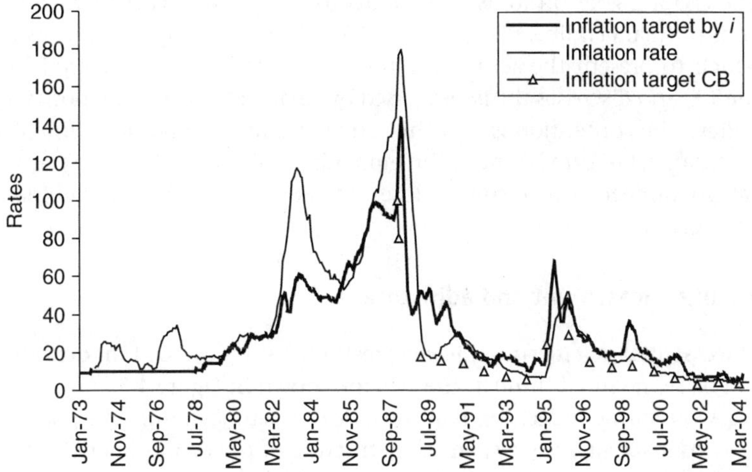

Figure 4.3 Inflation target given by interest rate*

* Inflation rates (measured by the National Consumer Price Index) and the 28 days CETES (interest rates on Treasury bonds) are monthly figures. Inflation targets are the targets that El Banco de México declares to Congress at the beginning of every year.

Source: Produced by the author based on data reported in *Economic Indicators*, Bank of Mexico, (1970–2004).

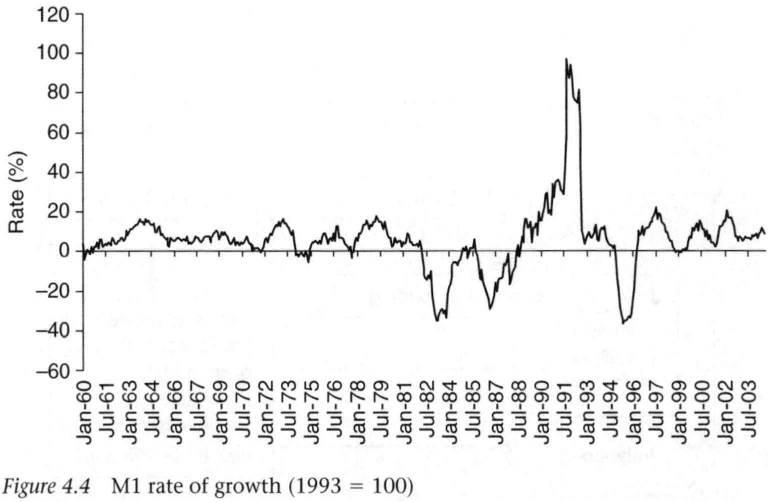

Figure 4.4 M1 rate of growth (1993 = 100)

Source: Produced by the author based on data reported in *Economic Indicators*, Bank of Mexico, 1970–2004.

The chapter goes on to use the model to analyze the particular experience of financial liberalization in the Mexican economy, as a means by which to present the actual working of the monetary policy model of the TA, and discusses the issues raised by financial reform and monetary policy. The contention is that the actual and more important difficulty for financial reform has been the monetary policy model of the tyrannical auctioneer. The chapter closes by advancing some preliminary conclusions.

Pricing, investment and adjustment

The essential macroeconomic view rests on a simple circuit model,[6] that can be represented through the scheme shown in Figure 4.5.

The investment decision is at the core of the model, from the point of view of macro aggregates, and the structure of prices and financial proficiency. The economic policy framework is, however, set by monetary policy.

Pricing responds to an investment decision that assesses the possibilities of recovering the capital advanced, given the basic price vector sent by the TA, (*E, i, w*). The pricing model is equivalent to the model in Ortiz (2003). There, a pricing model is set where the price of any commodity depends on the basic price vector received from the central bank. Firms adjust their prices and quantities right at the beginning: that is, at the

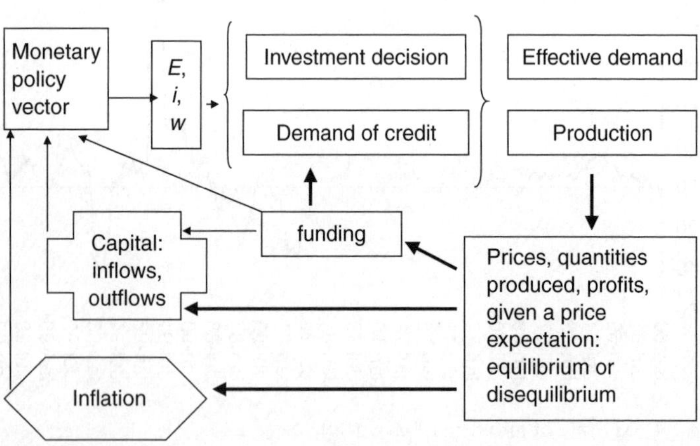

Figure 4.5 Monetary policy and circuit theory

moment they make a decision about how much to invest and to take credit. The market process is sequential after the decision on investment and production, and the whole issue is whether the expectations on prices and quantities to be sold can be fulfilled. In this chapter, the key questions concern the alternative paths for adjustment that firms can have.

For example, a devaluation $dE > 0$, will impact the rate of interest and the rate of profit. Real and monetary prices will show the adjustment capabilities, given the elasticity to obtain finance to stay in the market. Nevertheless, we have different trajectories for each price function, because prices react to different import and financial elasticity coefficients, and the impact on any sector might be higher or smaller than on any other. Consequently, for each sector we might have different impacts of a devaluation on profitability. From experience, we know that a devaluation would be effective to close the balance of trade deficit only if, besides fulfilling the Marshall–Lerner condition, overshooting of domestic prices can be controlled. Then, the situation will not develop into an inflationary spiral. Therefore, a successful adjustment demands that price adjustment is kept in control. This last condition usually is met by inducing a deterioration in profitability through the introduction of a wage contraction and a recessive monetary framework.

The relationship between *di* and *dE* will generally be negative (see Figure 4.6). Nevertheless, in a sectoral model with different structural coefficients, the trajectories of *dE* into *di* will generally be in a different form, because the possibility that they might have the same direction

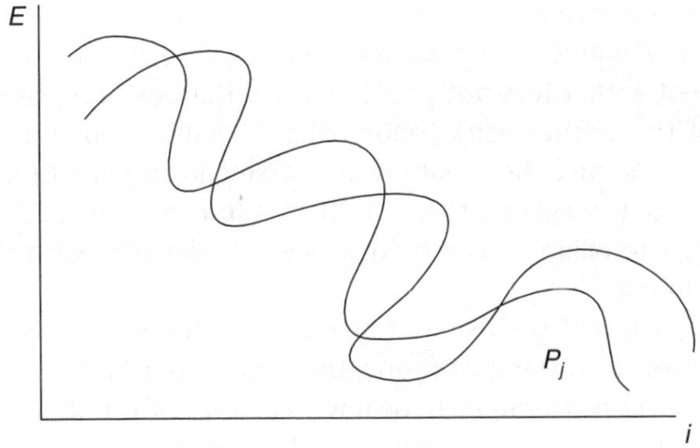

Figure 4.6 Price lines in (*E*, *i*)

of movement within particular tracts is not excluded. Therefore, the mapping of pricing behaviour in response to changes in the basic price vector may appear as in Figure 4.6, as shown in Ortiz (2003).

Price lines show that changes in nominal and relative prices will thus be the most visible impact of monetary policy. The shape of the price curves can have any form, not necessarily those traced here, and may give rise to all sorts of solutions. Thus, the neutrality of monetary policy is only conceivable in a world in which not only production structures, but also production functions are totally homogenous. Also required are the homogeneity of inputs, means of production and labour, and imported inputs. But even that would not be sufficient. Firms must also have the same k_i; that is, the same financial behaviour in the face of a specific monetary policy. Neutrality of monetary policy is meaningless unless agents were to have the same pattern of reaction to whatever pair (E, i) that comes from the monetary authority or from the market. In fact, that would be the standard assumption in Mundell–Fleming models[7] and in New Classical and New Keynesian models, as in Clarida *et al.* (2001).

It is within this context that the impacts of monetary policy can be traced back to its very source; that is, within the pricing structure of the productive sector. Private agents may have three fundamental forms of adjustment in the face of a particular basic price vector:

- Adjusting prices and quantities, either real or nominal.
- Adjust the level of investment.
- Adjust its real vector of activity, introducing changes to improve productivity and growth.

Furthermore, the presumption of a neutral monetary policy is that somehow it means that fulfilling the TA targets would be associated with some notion of equilibrium for every agent in the economy. The core of our argument is that it is not possible to say that, ex-ante, clearing the balances of the central bank (trade balance, public deficit and banks' balances) or reaching the inflation rate targeted can guarantee equilibrium for productive agents. This introduces a fourth form of adjustment, which is that imbalances can be displaced temporarily with the accumulation of debts.

Which adjustment path should be chosen? The right answer should pass through the working of monetary policy. To a large extent firms may have a long-run strategy to deal with adjustment. But it is also true that the context in which to make the right choice is set by monetary policy. Our model shows that the dynamics of disequilibrium do not necessarily converge to a permanent state of general equilibrium for the central bank and concerned agents, particularly firms.

From financial repression to financial regression: Mexico

The core issue arises from the standard view on financial liberalization. The argument emphasized in the early 1970s by McKinnon (1973), was the need to improve the allocation of capital, giving agents and the market the freedom to move to whichever activity was more profitable. Efficiency in the allocation of capital would then be associated with better performance and a higher rate of expansion of savings and investment. Financial liberalization would also lead to a reduction in prices and the rate of interest. The main condition needed for the model to work was to eliminate the pressure that would come from an outstanding public deficit calling for financial resources. In such a world, monetary policy should have more room for manoeuvre and enhanced capabilities to direct the economy.

The move to liberalize the capital market in Mexico started early in 1978 with the introduction of public debt instruments that in 1983 could be traded, opening the market for bids that could have an impact on rates of interest. Later, in 1988, direct controls on resources allocated to particular sectors were removed, Aspe (1993). The reduction of the fiscal deficit helped to reduce pressure in the capital market and the elimination of the reserve requirements system was modified in 1989. The market was also opened to new non-bank financial instruments. The institutional context was also modified considerably with the reform on the Law of Credit between 1989 and 1990, and legislation on the stock market in 1990, creating a more transparent condition for investment by the private sector. It is only then that banks were turned back to private concerns. The emphasis of the reform was on creating guaranties of entrance and confidence to invest in the new competitive environment.

But the end result is also important, and we cannot ignore the fact that the process evolved into the financial crisis in 1995, although that crisis cannot be simply be attributed to financial reform. That would overshadow some important aspects of monetary policy. Let us consider in more detail some of its results.

Figure 4.7 presents the overall performance of finance and bank credit in Mexico from 1933 to 2003. Let us emphasize that the main expansion from 1950 to 1978 corresponds to what McKinnon labelled the repressed period, while the contraction from 1995 to 2003 corresponds to his liberalized phase.

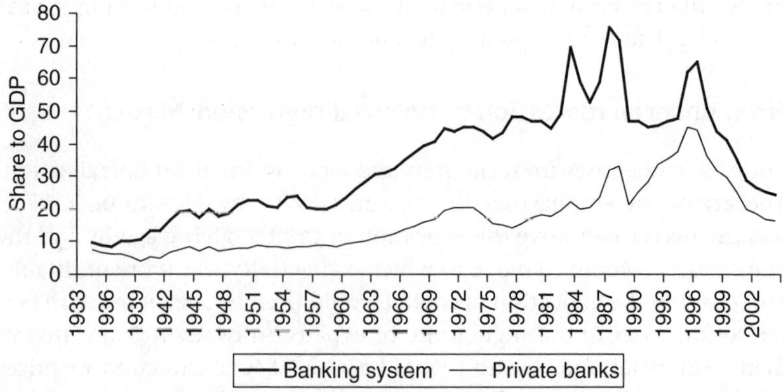

Figure 4.7 Total finance and private banks' credits

Sources: Produced by the author based on data provided by *Economic Indicators*, Bank of Mexico, 1960–2004, and *Historical Financial Records*, Bank of Mexico (1895–1980).

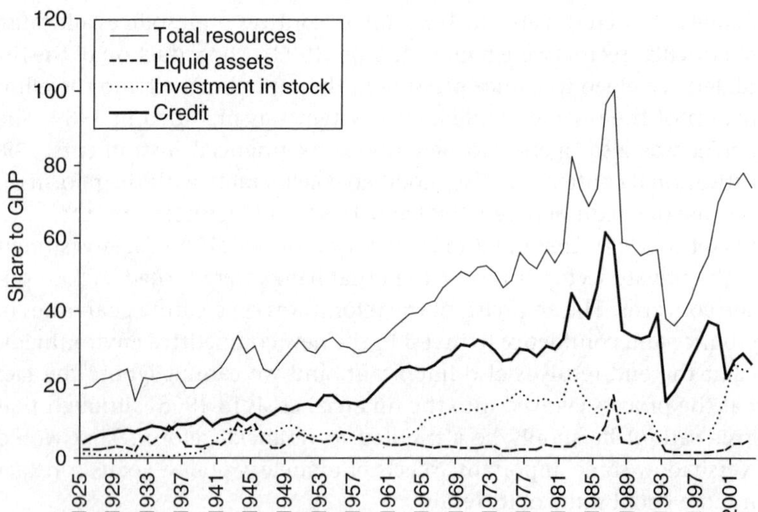

Figure 4.8 Private and development banks, resource structure, 1925–2003

Sources: Produced by the author based on data reported in *Economic Indicators*, Bank of Mexico, 1960–2004, and *Historical Financial Records*, Bank of Mexico, 1895–1980.

The rate of expansion of credit between 1950 to 1978 was over 13 per cent in real terms, twice the rate of growth for the economy, at that time 6.5 per cent. But the structure also changed with an increasing proportion of investment in assets and a diminishing share of credit, as can be observed in Figure 4.8.

That also led to a fundamental change of participation of the private banks from 1988 with financial reform, at the expense of development (public) banks and the central bank, as can be appreciated in Figure 4.9. This in turn helped to direct more resources to the private sector, at least until 1995.

Financial reform no doubt almost eliminated finance of development (national) banks and of the central bank. But one of the main purposes of reform was to create new venues for non-bank finance, and no doubt the reform created the stimuli for new forms and instruments of finance to be introduced into the market. However, non-bank finance, from its inception, has not performed very well, except for a very short period in 1994. But to my mind one of the important signs of regression is the spectacular growth of external debt in private firms, which grew from 1 per cent to nearly 10 per cent of GDP. This expansion is coincident with the contraction of bank finance from 35 per cent to 18 per cent of GDP.

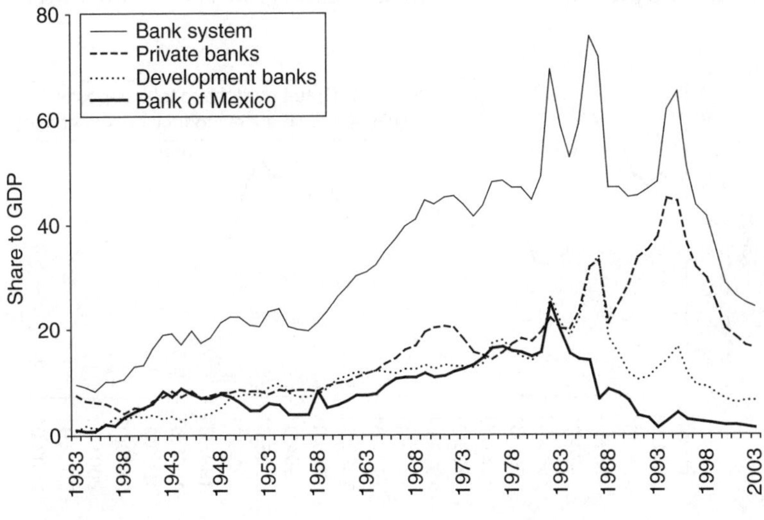

Figure 4.9 Structure of finance by institutions, 1933–2003

Sources: Produced by the author based on data reported in *Historical Financial Records*, Bank of Mexico, 1895–1980, and *Financial Monetary Series*, International Monetary Fund, 1980–2004.

Undoubtedly, large firms find cheaper credit in the international market than in the domestic market, and it is also true that an important part of it can be obtained via the sale of bonds. Nevertheless, it can hardly be considered an advance of the system altogether because, in fact, it shows one of its weaknesses; that is, its inability to provide credit.

Financial reform, and its aftermath with the financial crisis, has severely affected the structure of the banking system. This can be observed in a few standard criteria; for example, liquidity coefficients (credit portfolio to total deposits or liquid assets to total gross deposits), leverage (deposits to total resources or capital to resources), hedge (reserves to default portfolio), solvency (credit portfolio to total bank deposits or non-defaulted portfolio to total bank deposits), and default accounts (default portfolio to credit bill). There is no doubt that the reform, and the subsequent crisis, turned the system illiquid. Nevertheless, financial reform meant the systematic deterioration of the financial conditions of the entire banking system, as can be observed in the Figures 4.10–4.13.

In spite of the drastic reform and a very burdensome rescue package, the level of defaulted portfolio is still very high, liquidity is very short and the extreme coverage seems insufficient to cover the expanded credit. Furthermore, it seems that the defaulted portfolio grew with reform and privatization, and it looks to have grown even more with the

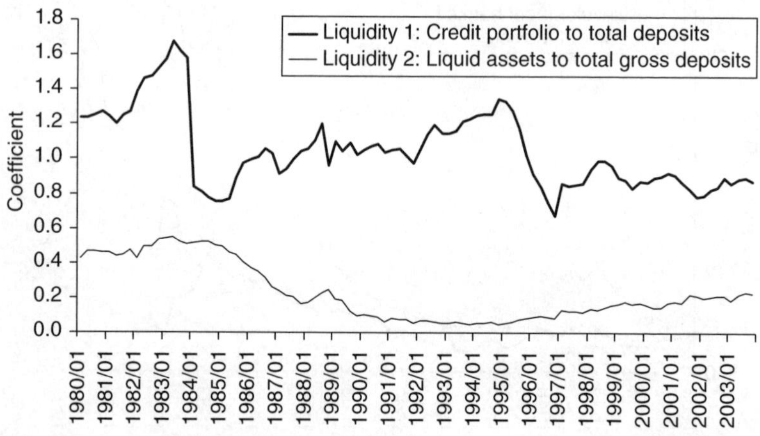

Figure 4.10 Structure of assets and liabilities of private and development banks (liquidity coefficients), 1980–2003

Source: Monthly records, *Economic Indicators*, Bank of Mexico, 1980–2004.

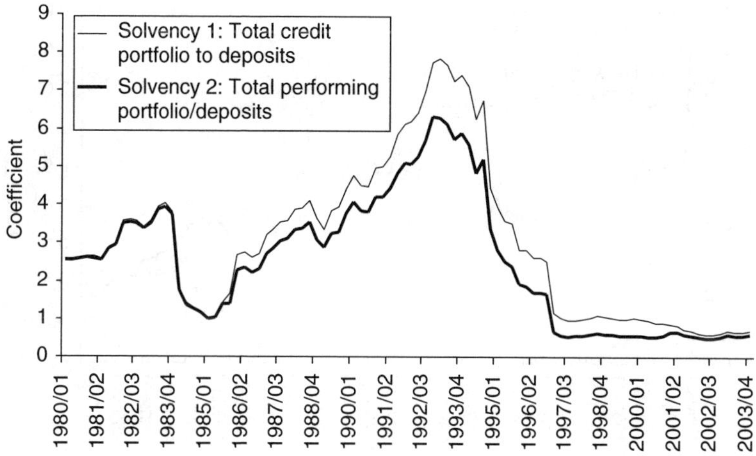

Figure 4.11 Structure of assets and liabilities of private and development banks (solvency coefficients), 1980–2003

Source: Monthly records, *Economic Indicators*, Bank of Mexico, 2004.

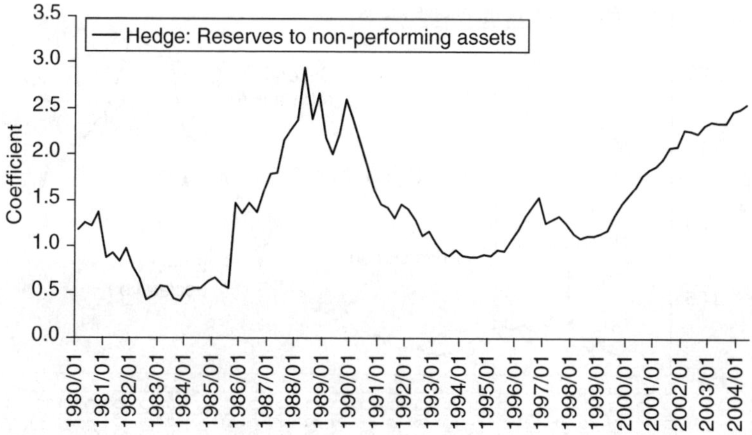

Figure 4.12 Structure of assets and liabilities of private and development banks (hedge coefficients), 1980–2003

Source: Monthly records, *Economic Indicators*, Bank of Mexico, 1980–2004.

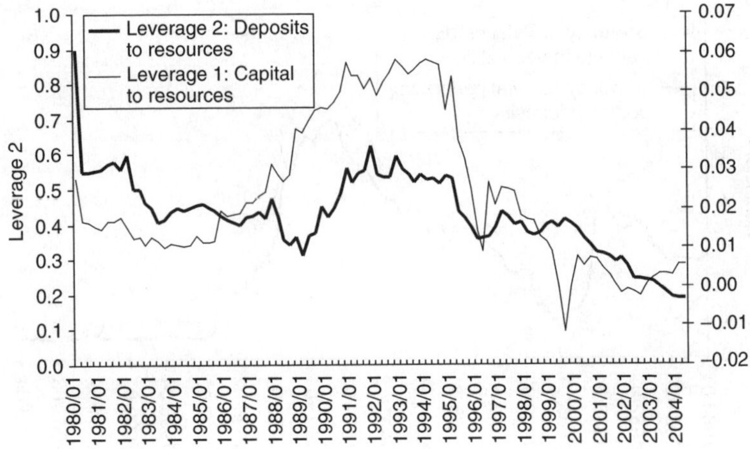

Figure 4.13 Structure of assets and liabilities of private and development banks (leverage coefficients), 1980–2003

Source: Monthly records, *Economic Indicators*, Bank of Mexico, 1980–2004.

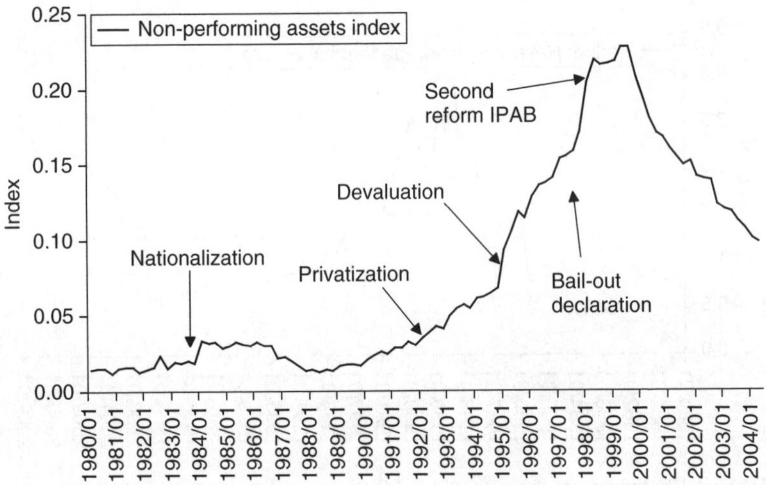

Figure 4.14 Index of non-performing assets, 1980–2003

Source: Produced by the author based on data reported in *Economic Indicators*, Bank of Mexico, 2004.

announcement of the reform package and with the adjustment programme after devaluation. In spite of the fact that leverage coefficients had been falling, credit to private firms has not been restored, as is evident from Figure 4.14.

The second round of reform, after the bail-out package, aimed at restoring an institutional framework more concerned with safety and stability, does not seem to have had any effect on the poor solvency of the system, nor its readiness to advance finance for investment.

Since financial liberalization is associated with greater mobility of capital, the general perception is that the Mexican case to some extent reflects a significant move towards greater mobility (Weintraub 2000). Nevertheless, the essential result of this process has been a significant contraction of the capital market, with at least four notorious distortions:

- There is a violent contraction of bank and non-bank finance to private firms, which has only partially been replaced with external finance.
- There is a significant move to investment in public financial instruments and only marginally in equity.
- Banks, and therefore the capital market, depend heavily on a form of indirect subsidy, which is tied to the public funds directed to restore capital and liquidity to the financial system. In spite of this, banks are still at the limit of their solvency.
- The banking system, after seven years of subsidies, has still not recovered conditions enabling it to stand on its own in the capital market.

Is there any change in prices and stability? Initially, the real rate of interest certainly increased with reform. Once the Mexican interest rate was allowed to be determined by the market, it increased from being 1.2 times higher than the real interest rate in the USA in 1981 to over 4.7 times higher in 1988. But, as can be seen in Figure 4.15, volatility also increased considerably. Figure 4.15 presents the real rate of public bonds in Mexico (bank deposits and CETES (from 1978)) as multiples of the US 28 days prime rate, and its trend (nvtimustrend) as projected by the Hodrick–Prescott filter. This is a monthly series from 1970 to December 2003.

The trend shows a slow but consistent decline of the real rate to an average of 0.6 in 2003. At the time of the crisis it was around 1.4, not much different than before liberalization in 1988. A reduction of volatility is also evident, which is also present in nominal estimates. How can

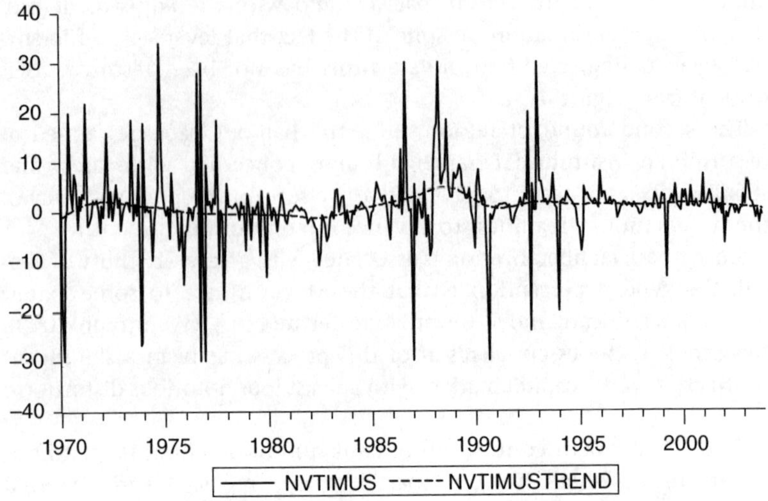

Figure 4.15 Real interest rate in Mexico as multiples of the US (28 days prime rate), time series and Hodrick–Prescott trend

Notes: NVTIMUS = Mexican real interest rates (measured by bank deposits between 1970–1978 and CETES from 1978 onwards) as multiples of the US 28 days prime rate. NVTIMUSTREND = trend of NVTIMUS.

Source: Produced by the author based on data reported in *Economic Indicators*, Bank of Mexico, 2004.

it be interpreted? There are four elements at play:

- Financial liberalization
- Reduction of credit
- Reduction in the real rate of growth of the economy
- A new monetary policy approach, acting through the basic price vector.

It would be difficult to justify any one of them as being determinant of the whole process. The standard presumption was that given the first within the framework of a comprehensive process of structural change, the second and third items should have been the opposite; namely, the expansion of credit and a faster growth process. The contention of this chapter is that the last element has been outstanding and has dominated all the others.

What is the rationale of this situation? Is it embedded in the approach to financial reform by itself, or is it in the monetary policy model?

Overall, the package for financial reform was comprehensive and well integrated, according to standard orthodox practice. According to one of its leading actors, Dr Aspe (Minister of Finance – 1993), institutional, fiscal and central bank reforms covered every aspect needed for the reform programme to be successful. Following the crisis, attention has been directed to rules of supervision and central bank independence. Nevertheless, the monetary policy package has remained almost the same, except for the fact that exchange rate policy is more flexible, although recreating again and again conditions of overvaluation.

There are three very important facts as a result of the monetary policy:

- Export performance has come to a standstill, to a large extent due to the overvaluation effect, but also for the long-run effect of the possibilities of encouraging real competitive capabilities, inhibiting productivity growth.
- There is a fall in the rate of investment.
- In the meantime, the possibilities of adjustment rest on access for external capital flows in any form.

The stability of the whole model then rests on the ability to sustain a flow of external capital that sooner or later may come to an end because, being as successful as it is, it has been increasing the weight of external debt, particularly the private debt.

From financial repression to financial regression: the case for debt lead growth

When discussing adjustment paths, we cannot ignore that there is one particular form to deal with imbalances by any agent or the economy – the issuance of debt. Let us depart from a condition in which the central bank can manage to fix a basic price vector such that inflation is zero and the deficits concerned (trade balance, public deficit and banks balances) also are zero. Then, the TA would consider it is in equilibrium. But all these conditions might be fulfilled without firms being able to clear their balances with banks, in spite of the fact that the rationale of financial liberalization was to forge a strong capital market that would ease the possibilities for adjustment in the economy. The standard conditions for the development of the capital market have generally been reduced to the idea that if the central bank can clear its balances, it is therefore inferred that firms should also be able to clear theirs.

Whatever the rationale about financial liberalization, it is peculiar that the literature on the actual experiences of liberalization (Caprio *et al.* 2001) recognizes that the initial impact of getting rid of controls on the rate of interest is a sudden increase in rates and volatility. This indeed was also the experience in Mexico. It is also recognized that the weaker the institutional set up, the higher the probability that it may evolve into an over-borrowing crisis. If, on top of that, the macroeconomic environment is not entirely stable, as was the case in Mexico from 1983 to 1996, there is no question that the more likely result should be a call for disaster. Nevertheless, almost nothing is said about the relationship of the difficulties with financial liberalization and monetary policy. The presumption is that ex-ante monetary policy set a scenario of neutrality, and that is a fundamental mistake.

Generally I would argue that in a capitalist economy, adjustment paths depends on the relationship between capital markets and the firms, and that, as was stated before, they may have four fundamental venues: (i) price adjustment: either real and/or nominal; (ii) capital flows adjustment, which might turn to real adjustment in quantities produced and prices; (iii) growth path adjustment, which relates to changes in productivity and investment; and (iv) adjustment through the accumulation of debts.

The first is ambiguous because it involves a real and/or a nominal adjustment. Orthodox theory generally deals with it in separate modelling structures, given all the weaknesses it has in price and monetary theory.[8] The second is closely related and rests on a logically flawed model that assumes the mobility of capital should work towards equilibrium, though the movement to such an equilibrium in a market economy has not been actually deducted from decentralized agents in disequilibrium. Paradoxically, it is within the framework of classical-Marxian dynamic models that we can find some advances in this direction.[9]

The third has been actually the more important path of adjustment for growing economies. It introduces the opportunity for firms to introduce dynamic responses – either technological, organizational and financial – to respond to disequilibria. From a dynamic perspective, it creates the virtuous circle of productivity and accumulation that is at the roots of a well ordered and reasonably well operating capital market. Nevertheless, it is very sensitive to the long-run incidence of monetary policy.

The core of our argument is that monetary policy is actually decisive in creating a bias to look for one particular adjustment path, the issuance of debt. Let us analyze it from the model presented in the second section.

The rationale is that at any price vector (*E, i, w*) some agents might be in equilibrium; that is, they can pay their debts and obtain the standard rate of profit on the invested capital. Some others might do even better, but it is unavoidable that some might make a loss and fail to pay off their debts. Excess profits might compensate for losses, of course, on average, though that would only occur as a fluke, although there is no reason to suggest that firms in default could outnumber those making higher profits. The real issue is the relationship between the disequilibria generated by a particular price vector (*E, i, w*) and the real possibilities of adjustment open to common firms.

To put the questions in a different format: What conditions should prevail in the economy in order for firms to be able to meet their debts? If such conditions are fulfilled, their capital value will be made up and the capital market can grow reasonably well. Evidently it depends on firms being able to be profitable; though the initial impact of any basic price vector is on profitability. The competitive process would reduce funds for firms making a loss and increase investment and capital values for those making excess profits. That is acceptable for textbook standards, but it is too mechanical. Real firms, even if they do not receive additional funds, are already engaged with fixed investments and a number of resources are committed or indebted. How can they adjust, given their outstanding debts? The standard text book assumes they disappear. But, in fact, they can also draw back on the bank, even if they are showing a loss, extending their outstanding debts. This has been an important means of adjustment induced by financial reforms, not because firms hide information from banks (Stiglitz 1994), but because banks might also be interested that the public do not realize that their assets are getting weaker. This is the source of the over-borrowing syndrome.

In terms of the model of the tyrannical auctioneer, price lines in Figure 4.6 trace the opportunities open for firms, given their technological and financial conditions. In small open economies, generally, we would have only one rate of exchange. The diagram shows that then the economy would be open to work with several rates of interest, not because they would tend to equalize considering differences in maturity, risk or any other consideration. They would differ because the market is open for differentiation, given the slopes of price lines, and oligopoly pricing seems to be the rule. That opportunity is reaped by banks, because banks can differentiate conditions for their clients. Consequently, in a fully flexible competitive economy (i.e. open to capital flows) price signals for commercial banks sent by the central bank (in his role of the TA) do not necessarily work in the same direction as they do for firms. Consequently, their adjustment paths may not be convergent.

The initial condition is that some firms are paying more for credit than other firms. Intuitively, we can infer that the former generally are weaker in negotiations with banks, perhaps because they might not have any other form of access to the capital market. But the initial problem is that the excess financial cost for some firms is transformed into excess profits for banks, if price adjustments are not an option for firms, given that part of the package is that the economy is fully open for trade; the particular price vector (*E, i, w*) might be particularly sensitive for an important number of firms in the economy. Therefore, even if the balances of the TA were in equilibrium and the rate of inflation is under control, any price vector extremely oriented to control inflation (an overvalued *E*, and a very high *i*, with a *w* working as the actual lever on the inflation rate), should put an important fraction of the economy on the brink of collapse, or at least facing low rates of profit than cannot stimulate the growth of productivity and attract investment. Consequently, we come to the conclusion that the scope for price adjustment is reduced because monetary policy sets a very limited path within which firms are able to find an alternative.

Under these conditions, export performance has been jeopardized, unable to reap the benefits of trade liberalization. This might be difficult to observe, but the case of the Mexican economy is illustrative of one of its more subtle characteristics. We can have an incredible gross performance on exports with almost no positive impact for the economy. This is so because overvaluation encourages export performance to rest on the flows of imported inputs. Therefore, the linkage with the rest of the economy breaks and there is no way to have an increase of domestic value added, as can be observed in Figure 4.16.

Successful cases of export led growth present a value added line well above the nominal growth of exports and imports, such as in the cases of South Korea, China and Singapore.[10] It is remarkable that at the point where the value added curve twisted downwards in 1994, the economy went into crisis. The second downturn in 2000 also put the economy in a situation of stagnation. In both cases, the sole form of adjustment left was to obtain more capital from abroad, with both parties (borrowers and lenders) knowing that otherwise their capital value would be untenable. In a way, both parties have come to terms in a common understanding to extend non-performing debts as in a Ponzi situation.

The standard assumption is that competition should bring some form of capital mobility that moves towards equilibrium.[11] But the history of

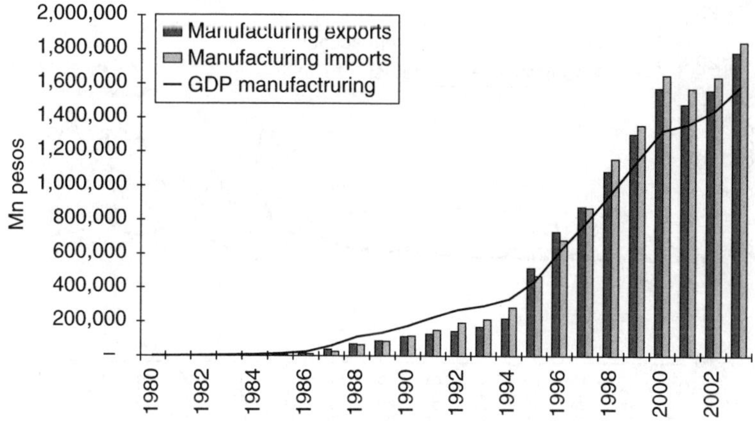

Figure 4.16 Exports and imports vis-à-vis manufacturing value added

Sources: Produced by the author based on data reported in *Economic Indicators*, Bank of Mexico, 1980–2004, and *National and Income Accounts*, INEGI, 1970–2003.

financial crisis is always associated with a condition in which capital cannot move in or out of a particular economy, or sudden movements may well bring the economy to its knees. Nevertheless, a model of financial crisis that rests on rigidities of the capital market is not necessarily a good model. Therefore, our initial proposition is built upon the condition that capital has full mobility. The question arises as to whether the policies followed by the TA are consistent with the opportunities of adjustment of the real economy and the capital market.

This is particularly the case when the central bank is forced to create special conditions to attract capital just to cover the external debt service. This is certainly the case of the Mexican economy, and any other case of recent financial crisis. The argument is irrespective of whether the debts are public or private, they need to be served punctually at all times. The capital that flows in should cover three component parts: amortization, interest payments on debt and balance of payments deficits. For the Mexican economy, these three components in 2003 amounted to US$65 billion, around 10 per cent of GDP, and kept increasing every year, even though the economy had not been growing at all, and its capacity to pay had been reduced by trade conditions. Therefore, even if attracting capital inflows is not declared as an important task for monetary authorities, they simply cannot manage to cover the debt and balance of payments deficit without it. This condition forces the central bank to pursue a policy that permanently pegs the interest rates to a

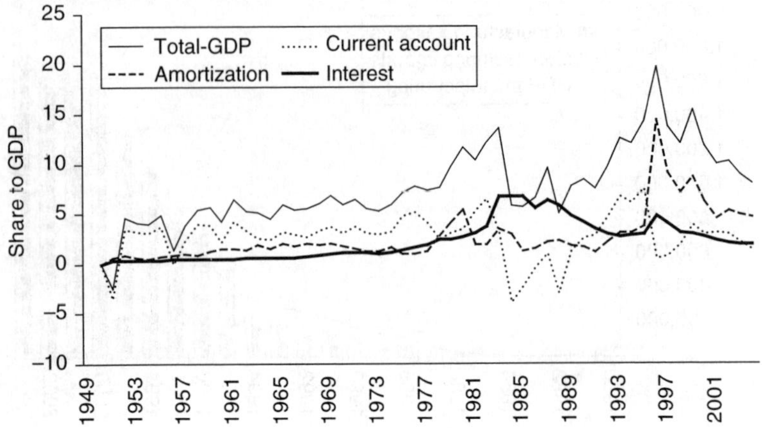

Figure 4.17 Total requirement for external savings, 1950–2003
Source: Produced by the author based on data reported in *Balance of Payments*, Bank of Mexico, 1960–2004.

level usually associated with an overvalued exchange rate, because otherwise the country risk premium will increase (see Figure 4.17).

It has been argued that the public debt component has been reduced, given that private firms or banks now are able to get credit in the international market. In fact, net public external debt amounts to nearly 60 per cent of external indebtness. It is also true that direct external debt has been reduced from US$ 170 billion in 1995 to US$ 133 billion in 2003. Apparently that is the correct magnitude. However, the actual magnitude of external commitments has also to consider other forms of liabilities with external creditors in the form of FDI in the money and capital market that has accumulated to nearly US$ 230 billion in 2003, an increase of US$ 130 billion from 1995. If half of it is already considered in the private debt balance, we should have to add another US$ 65 billions to the external liabilities to a total of around 200 billions. We cannot ignore that in our historical experience, private debts in crisis periods are turned into public debts. This has been the case in the 1976, 1983 and 1995 crises.

It is indeed paradoxical that either mistakes in the design or sequencing of financial reform or in monetary policy have led to a model that has a consistent trend for the development of already established capital markets in the developed economies, while reducing the scope for the development of emerging capital markets in developing countries. The reason is that the model has come to rest on the opportunities to engage in more debt, while not creating the conditions to repay those debts. This has been identified as a debt lead growth model and not as an export lead growth model (Kregel 2003).

Therefore, what we actually find is that monetary policy formed from a particular price vector (E, i, w), although is particularly directed to work within the first two adjustment mechanisms, is systematically biased for a rather poor performance on the productivity path. What is even more paradoxical is that monetary policy, presumably, was oriented to work through the price adjustment and the capital reallocation paths. This has not been the case given the poor productivity performance, such that necessarily diminishes or even destroys the third path of adjustment, which actually is the more important in the long run, and necessarily the path with the greater potential to create a real and strong capital market.

The positive relationship between growth and the expansion of the capital market derives from a historical perspective and a basic reading of Post Keynesian growth theory. In this, the positive relationship between investment decision and productivity allows the rate of growth of productivity (and therefore exports) to be sustained and is associated with a virtuous performance in the capital market, as in Kaldorian growth models.[12] The relationship, nevertheless, is not reversible.

We might end this chapter in agreement with Caprio *et al.* (2001): Few lament the demise of financial repression – though not with their analysis of the nature of the different ongoing experiences of financial reform, and even less on what is to be done now to recover the perspective of structural reforms. Mainstream literature has highlighted the notion that sequencing in financial reform is the key issue (McKinnon and Pill 1995, McKinnon 1999). Others have called attention to difficulties inherent to financial activities at all times (Stiglitz 2002). But only partially they have questioned the monetary policy framework (Stiglitz 1999).

The main issue, from the point of view of the needs for a new reform, is that the approach already launched on financial reform and the present policy framework has spelled disaster for the financial system. The essentials of financial reform cannot be reduced to freer markets, in the face of such a gruesome contraction of credit and finance.

Undoubtedly, an essential ingredient for structural reform is the development of competitive, expanding capital markets. What is not evident is that the way to create them is independent of monetary policy, as if it were a neutral box of tools. But the reconstruction of a sound capital market rests on the possibility that capital becomes productive, therefore competitive, and is able to adjust to the signals of competition. This is essential for a positive drive for manufacturing exports to give the right feedback to the domestic capital market.

The independence of central banks does not guarantee that monetary policy is neutral or that it can be run as in a vacuum. The current policy model has turned monetary policy in an extremely important component of everyday decision making. In a democratic society it cannot be given up to a group of 'wise men' on the grounds of banks' independence, while the whole economy is not independent of monetary policy. The tyrannical auctioneer should be accountable in all situations, given the increasing policy capabilities that have been granted.

The policy agenda is now open to rethinking the institution of the central bank and the way in which monetary policy should also work to create conditions for the growth of productivity and employment.

Notes

1. Patinkin (1965) put it clearly. Either the solution of the real and monetary side is only relevant in partial equilibrium, or money is expelled from the system (Benetti 1992). If expectations are introduced, for example in overlapped generations models, the solutions rest on a peculiar condition: future income is always a given, and known in advance (Hahn and Solow 1998). Therefore, the actions of agents and monetary policy cannot influence the equilibrium position, which in fact amounts to introducing a pseudo money and no actual capital market at all. Accumulative effects, in those sorts of model, are impossible to consider (Hahn and Solow 1995).
2. See Bernanke and Mishkin (1997) and Alvarez *et al.* (2001).
3. The wage rate is introduced here for the sake of completeness, though not fully considered in this chapter. In fact, the wage rate gives way to a broader consideration of a macroeconomic model.
4. Bernanke and Mishkin (1997) and Taylor (1993, 2001).
5. An important literature exists questioning the relevance of this result, because it gives rise to an equilibrium that might not consider monetary transactions.
6. A general view about the actual relevance of circuit theory is found in Rochon (1999).
7. For example, as in Pentecost (1993).
8. There is a vast literature on the difficulties of integrating money in the basic pricing framework. Patinkin (1962), Hahn (1985), Benetti (1992) and Hahn and Solow (1998).
9. See Nikaido (1983), Dumenil and Levy (1987), Flaschel and Semmler (1987) and Ortiz (1997).
10. Evidence on export performance and manufacturing value added is in the Trade and Development Report (2002) by UNCTAD.
11. The rationale for this proposition rests on a proposition that for no reason has been called a 'theorem', although it does not have the logical structure

necessary for such a name (the Modigliany–Miller proposition that rates of profit tend to equalize with rates of interest).

12. See Kaldor (1957), Kaldor and Mirrlees (1962) and Thirlwall (2003).

References

Alvarez, F., Lucas, R. and Weber, W. (2001) 'Recent Advances in Monetary-Policy Rules', *American Economic Review*, Papers and Proceedings.

Aspe, P. (1993) *El camino Mexicano de la transformación económica* (Fondo de Cultura Económica: México).

Balassa, B. (1985) *Change and Challenge in the World Economy* (Washington, DC: World Bank).

Ball, L. (2001) 'Policy Rules for Open Economies', in J. Taylor (ed.), *Monetary Policy Rules* (Chicago: NBER Business Cycles Series Vol. 31).

Ball, L. (1997) 'Efficient Rules for Monetary Policy', NBER Working Papers, No. 5952 (Cambridge, Mass.: National Bureau of Economic Research).

Bank of Mexico *Economic Indicators* (1980–2004) (Mexico City).

Bank of Mexico (1985), *Series Históricas y Financieras, 1895–1980,* Mexico City, also in Economiá Mexicana en Cifras, NAFINCA, 1994.

Benetti, C. (1992) *Moneda y Teoría del Valor* (Fondo de Cultura Económica: México).

Bernanke, B. and Gertler, M. (2001) 'Quantitative Policy Implications of New Normative Macroeconomic Research: Should Central Banks Respond to Movements in Asset Prices', *Amercian Economic Review*, Papers and Proceedings: 253–7.

Bernanke, R. and Mishkin, F. (1997) 'Inflation Targeting: A New Framework for Monetary Policy?', *Journal of Economic Perspectives*, Spring, 11(2), 97–116.

Blinder, Alan (1998) *Central Banking in Theory and Practice* (Cambridge, Mass: MIT Press).

Caprio, G., Honohan, P. and Stiglitz, J. (2001). *Financial Liberalization. How Far, How Fast?* (Cambridge: Cambridge University Press).

Clarida, R., Galí, J. and Gertler, M. (2001) 'Optimal Monetary Policy in Open versus Closed Economies: An Integrated Approach', *American Economic Review*, Papers and Proceedings.

Clower, R.W. (1967) 'Foundations of Monetary Theory', in *Money and Markets: Essays by R.W Clower* (Cambridge: Cambridge University Press), reprinted in R. W. Clower (ed.) (1970), *Monetary Theory* (Baltimore: Penguin).

Duménil, G. and Lévy, D. (1987) 'The Dynamics of Competition: A Restoration of the Classical Analysis', *Cambridge Journal of Economics*, 11: 133–53.

Eichner, A. (1984) 'A General Model of Investment and Pricing', in E. Nell, *Growth, Profits and Property. Essays in the Revival of Political Economy* (Cambridge, Mass: Cambridge University Press).

Fisher, F. (1999) *Competition* (Cambridge: Cambridge University Press).

Flaschel, P., Reiner, F. and Semmler, W. (1997) *Dynamic Macroeconomics. Instability, Fluctuations, and Growth in Monetary Economics* (Cambridge, Mass: MIT Press).

Flaschel, P. and Semmler, W. (1987) 'Classical and Neoclassical Competitive Adjustment Processes', *The Manchester School*, March, 13–37.

Hahn, F. (1985) *Money, Growth and Stability* (Oxford: Basil Blackwell).

Hahn, F. and Solow, R. (1998) *A Critical Essay on Modern Macroeconomic Theory* (Oxford: Blackwell).

IMF, *Financial Monetary Series*, 1980–2004 (Washington, DC).

Kaldor, N. (1957) 'A Model of Economic Growth' *Economic Journal*, December.

Kaldor, N. and Mirrlees, J. (1962) 'A New model of Economic Growth' *Review of Economic Studies*, 29,3.

Kregel, J. (2003) 'An Alternative View of the Argentine Crisis: Structural Flaws in Structural Adjustment Policy', in *Investigación Económica*, 243, 15–49.

Krueger, A. (1995) 'Policy Lessons from Development Experience Since the Second World War', in J. Behrman and T.N. Srinivasan (eds) *Handbook of Development Economics, Vol. III*, 2497–550.

McKinnon, R. (1999) 'The Overborrowing Syndrome', mimeo.

McKinnon, R. (1973) *Money and Capital in Economic Development* (Washington, DC: Brookings Institution).

McKinnon, R. and Pill, H. (1995) 'Credible Liberalizations and International Capital Flows', mimeo, Department of Economics, Stanford.

Nikaido, H. (1983) 'Marx on Competition' *Zeischrift für Nationalokonomie*, 43 (4).

Ortiz, C.E. (2003–4) 'Pricing in a Small Open Monetary Economy. A Post Keynesian Model', *Journal of Post Keynesian Economics*, Winter 2003–04.

Ortiz, C.E. (1997) 'Disequilibrium Pricing, Critical Equilibrium and the Real Cycle', in P. Davidson and J.A Kregel (eds), *Improving the Global Economy* (Cheltenham: Edward Elgar).

Patinkin, D. (1965) *Money Interest and Prices. An Integration of Monetary and Value Theory* (New York: Harper & Row).

Pentecost, E. (1993) *Exchange Rate Dynamics* (Cheltenham: Edward Elgar).

Rochon, L. (1999) *Credit Money and Production* (Cheltenham: Edward Elgar).

Snowdon, B., Vane, H. and Wynarczyk, P. (1996) *A Modern Guide to Macroeconomics* (Cambridge, Mass.: Edward Elgar).

Stiglitz, J. (1994) 'The Role of the State in Financial Markets', in *Proceedings of the World Bank Annual Conference on Development Economics*, 1993 (Washington: World Bank).

Stiglitz, J. (1999) 'Knowledge for Development: Economic Science, Economic Policy and Economic Advice', Address to the World Bank Conference on Development 1998 (Washington, DC: World Bank).

Stiglitz, J. (2002), *Globalization and its Discontents* (London: Penguin).

Taylor, J. (2001) 'The Role of Exchange Rate in Monetary-Policy Rules', *American Economic Review*, Papers and Proceedings.

Taylor, J. (1993) 'Discretion versus Policy Rules in Practice', Carnegie-Rochester Conference Series on Public Policy, December, 39(0) 195–214.

Thirlwall, A.P. (2003) *Growth and Development. With Special Reference to Developing Economies*, 7th Edn (Basingstoke: Palgrave Macmillan).

UNCTAD (2002) *Trade and Development Report* (New York: UNCTAD).

Weintraub, S. (2000) *Financial Decision-Making in Mexico. To Bet a Nation* (Pittsburgh, PA: University of Pittsburgh Press).

Woodward, M. (2001) 'The Taylor Rule and Otimal Monetary Policy', *American Economic Review*, Papers and Proceedings.

5

Inflation Targeting and Exchange Rate Risk in Emerging Economies Subject to Structural Inflation

Guadalupe Mántey

Introduction

For more than three decades, conventional models of central banking have been informed by the quantity theory of money and the monetarist approach to the balance of payments, which assume that: (i) inflation is a monetary phenomenon; (ii) purchasing power parity determines exchange rates in the long run; (iii) real interest rates cannot be affected by monetary variables in the long run; and (iv) money supply is an exogenous variable under central bank control.

Following this paradigm, during most of the 1970s and 1980s central banks established their intermediate objectives in terms of targets on selected monetary aggregates, or rules. In the last decade, however, growing dissatisfaction with the quantity theory of money and the monetarist approach to the balance of payments led to an alternative explanation of inflation, giving rise to a new regime for monetary control based on inflation targeting.

Empirical research on money market behaviour, carried out in the 1990s with the aid of new econometric methods, eroded the foundations of the monetarist approach, by demonstrating that inflation is a super-exogenous variable in stable money demand functions (i.e. prices do not depend on past values of the money supply); so that the stability of demand functions should be explained by money supply accommodating to money demand (Hendry and Ericsson 1991).

Endogenous money theory, based on institutional economics contributions (Chick 1989, Niggle 1991) and empirical research on commercial banking practices (Kaldor 1970, Wray 1990) reached the same conclusion, and provided two explanations for the phenomenon, which are not mutually exclusive:

- Money supply is the result of money demand (debts) which originates with the production process itself
- Base money is endogenous due to central bank responsibility for payments system safety.

One obvious implication of endogenous money theory is that inflation cannot be considered a monetary phenomenon in the way quantity theory envisaged; that is, the price level being the variable that balances money supply and demand.

Backing the endogenous money approach, central bankers substituted a theory that explains present inflation as a function of expectations regarding future inflation for the quantity theory of money.

In this model, monetary policy retains its influence on the level of prices in an indirect way, through the process of forming expectations. Since expectations on future inflation depend on conventional beliefs, which are still based on the monetarist paradigm, orthodox monetary policy measures are expected to have an effect on inflation by means of self-fulfilling prophesies. Consequently, under this regime the transmission mechanism of monetary policy remains hidden.

Inflation targeting has been successfully applied in industrialized countries, and has been recommended by multilateral financial institutions to central banks of developing countries.

This chapter examines the appropriateness of this regime for monetary control in developing countries subject to structural inflation. Structural inflation is understood to be a magnified response of the inflation rate to exchange-rate variations, characteristic of developing economies, brought about by technological dependence, oligopolistic competition and unequal international trade.

Mainstream open economy macroeconomics assumes developing economies behave like industrialized ones, and inflation targeting relies on the same assumption. We shall argue that dualism affects the inflationary process and, to be effective, price stabilization policies in semi-industrialized economies must be directed to lower the exchange rate pass-through, taking into account the structural origin of trade imbalances.

The chapter is organized in seven sections. The next section deals with the theoretical arguments and empirical findings which account for the debasement of the quantity theory of money, and the substitution of inflation targeting for the control of monetary aggregates.

The third section presents a brief overview of structural inflation theory and its application to stabilization programmes in Latin American countries. The fourth section examines the opposite phenomenon in industrialized countries (i.e. incomplete exchange rate pass-through) and extends the model proposed by Arestis and Milberg (1994), by incorporating assumptions of unequal trade and dependence, in order better to analyze structural inflation in developing economies.

In the fifth section, we use the enlarged model to explain the magnified exchange rate pass-through in Mexico and Brazil, and its decline after the implementation of trade liberalization policies during the last decade. These effects are measured by means of two cointegration and error correction models of the inflation rate estimated for Mexico and Brazil. In this section we also show that exchange-rate depreciation is an inefficient tool for stabilizing the trade balance, due to the high income elasticity and low price elasticity of imports demand in both countries, as well as to the detrimental effect of currency devaluation on real wages and employment.

The sixth section analyzes differences in exchange rate determinants in developed and developing countries, and debates the effectiveness of inflation targeting and interest rate policy in stabilizing the trade balance and the exchange rate in emerging countries affected by structural inflation. It also warns of the systemic risks a developing economy faces when its central bank policy is conditioned by volatile expectations of international investors.

The last section summarizes the main conclusions, and highlights the merits of the stabilization strategy recommended by early Latin American structuralists and inferred from Thirlwall's law in balance-of-payments constrained growth models.

The debasement of quantity theory of money

For many years, central banking policy models were informed by the quantity theory of money. The models assumed that the nominal quantity of money was exogenously determined by (a) a central bank's supply of reserves and a stable money multiplier; (b) base money increases being dependent mainly on fiscal deficits; (c) a stable demand for cash balances; (d) the real rate of interest being independent from monetary phenomena; and (e) the price level variable that cleared the money market.

These models also assumed perfect competition prevailed in factor and product markets; but since labour contracts were settled in nominal terms, prices tended to rise whenever wages increased more than labour productivity.

In the short-run, anti-inflationary monetary policy was usually framed in the expectations augmented Phillips-curve model, which related wage inflation to the level of unemployment. This approach implied that a high level of unemployment was caused either by inflationary expectations or by institutional constraints to a low natural rate of unemployment. If central bank policies were credible, a higher level of employment could only be attained by structural reforms in the labour market (e.g. abolition of minimum wages, reduction of social security and unemployment benefits, etc.) which would reduce unit labour costs.

Based on the monetarist approach, which recommended a constant rate of growth in the quantity of money to satisfy a stable demand for real cash balances, these models supported monetary regimes based on rules for monetary expansion and central bank independence, as a way to enhance central bank credibility and reputation (Friedman 1968, 1981, Barro and Gordon 1983, Rogoff 1985). Rules were expressed in terms of aggregate monetary targets.

The instability that began to appear in estimated money demand functions during the late 1970s and early 1980s, when innovations and deregulation in financial markets brought about a decline in the income velocity of money, undermined the foundations of the quantity theory of money (Laidler 1990, Fisher 1995). At the same time, developments in institutional economics, and empirical research on commercial bank behaviour, led to the conclusion that the quantity of money was demand determined, with the obvious implication that the price level was not the variable that equilibrated the money market (Kaldor 1970, Wray 1990).

From then on, endogenous money theorists maintained that central banks are unable to determine the supply of money, since the latter depend on production decisions and credit demands, which are influenced only indirectly. Therefore, any attempt to establish target values for monetary aggregates is bound to fail, since central banks can only limit their supply of reserves at the cost of generating liquidity crises in the banking system (Arestis and Eichner 1988, Chick 1989, Padoa-Schioppa 1994, Lavoie 1996).

In the early 1990s, the advancement of econometric techniques enabled economists to estimate money demand functions with stable parameters, by means of cointegration and error correction models (Hendry and Ericsson 1991). The empirical research on money demand in the United Kingdom and the United States, however, revealed that the rate of inflation was not only a weakly-exogenous variable in the models, but also super-exogenous,[1] and thus equations could not be inverted to represent models of price determination. The resulting conclusion was that the supply of money depended on the same variables that determined its demand, thus providing additional support to endogenous money theory.

The questioning of quantity theory, and the need to speed up economic growth, led to the abandonment of unconditional rules on monetary aggregates in many developed countries in the late 1980s and early 1990s. Nevertheless, the institutional framework of the previous monetarist regime, with its emphasis on central bank credibility, accountability and transparency, remained a cornerstone of the new monetary control regime based on inflation targeting.

Inflation targeting focuses on the medium term, and leaves room for central bank flexibility to respond to unpredictable shocks. Thus, inflation targeting hopes to provide an anchor for expectations, while enabling central bankers to exercise discretion (Le Heron and Carre 2004).

Inflation targeting departs from mainstream monetary theory in four important ways. It:

(i) admits money is endogenous;
(ii) holds that the real interest rate is a central bank policy variable;
(iii) is not supported by the quantity theory of prices;
(iv) does not explain the transmission mechanism of monetary policy.

Today, the typical reaction function of a central bank takes the form of Taylor's rule, in which the nominal interest rate minus the expected inflation (determined by opinion surveys) is explained by variables such as the difference between actual inflation and the target rate, the product gap, the current account deficit, the rate of unemployment and so on, the weights on each reflecting the importance attached to each policy objective by the monetary authority.

The new regime assumes that the central bank is aware of the true model of the economy, and behaves according to a stable reaction function whenever the economy departs from equilibrium. Hence, rather than a rule, such a reaction function is the mathematical expression of a discretional policy (Blinder 1998). Here, since money is endogenous, the explanation of inflation as a monetary phenomenon is ruled out. Hence, inflation targeting assumes that actual prices depend mainly on expectations about future prices. It centres attention on inertial or underlying inflation, and assumes that random inflationary shocks have only short-term effects that become white noise, because the economy operates with automatic stabilizers and under free competition.

Inflation targeting shuns explanations of the transmission mechanism of monetary policy. Central bank intervention influences economic activity and the level of prices because people trust the monetary authority, and are convinced it is doing what it should. Nevertheless, since people's beliefs often reflect the conventional wisdom that originated in the quantity theory of money and its flawed assumptions, transparency is understood to be common understanding, not absolute disclosure of the monetary policy model: 'Confidence emerges from uncertainty and indeterminacy about the model of the economy and the transmission mechanism ... [so that] An optimal degree of ambiguity is necessary to the confidence strategy. Total transparency can lead to counterproductive reflexivity between the central bank and financial markets' (Le Heron 2004).

In economies where contingent inflationary shocks have small and/or transitory effects, and actual inflation depends mainly on expectations of future prices, the announcement of multi-annual inflation targets by the central bank, and an adequate communication strategy between the latter and economic agents, are likely to induce a process of self-fulfilling prophesies, which strengthen central bank credibility and reputation in a virtuous circle. On the other hand, in economies where structural imbalances are the main cause of inflation, and markets do not stabilize automatically, tending rather to amplify the initial shock, inflation targeting may be a short-lived nominal anchor for the economy.

In the late 1980s, various Latin American economies implemented heterodox stabilization programmes which, by means of negotiated social agreements, reduced uncertainty about prices, wages and exchange rates, and successfully lowered inflation rates in the short run. Nonetheless, this strategy overlooked the structural imbalances in foreign trade that characterize developing economies, so that the nominal exchange rate anchor quickly led to unsustainable trade account deficits, giving rise to currency crises and mounting inflation.

This chapter attempts to demonstrate that inflation targeting in developing countries is bound to fail for the same reasons. It will be argued that fighting inflation by anchoring expectations of future inflation, without a consistent and realistic model of price determination, on the basis of eclectic conventional beliefs, leaves economic policy at the mercy of volatile foreign capital flows, induces recession, favours a redistribution of income from wages to profits and rents, and unavoidably leads to an exchange-rate crisis.

Inertial inflation and structural inflation

Mainstream exchange rate theory, rooted in the quantity theory of money and the law of one price, postulates that purchasing power parity between two currencies determines its long-run rate of exchange (Krugman and Obstfeld 1999). It assumes that the direction of causality goes from an excess money supply (usually as a result of government deficits) to the rate of inflation, and from there to the exchange rate.

The validity of this theory has been disputed in developing countries, where trade account imbalances arise mainly because the income elasticity of their exports demand is much lower than the income elasticity of their imports, due to their backward industrial structures. These countries are forced to withstand frequent currency devaluations, which lead to pronounced strong inflationary effects.

Early versions of the structural theory of inflation attempted to explain the hyperinflation that appeared in Germany after World War I, and also in Latin American countries in the 1950s, when the latter implemented import substitution strategies to foster industrial development.

In the early 1930s, a number of German economists contended that ongoing inflation in their country was not a monetary phenomenon, linked to fiscal deficits, but rather originated in a lack of foreign currency to pay for war reparations, forcing the government to carry out a series of exchange rate adjustments. They claimed that prices increased as a result of currency devaluations, and that the money supply merely adapted to the increase in money demand brought about by rising prices. For this reason, these German economists were amongst the forerunners of endogenous money theory (Camara and Vernengo 2001).

In the 1950s, a group of economists working for the United Nations Economic Commission for Latin America and the Caribbean (ECLAC) also posited that inflation in the region was not a monetary phenomenon, nor could it be explained by excess demand. They emphasized that dualism in the industrial structure and an unfavourable division of labour were the main sources of inflationary pressures in developing countries.

This theory, known as 'Latin American Structuralism', attempted to explain different behavioural patterns observed in developed and developing economies, as well as the asymmetric economic relationships between rich and poor countries, labelled the 'centre' and the 'periphery'.

Economists at ECLAC claimed that external and internal equilibrium in developing nations could not be achieved by means of relative price adjustments, as neo-classical economics postulate. Further, trade inequality was a result of technological dependence on industrialized economies, and poor countries' backward industrial structure, which could not be resolved by currency devaluation. Furthermore, these theorists argued that exchange-rate depreciation in Latin American countries would only bring about a sharp increase in the rate of inflation, and deeper recession.

The basic inflationary pressures in backward economies, they explained, arose from an inelastic supply of exportable primary goods, and their strong dependence on capital goods, technology and other industrial inputs imported from rich countries, where scientific research leading to technical progress occurs.

The low income elasticity of developed (centre) countries' demand for primary products, and the high income elasticity of developing (peripheral) countries demand for industrial goods, produced a secular fall in the terms of trade for the periphery. Currency devaluations would not lead to a substantial rise in exports for three reasons: (i) because raw materials and commodity prices were determined in hard currencies in international markets; (ii) because these products exhibited very low income elasticities of demand; and (iii) because their prices were influenced to such a degree by the quantity supplied that an increase in the volume offered would likely lead to a fall in export proceeds (Prebisch 1983). On the other hand, currency depreciation would have little effect on the volume of imports, since demand was price inelastic and depended mainly on income growth.

The inflationary effects of exchange-rate variations in peripheral countries, called 'structural inflation' by the Latin American economists, would only diminish as these nations progressed in their industrialization processes, and domestic manufactured products gradually substituted imports. This process would not unfold spontaneously, but required government intervention and leadership (Bielschowsly 1998).

Even though Latin American economists rejected the view that inflation originated in money market imbalances, they still believed that fiscal deficits, monetary expansion, and wage bargaining were important elements in the propagation of the basic inflationary pressures that arose from the inelastic supply of agricultural products and exchange-rate depreciation (Noyola 1957, Pinto 1975). This view held that inflation would reflect the way in which conflicting claims on income distribution among productive factors were eventually resolved. Since the inflation propagation mechanism was influenced by the social structure, structural inflation would differ from country to country given prevailing social and market structures and institutional frameworks. In countries where labour unions were powerful and/or export producers were well organized, exchange rate variations would have stronger inflationary effects. The degree to which monopolies existed in different markets would also influence inflation (Noyola 1957).

Summing up, the theory of structural inflation broke down price behaviour into two elements: (i) the exchange rate pass-through, which was explained by the structure of foreign trade and income elasticities of exports and imports; and (ii) inertia, which depended on the way distribution conflicts were resolved.

Neo-structuralist models have simplified the former element to a cost-push explanation of inflation; and have emphasized the distribution conflict, often relying on Kaleckian-type models of mark-up pricing under oligopolistic competition in product markets, even though competitive factor markets are assumed (Taylor 1983, 1992; Alberro and Ibarra 1987). By contrast, balance-of-payments constrained growth models focus attention on trade inequality and dependence, but they neglect imperfections in product markets as well as the distribution conflict (Thirlwall 1999).

Neo-structuralist macroeconomic models provided theoretical support to the successful heterodox price stabilization programmes implemented in various Latin American countries at the end of the 1980s. This strategy, exactly like contemporary inflation targeting, aimed at generating expectations of declining inflation.[2]

The mix of policy measures included wage and price freezes, elimination of indexation, balanced public finances, and exchange rate anchoring. The stabilization plan endeavoured to minimize uncertainty among economic agents, in order to avoid the usual defensive measures to preserve factor shares in income, through price increases and nominal wage rate bargaining (Alberro and Ibarra 1987).

Interestingly, these programmes included the prerequisite of a balanced budget and other tight monetary policies in the early stages of implementation, not because their proponents assumed a direct link between monetary conditions and the level of prices, as the quantity theory of money postulates, but rather to assure governmental commitment to the stabilization plan. Just as their forerunners, the ECLAC economists, Latin American neo-structuralists emphasized that the direction of causality was from prices to the quantity of money, and not the other way around, as monetarists held.

A general model of exchange rate pass-through

Structural inflation does not merely refer to the weighted cost-push effect of currency devaluation, due to higher prices of imported inputs expressed in local currency; it involves a disproportionate price response to exchange rate depreciation, which could be called a magnified exchange rate pass-through. In developed countries, the analysis of exchange rate pass-through concerns the effects of exchange rate variations on the prices of exportable commodities. In a developing economy, this aspect of exchange rate pass-through is not as relevant, since most of its export revenues comes from products that are priced in foreign currencies, in international markets. The effects of exchange rate movements on domestic prices of imported goods and on the domestic inflation rate are more important.

Conventional theory of international trade anticipates no exchange rate pass-through in a closed economy, but full pass-through when the country is completely open to foreign trade. Krugman and Baldwin (1987) have shown, however, that firms engaged in international trade might not charge production costs fully to selling prices, when they perceive an elastic demand for their products.

Arestis and Milberg (1993) created a model to explain incomplete exchange rate pass-through, in an economy where domestic and foreign firms participate in oligopolistic competition. They assumed that prices were determined by a mark-up over variable costs and, building on Eichner's theory, they explained the mark-up as a function of the amount of internal finance required to implement investment projects that assure the firm's survival (Eichner 1973).

They defined the average unit price for the domestic firm as the sum of the average variable cost, plus average fixed costs at the normal utilization of capacity, which include internal funds needed to carry out planned investment (i.e. the corporate levy):

$$P = AVC + \left[(FC + CL)/(SOR^{*}ERC)\right]$$

where *P* is the average price; *AVC* is the average variable cost; *FC* is total fixed costs; *CL* is the corporate levy; *SOR* is the standard operating ratio; and *ERC* is the engineering rated capacity.

Following Eichner, they assume that the corporate levy depends on three elements: the profitability of new investment; prevailing conditions in financial markets; and the costs involved in raising the mark-up, such as demand substitution effects and a fall in sales, as new competitors enter the market.

For foreign firms that compete in the same market, the same price equation holds, the only difference being that the right-hand side is multiplied by the exchange rate, so that:

$$Pf = \{AVC + [(FC + CL)/(SOR^{*}ERC)]\}e$$

where *Pf* is the average price for the foreign firm, and *e* is the relevant exchange rate.

Within this analytical framework, the authors explore what the foreign firm's pricing behaviour would be if the local currency depreciated; and they conclude 'The greater the sensitivity of funds generation to the exchange rate change, the smaller will be the mark-up change and the more limited will be the degree of exchange rate pass-through' (p. 178).

Arestis and Milberg's model could also explain the opposite phenomenon; that is, the magnified effect of exchange rate variations on the inflation rate, or 'structural inflation', provided two additional assumptions are introduced. The first concerns the dependence on foreign technology and imported capital goods, which is characteristic in semi-industrialized economies; the second refers to the causal relationship between technical progress and market power.

Assuming that technical innovations are the main source of market power, and originate in scientific research largely financed out of the monopoly rents generated by technical progress, a virtuous circle would give a dynamic advantage to developed countries in world trade. If foreign firms were the price leaders in developing countries, exchange rate pass-through would differ more in the periphery than in the centre.

In developed countries, where domestic and foreign firms compete on equal footing, exchange rate depreciation gives domestic producers a competitive advantage, which forces foreign competitors to lower their mark-ups over variable costs. By contrast, in the developing economy, where foreign producers would be the price leaders due to their technological leadership, an exchange rate adjustment that increased their average unit cost in local currency would establish the new market price, and would give domestic producers the opportunity to raise their mark-ups. This may explain why in developing economies that exhibit structural inflation, the exchange rate elasticity of prices is near unity, even though imports of goods and services are less than one third of GDP.

Domestic producers would not dare bid below the foreign producers' price for two reasons that usually accompany exchange rate adjustment in developing economies. First, is the rise in interest rates that the central bank would initiate, following mainstream monetary theory, to temper the inflationary effect of the exchange rate adjustment; and second, is the fall in economic activity that would result from a lower import capacity and higher interest rates.

The generalized model anticipates that, as the developing economy becomes more open and integrated into global markets, the magnified effect of exchange rate adjustments will tend to decline, since foreign producers endeavour to compete with local producers in order to enlarge their markets, and domestic firms are compelled either to lower their mark-ups, or reduce unit labour costs, in order to penetrate foreign markets.

In the following section, we present statistical evidences from two developing countries subject to structural inflation that support these hypotheses. Two models of price determination, estimated for Mexico and Brazil, reveal that the opening-up processes in these economies lowered the exchange rate pass-through domestic inflation; but at the same time, foreign competition increased the income elasticities of their imports, and negatively affected domestic employment and real wage rates.

Trade liberalization and exchange rate pass-through in developing countries

Brazil and Mexico are two typical cases of countries subject to structural inflation. Inflation rates and exchange rate variations are highly correlated (see Figures 5.1 and 5.2), and Granger causality tests systematically indicate that exchange rate variations precede price changes, not the other way around, as conventional open economy macroeconomics postulates (see Table 5.1).

In both countries, the exchange rate pass-through is disproportionate to the import content of domestic output, and to the ratio of foreign trade to income. During the past decade, these two emerging economies had similar economic policy strategies, in order to rein in hyperinflation brought about by succeeding currency depreciations. Their stabilization plans shared four common elements:

- an exchange-rate crawling-peg regime
- international trade was liberalized
- foreign investment was actively sought
- central governments balanced their budgets before pegging the exchange rate.

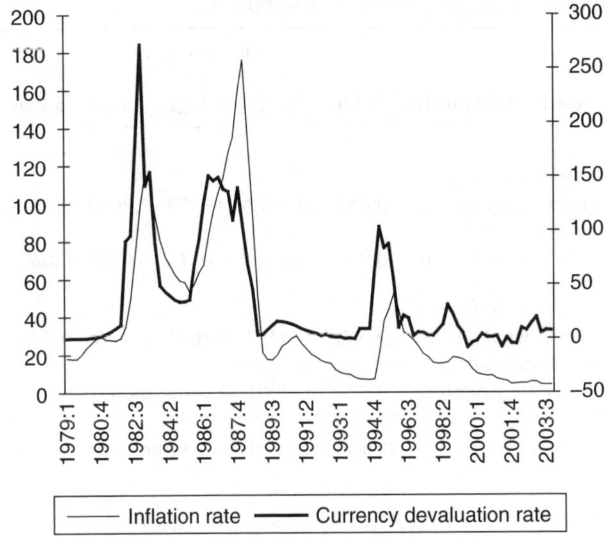

Figure 5.1 Mexico (inflation and rate of currency devaluation)

Source: Author's calculations based on data reported in Bank of Mexico, 2004.

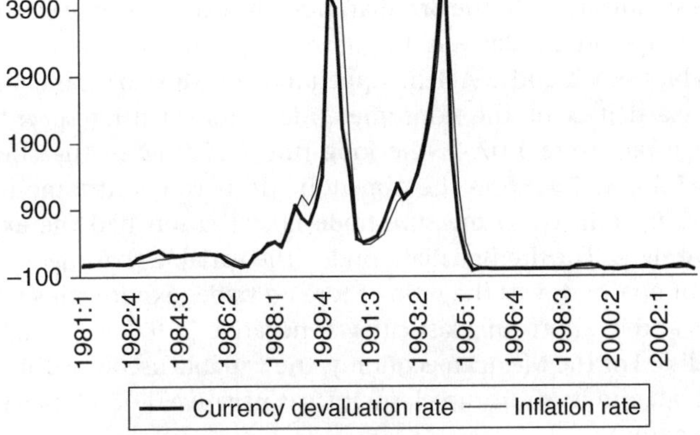

Figure 5.2 Brazil (inflation and rate of currency devaluation)

Source: Author's calculations based on data reported by the IMF, *International Financial Statistics*, various issues.

Table 5.1 Granger causality tests (1980.3–2003.2)

	F Probabilities					
Null hypothesis and country	**1 lag**	**2 lags**	**3 lags**	**4 lags**	**8 lags**	**12 lags**
Brazil						
Inflation does not Granger cause currency devaluation	0.0427	0.1678	0.8253	0.7063	0.5583	0.5442
Currency devaluation does not Granger cause inflation	0.0001	0.0027	0.0113	0.0350	0.0633	0.1092
Mexico						
Inflation does not Granger cause currency devaluation	0.0031	0.3972	0.4031	0.4976	0.5480	0.7143
Currency devaluation does not Granger cause inflation	0.0001	0.0001	0.0001	0.0001	0.0015	0.0002

Source: The values are the author's calculations, based on data from Bank of Mexico.

The exchange rate nominal anchor and trade liberalization led to a rapid drop of inflation rates in both economies, as anticipated by the enlarged model of our previous section.

In Mexico, inflation rates fell from an average annual rate of 123 per cent in 1987–88, to 20 per cent in 1989, and 7 per cent in 1994; in Brazil, inflation fell from an annual average rate of 1,430 per cent in 1990–93, to 16 per cent in 1995, and 3 per cent in 1998.

Price functions estimated for both countries in 1980.1–2002.4 enable us to infer that the crawling-peg exchange rate regime implemented in both economies, and trade liberalization, were the main determinants of price stabilization. In the Brazilian case, the exchange rate elasticity of the consumer price index was 0.96 in the long run, and 0.69 in the short run (Tables 5.A.2 and 5.A.3 in Appendix). In Mexico's case, the estimated elasticities of the consumer price index with respect to the exchange rate were 1.07 in the long run, and 0.15 in the short run (Tables 5.A.4 and 5.A.5 in the Appendix). In both country models, the variables introduced to measure trade liberalization had the expected negative signs. For the Brazilian model, the variable that measured the degree of openness was the ratio of foreign trade (exports plus imports) to GDP; and its short-run elasticity was negative 0.19 (Table 5.A.3 in the Appendix). For the Mexican economy, the variable used was the import coefficient, and its short run elasticity was negative 0.07. (Table 5.A.5 in the Appendix).

Two additional results deserve attention. First, in the Brazilian model, credit availability was found to be inversely associated with the rate of inflation, with an estimated short-run elasticity of negative 0.27. This outcome, which would be untenable in mainstream macroeconomics, is however reasonable under the assumptions of our model: we recall that the latter was built upon Eichner's theory of mark-up pricing under oligopoly, wherein the corporate levy is inversely associated to financial market conditions.

Second, in the Mexican model, the institutional minimum wage played a small but significant role in price behaviour. The estimated short-run elasticity was 0.07, being equal in absolute value to the elasticity of the import coefficient. This result is interesting because in Mexico the institutionally determined minimum real wage has fallen steadily since the debt crisis in early 1980, at the same time that the economy underwent a hasty opening up process (see Figure 5.3). This suggests that the minimum wage and the exchange rate have also been used as a nominal anchor for the economy.

In the early stages of implementation, stabilization policies in these two countries brought about huge inflows of direct foreign investments and short-term credit, which made it easy for central banks to maintain the crawling peg. From 1989 to 1994, Mexico received a net capital inflow

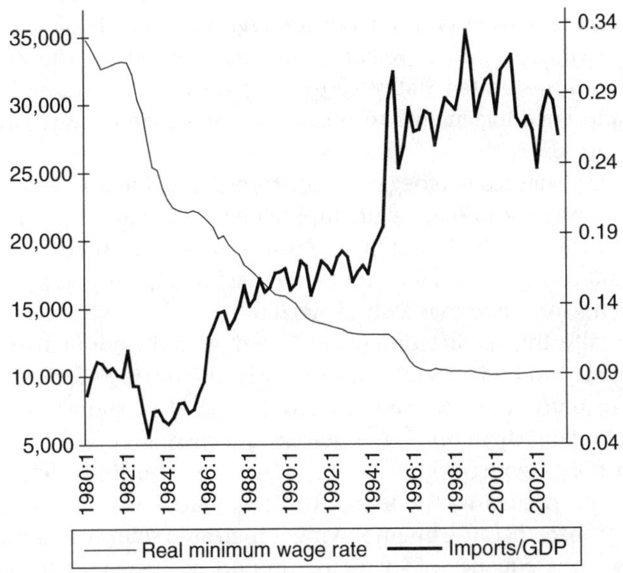

Figure 5.3 Mexico (imports/GDP and real minimum wage)

Source: Author's calculations based on data reported in INEGI and Bank of Mexico, various issues.

of US$ 89 billion, and Brazil US$ 124 billion from 1994 to 1999. Structural reforms reduced the perceived country risks in international financial markets, and price stability strengthened international investor confidence, in an apparent virtuous circle (Cambiaso 1993, Averbug 2002). The exchange-rate peg, however, involved a bias towards currency overvaluation; but central banks, mainly concerned with price stability, behaved with benign indifference as the real exchange rate fell supported by vast capital inflows. Banks even showed satisfaction insofar as inflows reflected international investors' credibility in their policies. Currency overvaluation was also considered a minor disadvantage, as non-hedged corporate indebtedness in foreign currency grew significantly in both countries when prices stabilized (Cinquetti 2000, Lecuona 2000).

In Brazil, politicians were aware of the risks involved in the exchange peg, especially regarding the falling competitive advantage of Brazilian exporters, but they expected to compensate for the decline in the real exchange with structural reforms that raised labour productivity, and with a fall in prices in the non-tradable goods sector, as a result of restrictive monetary and fiscal policies. In addition, the country struggled to increase its share in international primary commodity markets, where it is a price taker, by investing in capital intensive technology and competing on the basis of very low profit margins (Katz 2000).

In Mexico, the political weakness of labour unions and its common border with the United States led to competitive strategy based on low wages and encouragement to subcontracting in labour intensive productive processes.[3]

Both strategies led to a negative redistribution of income, as a result of the fall in wages and soaring unemployment (see Figure 5.4). Industrial development also took a step backwards, since the shares of capital goods and consumer durables industries declined in output, and import coefficients increased markedly (Katz 2000).

Eventually, this stabilization policy, based upon the nominal exchange rate anchor and trade liberalization, collapsed. The trade account deteriorated in both countries, and caused a reversal of short-term capital flows, plunging them into an exchange rate crisis.

But if the crawling-peg exchange-rate regime had limits imposed by trade deficit financing, the falling real wage rate has not had an automatic stabilizer, because unemployment increased sharply in both countries, as a consequence of increasing import coefficients and recessive monetary and fiscal policies. In Brazil, the average real wage rate in manufacturing industry in 2001 was half the wage rate observed in

Figure 5.4 Brazil (imports/GDP and unemployment)

Sources: Author's calculations based on data reported by the IMF in *International Financial Statistics*, ILO, and *LABORSTA Labour Statistics*, various issues.

1985; in Mexico, in 2002 it was still below the real level in the early 1980s, before the external debt crisis.

Figure 5.5 shows the dramatic increase in the import coefficient of the Brazilian economy during the 1990s, notwithstanding the falling trend in real wages, and the wide fluctuations observed in the real exchange rate, particularly its rising trend from 1999 onwards, when the crawling peg was abandoned.

In Mexico, the import coefficient has risen by incremental steps in the last two decades, as the economy was opening up (see Figure 5.6); and, as in the Brazilian case, it has not been noticeably affected by the real exchange-rate behaviour, nor by the real wage rate. This evidence suggests that product differentiation in international trade precludes balance-of-payments equilibrium at lower real wage rates and higher real exchange rates in developing countries. If this is so, trade liberalization and exchange rate flexibility do not resolve the structural imbalance in foreign trade that is characteristic of their economies, but rather tend to aggravate it. Those were the main preoccupations of the early Latin American structuralists, and presently they constitute the core of balance-of-payments constrained growth models.

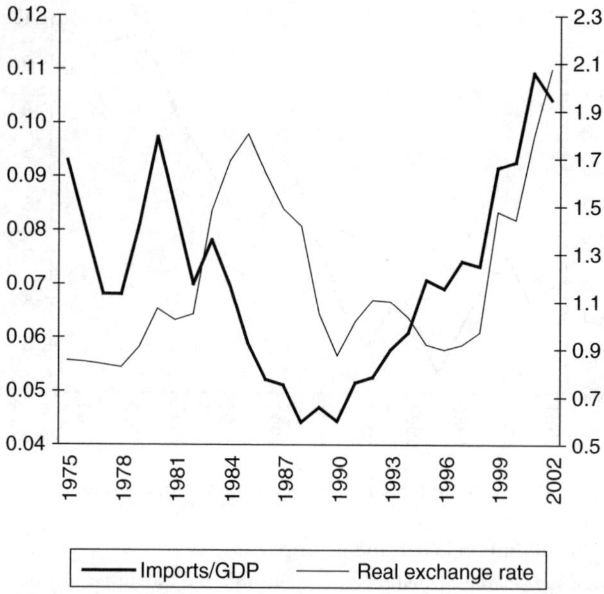

Figure 5.5 Brazil (imports/GDP and real exchange rate)

Source: Author's calculations based on data reported by the IMF in *International Financial Statistics*, various issues.

Macroeconomic stabilization policies in developing countries have disregarded the need to reduce the income elasticity of imports, and to raise the income elasticity of exports, as one (if not the only) way to overcome the external sector structural imbalance. Paradoxically, many of the structural reforms implemented to promote exports have worked against this goal, not only by overvaluing the currency, but also by hindering industrial development based on increasing domestic linkages and conducive to improvements in the terms of trade.

Inflation targeting and interest rate policy in emerging economies

The 1994 Mexican exchange rate crisis put an end to the crawling peg regime that anchored the economy for seven years. Similarly, the Brazilian crawling peg lasted for six years but ended in an exchange-rate crisis in 1999. After the crises, a new monetary regime based on announcements

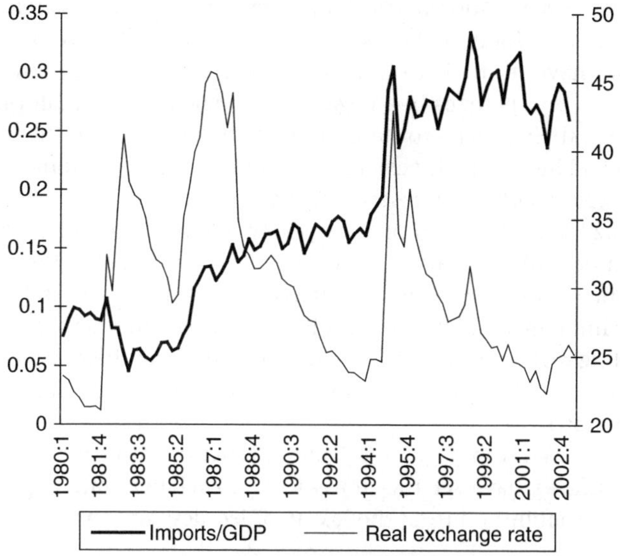

Figure 5.6 Mexico (imports/GDP and real exchange rate)
Source: Author's calculations based on data reported by Bank of Mexico, 2003.

from the central bank regarding multi-annual inflation targets was institutionalized in both countries.

In this section, we will argue that this regime, which has successfully lowered inflation in industrialized countries, is bound to fail in emerging economies for three reasons: (i) because in a developing country, monetary policy implemented through open market operations is insufficient to stabilize the trade balance; (ii) because central bank policy measures are unable to influence international capital flows, so that currency convertibility, and the exchange rate, eventually depend on international financial market conditions and foreign investors' expectations; and (iii) because country-risk evaluations depend heavily on trade and fiscal balances, which inevitably deteriorate when price stability is achieved by anchoring the nominal exchange rate and rising interest rates.

In a country with a reserve currency, central bank intervention through open market operations may influence the exchange rate, because the latter depends on the variety of financial assets offered in that currency, and on their liquidity, which is affected by central bank interest rate policy. In weak currency countries, by contrast, it is the balance of payments that determines national currency convertibility and, therefore, the exchange rate (Toporowski 2004). Since central bankers of developing countries have no tools to influence international money and capital markets (except perhaps in a negative way when they default on external debts), their policies to stabilize the exchange rate and the inflation rate depend heavily on investors' expectations in international markets, and monetary policies in reserve currency countries.

In Brazil and Mexico, monetary policy has been conditioned by the ebb and flow of international speculative capital, for the three reasons mentioned above: (i) because their economies depend heavily on foreign technology and imported capital goods; (ii) currency depreciation and falling real-wage rates do not significantly lower their import coefficients; and (iii) exchange rate increases have a strong effect on their inflation rates.

It can be seen from Figures 5.7 and 5.8 that in both countries foreign capital inflows have set the limits to real exchange rate appreciation (and price stability) during the last two decades; and that the size and

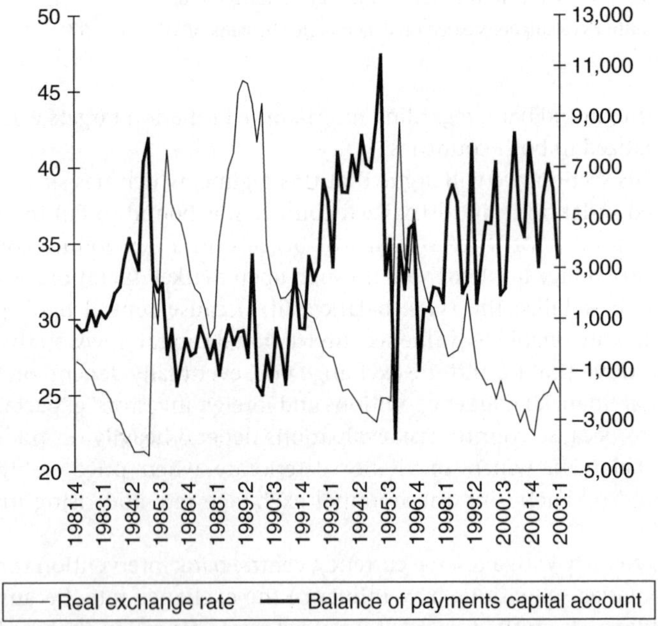

Figure 5.7 Mexico (real exchange rate and capital account of balance of payments)

Source: Author's calculations based on data reported by Bank of Mexico, various issues.

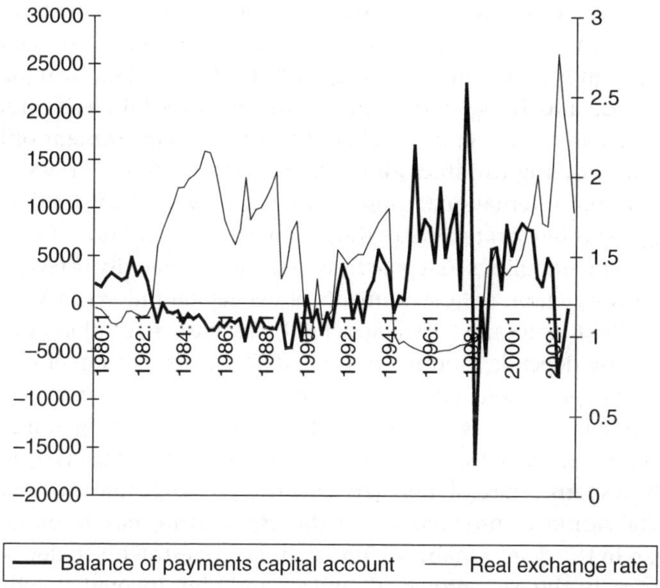

Figure 5.8 Brazil (real exchange rate and capital account of balance of payments)
Source: Author's calculations based on data reported by the IMF in *International Financial Statistics*, various issues.

volatility of these flows have increased markedly in the last decade, thereby imposing constraints to other economic policy objectives beyond price stability.

Inflation targeting enables monetary policy to react quickly to foreign investors' changing moods; but since it involves interaction between the central bank and the markets, it is difficult to know who decides (Le Heron and Carre 2004). Central bank reaction functions estimated for Mexico indicate that the most significant variables that influence the money market rate are the Mexican Brady Bond yield differential with respect to the US government bond, and the exchange rate (Castellanos 2000). They also reveal that causality goes from the exchange rate to the money market rate, and not the other way around, as interest rate parity theory postulates. Similarly, the Taylor rule estimated for Mexico by Martínez *et al.* (2001), in the years following the exchange rate crisis, showed the product gap was not significant; and the main determinants of central bank monetary policy were lagged exchange rate variations, and changes in the yield on Mexican government bonds placed in international financial markets.

These results corroborate the assertion that independent central banks in developing economies have become more interested in achieving credibility in international financial markets, than in their own jurisdiction (Aybar and Harris 1998); and it also justifies Blinder's criticisms regarding banks' reluctance to obey the orders of government officials, while succumbing to international bond dealers (Blinder 1998). Note, however, that international capital does not flow to countries that offer the highest interest rates, but to those that exhibit conditions for growth and implement policies that guarantee free capital mobility (Kregel 1998).

In his research on the determinants of net capital inflows to Mexico in the late 1980s and early 1990s, Ros (1993) observed that inflows were not significantly dependent on interest rate differentials, but rather on other indicators of governmental commitment to exchange rate stability and free capital mobility, such as the fiscal balance, privatization programmes, the level of international reserves, policies that enhance free markets operation, and the responsiveness of monetary policy to exchange rate movements.

Globalization of production, on the other hand, has accounted for changes in the determinants of foreign direct investments in developing countries. In the past, protected markets and high-income growth rates in developing countries were the main incentives for direct investments. Now, the fragmentation of production processes, and free trade, drive this capital flow to countries that offer lower labour costs and cheap raw materials (Kregel 1994).

The policies demanded by international investors, however, do not guarantee long lasting stability. The policy mix implemented in Mexico and Brazil in the past decade, composed of nominal exchange-rate stability (which involves currency overvaluation), trade liberalization, primary fiscal balance, and tight monetary policy, has led to similar results in both countries: a voluminous inflow of short-term capital, a decline in economic activity, a consumption boom, a growing trade deficit, a surge of bad loans in commercial banks' balance sheets, a mounting public debt (despite a decrease in government non-financial expenditures as a percentage of gross domestic income), a dramatic fall in real wages, and a pervasive rise in unemployment. These results indicate that a developing economy, exposed to cyclical trade imbalances, can sustain convertibility and exchange rate stability by means of capital inflows only in the short run. Empirical evidence indicates that growing short-term external debts and rising fiscal deficits trigger short-term capital flow reversals, and lead to exchange rate crises (Kaminsky *et al.* 1998).

Inflation targeting overlooks the structural imbalance in the trade account of the developing economy. Hence, its role in giving the right direction to inflation expectations is constrained by the same factors that led to the break down of the previous exchange-rate crawling-peg regime. Foreign investors' expectations of central bank management will eventually have to confront reality; and rising current account and fiscal balances will, in the end, bring about the reversal of short-term capital flows on which short-term price stability was based.

Conclusion

In emerging economies subject to structural inflation, independent central banks concerned mainly with price stability show a bias towards stabilizing the nominal exchange rate, either openly through a crawling peg, or (more subtly), through inflation targeting, and a discretional monetary policy heavily dependent on international market evaluations of country-risk. Both modalities are bound to fail in the medium term, for at least two reasons. First, because they overlook the structural origin of trade-account imbalances, and rely heavily on interest rate policy, which is ineffective in lowering the income elasticity of imports. Second, because they eventually conduce to fiscal imbalances, due to increased cost of government domestic debt, which is an important indicator of country risk in evaluations made by international investors.

The remedies to exchange-rate instability in emerging economies posited during the last decade also disregard asymmetries in the economic behaviour of economies at different stages of development. It is generally assumed that an exchange-rate crisis arises from lack of credibility regarding central bank policies, and that free capital mobility contributes to exchange rate instability.

On the basis of this diagnosis, two extreme solutions are often recommended. One is to peg the national currency to a hard reserve currency, either by a currency board that substitutes for the central bank, or by straight unilateral dollarization. The other is to put limits on short-term international capital mobility. Regardless of the soundness of reducing the volatility of short-term capital flows, none of these measures solves the basic problem that brings on the cyclical trade imbalance in emerging economies and, consequently, exchange rate instability.

Balance-of-payments constrained growth models seem to be better equipped to resolve financial instability in these economies, since they focus on the growth constraints that arise from unequal trade and dependence. Recalling Thirlwall's law:

$$g/z = \varepsilon/\pi$$

where g is one country's growth rate relative to others z, ε is the income elasticity of demand for the country's exports, and π is the income elasticity of its demand for imports, those models anticipate that unless an emerging country raises ε (by means of industrial development) or lowers π (through import substitution policies), higher rates of growth with balance-of-trade equilibrium and stable prices are unattainable.

Interestingly, in South Korea and other South-east Asian countries that exhibited structural inflation in the early 1960s, this phenomenon disappeared a few years after they initiated an export-oriented industrial development strategy. Their plans, in accordance to Thirlwall's law, aimed to raise the income elasticity of exports and to accelerate import substitution. They were implemented to a great extent through very selective credit allocation guidelines, backed by consistent monetary, fiscal and exchange rate policies, which eventually led to a positive relationship between credit expansion and the trade balance (Levy and Mántey 2001).

On these grounds, three conclusions may be derived from our analysis:

- Inflation targeting, just as its predecessor, the crawling-peg regime, is an inadequate strategy for monetary control in emerging economies subject to structural inflation
- Long-term price and trade-account stability in such economies require monetary and fiscal policies that increase the income elasticity of their exports, and decrease their import coefficients
- Monetary policy conducted through open market operations, and divorced from an industrial development strategy, is inadequate to tackle the problem of exchange-rate instability in a developing economy.

Appendix

This appendix presents the main results of two quarterly error correction models of the inflation rate estimated for Brazil and for Mexico. Data came from the IMF, *International Financial Statistics*; ILO, *LABORSTA Labour Statistics*, and Mexico's National Bureau of Statistics INEGI. The sample period was 1980.1 to 2003.2

Table 5A.1 Key to variables used in the models

Mexico's model	
IPC93	Consumer price index
TICI	Exchange rate
IMPIBC	Imports as a proportion of GDP
SALMIN	Minimum wage rate

IPC93RES2 Error correction mechanism
DUM88BIS Dummy to represent the effect of import duties reductions
DUM82BIS Dummy to represent the effect of a transient exchange control
DUM87 Dummy to represent exchange rate expectations after the 1987 crack
L Denotes logarithm
D Denotes first difference
DD Denotes second difference
(−1) Denotes one lag

Brazil's model

B62 Consumer price index
B11 Nominal exchange rate
B73 Balance of payments financial account
B41R Domestic credit in real terms
BAPERT Foreign trade as a proportion of GDP
B62RES2 Error correction mechanism
BDUM991 Dummy to represent the exchange rate crisis in the first quarter of 1999
BDUMARG Dummy to represent the effect of the Argentinian crisis
DUM831 Dummy to represent external debt crisis in 1983
L Denotes logarithm
D Denotes first difference
DD Denotes second difference
(−1) Denotes one lag

Table 5A.2 Brazil: price model cointegrating vector

Johansen cointegration test

Sample: 1980:1 2003:4
Included observations: 89
Test assumption: linear deterministic trend in the data
Series: B62LD B11LD B73L
Lags interval: 1 to 2

Eigenvalue	Likelihood ratio	5% critical value	1% critical value	Hypothesized no. of CE(s)
0.450200	68.42616	29.68	35.65	None**
0.146965	15.18630	15.41	20.04	At most 1
0.011610	1.039300	3.76	6.65	At most 2

*(**) denotes rejection of the hypothesis at 5% (1%) significance level
L.R. test indicates 1 cointegrating equation(s) at 5% significance level

Normalized cointegrating coefficients: 1 cointegrating equation(s)

B62LD	B11LD	B73L	C
1.000000	−0.964519	0.031971	−0.292267
	(0.02921)	(0.01382)	

Log likelihood 332.0914

Table 5A.3 Brazil: rate of inflation error correction model

LS // dependent variable is B62LDD
Sample (adjusted): 1980:3 2003:1
Included observations: 91 after adjusting endpoints

Variable	Coefficient	Std error	t-statistic	Probability
B62RES2(−1)	−0.952014	0.059165	−16.09083	0.0000
B11LDD	0.686449	0.029015	23.65831	0.0000
B41RLD	−0.267749	0.056588	−4.731578	0.0000
BAPERTLD	−0.132617	0.024428	−5.428864	0.0000
BAPERTLD(−1)	−0.056529	0.027221	−2.076682	0.0409
BDUM991	−0.192291	0.052258	−3.679644	0.0004
BDUMARG	−0.147445	0.052816	−2.791651	0.0065
BDUM831	−0.167457	0.052739	−3.175188	0.0021

R-squared	0.910390	Mean dependent variable	−0.001093
Adjusted R-squared	0.902833	S.D. dependent variable	0.164363
S.E. of regression	0.051234	Akaike info. criterion	−5.858879
Sum squared residual	0.217873	Schwarz criterion	−5.638144
Log likelihood	145.4556	F-statistic	120.4628
Durbin–Watson statistic	1.723600	Probability (F-statistic)	0.000000

Diagnostic Tests (F Probabilities):

Jarque–Bera	0.179
LM(1)	0.211
ARCH(1)	0.776
Ramsey(1)	0.817

Table 5A.4 Mexico: price model cointegrating vector

Johansen cointegration test

Sample: 1978:1 2003:4
Included observations: 98
Test assumption: no deterministic trend in the data
Series: IPC93LD TICILD
Lags interval: 1 to 4

Eigenvalue	Likelihood ratio	5% critical value	1% critical value	Hypothesized no. of CE(s)
0.160899	19.40652	12.53	16.31	None**
0.022348	2.214899	3.84	6.51	At most 1

*(**) denotes rejection of the hypothesis at 5% (1%) significance level
L.R. test indicates 1 cointegrating equation(s) at 5% significance level
Normalized cointegrating coefficients: 1 cointegrating equation(s)

IPC93LD	TICILD
1.000000	−1.068782
	(0.09230)
Log likelihood	425.5748

Table 5A.5 Mexico: rate of inflation error correction model

LS // dependent variable is IPC93LDD
Sample(adjusted): 1980:2 2002:4
Included observations: 91 after adjusting endpoints

Variable	Coefficient	Std error	t-statistic	Probability
IPC93RES2(−1)	−0.260904	0.021541	−12.11192	0.0000
TICILDD	0.150089	0.019844	7.563410	0.0000
IMPIBCLD	−0.070749	0.017884	−3.955916	0.0002
SALMINLDD	0.074790	0.014272	5.240147	0.0000
DUM82BIS	−0.089780	0.015886	−5.651405	0.0000
DUM87	0.064449	0.014791	4.357436	0.0000
DUM88BIS	−0.112686	0.015871	−7.100201	0.0000

R-squared	0.839525	Mean dependent variable	−0.000811
Adjusted R-squared	0.828062	S.D. dependent variable	0.035147
S.E. of regression	0.014574	Akaike info. criterion	−8.383254
Sum squared residual	0.017841	Schwarz criterion	−8.190111
Log likelihood	259.3147	F-statistic	73.24091
Durbin–Watson statistic	2.200061	Probability (F-statistic)	0.000000

Diagnostic tests (F Probability)	
Jarque–Bera	0.525
LM(1)	0.283
ARCH(1)	0.416
Ramsey(1)	0.840

Table 5A.6 Unit root tests

Variable	Critical value	1% ADF Test	Conditions
Brazil's model			
B62LDD	2.589	−7.865	No intercept, 2 lags
B62LD	−3.504	−2.185	Intercept, 2 lags
B11LDD	−2.589	−7.833	No intercept, 2 lags
B11LD	−3.504	−2.467	Intercept, 2 lags
B73LD	−2.589	−8.221	No intercept, 2 lags
B73L	−3.504	−0.388	Intercept, 2 lags
B41RLD	−2.589	−5.347	No intercept, 2 lags

B41RL	−3.504	−1.171	Intercept, 2 lags
BAPERTLD	−2.589	−7.101	No intercept, 2 lags
BAPERTL	−3.504	−2.859	Intercept, 2 lags
Mexico's model			
IPC93LDD	−2.589	−5.211	No intercept, 4 lags
IPC93LD	−2.589	−1.568	No intercept, 4 lags
TICILDD	−2.589	−5.296	No intercept, 4 lags
TICILD	−2.587	−2.224	No intercept, 4 lags
IMPIBCLD	−2.589	−5.499	No intercept, 2 lags
IMPIBCL	−3.504	−0.791	Intercept, 2 lags
SALMINLD	−3.499	−4.220	Intercept, 2 lags
SALMINL	−3.499	−2.453	Intercet, 2 lags

Notes

1. Super-exogeneity means that past values of the dependent variable do not affect the conditional process of the independent variable. In the particular case of a money demand equation, price super-exogeneity implies that changes in the quantity of money have not determined the rate of inflation.
2. One important difference between these two strategies, however, is that heterodox plans emphasized income growth as a necessary condition for price stability.
3. López and López (2003) investigated the effects of trade liberalization on real wages in the Mexican manufacturing industry, and found that in all branches of activity the share of exports in total sales was a significantly negative explanatory variable, whereas the rate of unemployment in the specific industry, and the gains in productivity, were both non significant. Hernández-Laos (2000) estimated that more than 80 per cent of labour share variations in Mexican manufacturing output were accounted for by changes in the ratio between real wages and real exchange rates.

References

Alberro, J.L. and Ibarra, D. (1987) 'Programas heterodoxos de estabilización: Presentación', *Estudios Económicos*, Special Issue, October.

Arestis, P. and Eichner, A.S. (1988) 'The Post-Keynesian and Institutionalist Theory of Money and Credit', *Journal of Economic Issues*, XXII, 4, December.

Arestis, P. and Milberg, W. (1993) 'Degree of Monopoly, Pricing and Flexible Exchange Rates', *Journal of Post Keynesian Economics*, 16, 2, Winter 1993–94.

Averbug, A. (2002) 'The Brazilian Economy in 1994–1999: From the Real Plan to Inflation Targets', *World Economy*, 25, 7, July.

Aybar, S. and Harris, L. (1998) 'How Credible are Credibility Models of Central Banking?', in P. Arestis and M. Sawyer (eds), *The Political Economy of Central Banking* (Cheltenham: Edward Elgar).

Barro, R.J. and Gordon, D.B. (1983) 'Rules, Discretion and Reputation in a Model of Monetary Policy', *Journal of Monetary Economics*, 0(12).

Bielschowsly, R. (1998) 'Cincuenta años del pensamiento de la CEPAL: una reseña histórica', en *Cincuenta Años del Pensamiento en la CEPAL: Textos Seleccionados* (Santiago: FCE-CEPAL).

Blinder, A. (1998) *Central Banking in Theory and Practice* (Cambridge, Mass.: MIT Press).

Camara, A. and Vernengo, M. (2001) 'The German Balance-of-payments School and the Latin American Neo-Structuralists', in L.P. Rochon and M. Vernengo (eds), *Credit, Interest Rates and the Open Economy* (Cheltenham: Edward Elgar).

Cambiaso, J. (1993) 'Síntomas del mal holandés por la vía de la cuenta de capital', *Monetaria*, XVI, 1.

Castellanos, S.G. (2000) 'El efecto del "corto" sobre la estructura de tasas de interés', Banco de Mexico, *Documentos de Investigación*, 2000–1, June.

Chick, V. (1989) 'The Evolution of the Banking System and the Theory of Monetary Policy', University College London, Discussion Paper 89–03, November.

Cinquetti, C.A. (2000) 'The Real Plan: Stabilisation and Destabilization', *World Development*, 28, 1, January.

Eichner, A.S. (1973) 'Una teoría de la determinación del margen de ganancia en el oligopolio', in J.A. Ocampo (ed.), *Economía Poskeynesiana*, Mexico 1988: Fondo de Cultura Económica, Serie Lecturas, 60.

Fisher, S. (1995) 'Central Bank Independence Revisited', American Economic Association Papers and Proceedings, May.

Friedman, M. (1981) *The Optimum Quantity of Money and Other Essays* (New York: Aldine).

Friedman, M. (1968) 'The Role of Monetary Policy', *American Economic Review*, 58, March.

Hendry, D.F. and Ericsson, N.R. (1991) 'An Econometric Analysis of UK Money Demand in "Monetary trends in the United States and the United Kingdom" by Milton Friedman and Anna J. Schwartz', *American Economic Review*, 81, 1, March.

Hernández-Laos E. (2000) 'Políticas de estabilización y ajuste y distribución funcional del ingreso en Mexico', *Comercio Exterior*, 50, 2, February.

ILO, International Labour Office Bureau of Statistics, Geneva, *International Labour Database*, LABORSTA, http://laborsta.ilo.org

IMF, International Monetary Fund, Washington, *International Financial Statistics*, various issues.

INEGI, Instituto Nacional de Estadística, *Geografia e Informática*, Mexico, Banco de Información Económica (BIE), http://www.inegi.gob.mx/inegi/default.asp

Kaldor, N. (1970) 'The New Monetarism', in A.A. Walters (ed.), *Money and Banking* (Harmondsworth: Penguin Education), 1973.

Kaminsky, G.L., Lizondo, S. and Reinhart, C.M. (1998) 'Leading Indicators of Currency Crises', IMF Staff Papers, 45, 1, March.

Katz, J. (2000) 'Cambios estructurales y productividad en la industria latinoamericana, 1970–1996', *Revista de la CEPAL*, 71, August.

Kregel, J. (1998) 'Flujo de capitales, fragilidad e inestabilidad financiera en el desarrollo económico', in A. Girón and E. Correa (eds), *Crisis Financiera: Mercado sin Fronteras* (Mexico: UNAM-El Caballito).

Kregel, J. (1994) 'Capital Flows: Globalization of Production and Financing Development', in *UNCTAD Review 1994* (Geneva: UNCTAD).

Krugman, P. and Baldwin, R. (1987) 'The Persistence of the US Trade Deficit', *Brookings Papers on Economic Activity*, I.

Krugman, P. and Obstfeld, M. (1999) *Economía Internacional: Teoría y Política* (Madrid: McGraw-Hill).

Laidler, D. (1990) 'The Legacy of the Monetarist Controversy', *Federal Reserve Bank of St. Louis Review*, March–April.

Lavoie, M. (1996) 'Monetary Policy in an Economy with Endogenous Money', in G. Deleplace and E. Nell (eds), *Money in Motion: the Post-Keynesian and Circulation Approaches* (New York: St Martin's Press).

Lecuona, R. (2000) 'Impacto del estancamiento y la crisis mexicana', in I. Manrique (ed.), *Arquitectura de la Crisis Financiera* (Mexico: UNAM-MA Porrúa).

Le Heron, E. and Carre, E. (2004) 'Credibilidad, confianza e inflación', in G. Mántey and N. Levy (eds), *Inflación, Crédito y Salarios: Nuevos Enfoques de Política Monetaria para Mercados Imperfectos* (Mexico: UNAM-MA Porrúa).

Levy, N. and Mántey, G. (2001) 'The Role of Institutional Factors on the Transmission Mechanism of Monetary Policy in Emerging Economies', in D. Kantarelis (ed.), *Global Business and Economics Review-Anthology 2001* (Worcester: B&ESI).

López, A. and López, J. (2003) 'Manufacturing Real Wages in Mexico', mimeo.

Martínez, L., Sánchez, O. and Werner, A. (2001) 'Consideraciones sobre la conducción de la política monetaria y el mecanismo de transmisión en Mexico', Banco de Mexico, *Documentos de Investigación*, 2001–2, March.

Niggle, Ch.J. (1991) 'The Endogenous Money Supply Theory: An Institutionalist Appraisal', *Journal of Economic Issues*, XXV, 1, March.

Noyola, J.F. (1957) 'Inflación y desarrollo económico en Chile y Mexico', *Panorama Económico*, 11, 170, July, reproduced in *Cincuenta Años del Pensamiento en la CEPAL: Textos Seleccionados* (Santiago: FCE-CEPAL).

Padoa-Schioppa, T. (1994) *Adapting Central Banking to a Changing Environment* (Washington, DC: IMF).

Pinto, A. (1975) *Inflación: Raíces Estructurales*, Lecturas del FCE No. 3, Mexico: Fondo de Cultura Económica.

Prebisch, R. (1983) 'Cinco etapas de mi pensamiento sobre el desarrollo', *Trimestre Económico*, 63(2), April–June 1996.

Rogoff, K. (1985) 'The Optimal Degree of Commitment to an Intermediate Monetary Target', *Quarterly Journal of Economics*, 100, November.

Ros, J. (1993) 'Mercados financieros y flujos de capital en Mexico', Kellog Institute for International Studies, University of Notre Dame, Working Paper 201, December.

Taylor, L. (1992) *Estabilización y Crecimiento en los Países en Desarrollo: Un Enfoque Estructuralista* (Mexico: FCE, Economía Contemporánea).

Taylor, L. (1983) *Structuralist Macroeconomics: Applicable Models for the Third World* (New York: Basic Books).

Thirlwall, A.P. (1999) *Growth and Development* (Hong Kong: Macmillan).

Toporowski, J. (2004) 'Limitaciones a la estabilización financiera por los bancos centrales', in G. Mántey and N. Levy (eds), *Inflación, Crédito y Salarios: Nuevos Enfoques de Política Monetaria para Mercados Imperfectos* (Mexico: UNAM-M A Porrúa).

Wray, L.R. (1990) *The Endogenous Money Approach: Money and Credit in Capitalist Economies* (Aldershot: Edward Elgar).

6

Credible Commitments and the Relevance of State Capacity: Mexico's Foreign Direct Investment under the NAFTA

Albert A. Gonzalez

Introduction

Whether to decrease reliance on foreign lending, or recover from economic crisis, a comparative advantage among other emerging markets that attracts foreign direct investment (FDI) can contribute significantly towards country development.[1] How do states make credible commitments to this end, especially those whose ability to implement policy is shaped by a recent democratic transition? Credible commitments are intended to mitigate the hazards of complex transactions over space and time.[2] Policies made by the state that prove effective and enforceable, such as economic or political reform, can accomplish this to the extent they reduce costs associated with economic activity.[3]

This chapter examines the political economy behind Mexico's ability to make credible commitments. It seeks to explain why, despite a competitive advantage to attract FDI through its membership in the NAFTA, Mexico's ability to attract FDI recently declined.[4] An explanation for this recent trend – one that is institutional by nature – will be offered which increases our understanding of the role state capacity in FDI recipient countries' plays in making credible commitments that would help attract FDI. This proposition is explored in an attempt to answer the research question: to what extent is Mexico's commitment in the NAFTA credible in attracting FDI? This chapter argues that Mexico's commitments in the NAFTA are strong determinants for attracting FDI; however, their effectiveness is weakened with a state capacity unable to make credible commitments or preserve the country-specific advantages the NAFTA meant to enhance.

Mexico is an exceptional case of a developing country's membership to a free trade agreement that, in addition to proximity to the US market and relatively cheap labour, captures trade-related incentives that can attract FDI. Despite a recent decline in FDI levels into Mexico, it is still a front-runner among developing countries as an attractive location for FDI.[5] However, as it relates to its recent decline in FDI, this chapter aims to identify the influence of state capacity on making credible commitments that may halt this trend.

This chapter views state capacity as the product of historical, institutionalized processes and interests that shape the state's ability to make and implement policy.[6] After briefly reviewing the political economy behind the state's current ability to make credible commitments, three detailed observations will be offered to support the argument of this chapter: (i) Mexico's state capacity to make credible commitments towards reforming its electricity sector, labour and tax systems – proposals currently stalled in Mexico's Congress; (ii) from a transaction costs perspective, credible commitments to reduce the high costs this translates into for foreign investors would allow Mexico to better compete for FDI in light of its country-specific advantages, such as the NAFTA; (iii) harmful to Mexico's ability to attract FDI is the yet unmitigated relationship between high transaction costs and delays in credible commitments meant to reduce them.

On institutions and regimes: the evolution of Mexico's state capacity to make credible commitments

Mexico's institutions changed dramatically during the 1980s and 1990s. After the 1982 debt crisis, the country reoriented the focus of its economic model for growth away from one that was inward looking and protectionist to one that is liberalized and oriented to international markets. This was achieved by a fundamental shift in economic policy towards market-oriented reforms; credible commitments were made in the domestic and international arenas that 'locked-in' policy to liberalize its trade and investment regimes. Mexico began to integrate with the global economy. Most significant among these commitments are: fiscal austerity measures immediately after the crisis to ensure macroeconomic stability, trade liberalization with the USA in 1985, entrance to the General Agreement on Tariffs and Trade in 1986, privatization of state-owned enterprises especially during the years 1988–93, entrance into the NAFTA in 1994, and the liberalization of foreign investment restrictions starting in 1984 but accelerating between 1989 and 1993.[7]

The instruments available to the Partido Revolucionario Institucional (PRI) – which governed Mexico in the 1980s and 1990s, as with most of the twentieth century – to enforce these major policy decisions came in many forms. Making credible commitments towards the restructuring of its economy was enabled largely by the authoritarian nature of the PRI-governed regime. Reform credibility, or policy implementation, was provided for by the PRI's influence over policy makers, sectors of society, and policy outcomes.

Structurally and institutionally, the depth of the PRI's control over policy outcomes enhanced the feasibility by which major shifts in economic policy could be made towards economic reform. This classic institutional arrangements for policy making reflected concentrated power at the presidential level. Additionally, the voice of interest groups such as labour, the peasantry and business were incorporated into governance itself, ensuring limited opposition to the PRI's top-down decision making procedures. This was to the PRI's advantage as credible commitments could be made in an almost streamlined fashion, with the ability to quell dissent. The PRI maintained the party-line in a vertically integrated system that operated by its own sanctioning.[8] It dominated Congress. Elected and appointed leaders, unions and other representative actors survived because of PRI funding, and the PRI existed in the capacity it did because the institutional arrangement made it all possible.

Mexico's economic, democratic transition: the beginning of change and transformation of institutions

For most of the twentieth century, Mexico was politically stable due to the one party dominance of a corporatist structure. Under a pretence of democracy, arrived at by the PRI and its supposed representation of constituent voices through incorporating them into government, Mexico reflected what Peruvian novelist Mario Vargas Llosa called 'the perfect dictatorship'.[9] But during the modern reforms of the 1980s and 1990s, the authoritarian politics that upheld this power arrangement softened as reform progressed.

The commitments to economic reform during this period, at times, relied on relied on the authoritarian nature of the PRI's classic institutional arrangement for enforceability.[10] However, economic reforms included simultaneous attempts at improving transparency and reducing corruption. The same regime attempting economic reform struggled to implement political reform that would mean changes to its classic institutional arrangements. It was almost a schizophrenic attempt at using economic reforms to help dismantle the corporatist, PRI machine while at the same time preserving the centrality of decision-making that made it all possible. Therefore, if authoritarianism provided credibility to commitments, this credibility was inherently reduced by the extent that political reform was successful.

An insightful illustration of this is the contrast between the PRI's support of political reforms while attempting to limit its actual influence on its power. The 1980s saw the PRI gradually support numerous political reforms. However, the presidential victory of Carlos Salinas de Gortari in 1988, for example, was essentially orchestrated by the PRI in this widely-disputed election.[11] After the election, Salinas needed to quell doubt on the election's credibility to ensure his own. He therefore pushed through various electoral reforms aimed at transparency that made it difficult for the PRI to again act in the coercive (and illegal) manner that got him 'elected'.[12] Almost a decade later, during the administration of Ernesto Zedillo (1994–2000), outcomes of electoral reforms helped plurality to emerge – the PRI lost its absolute majority in Congress for the first time in 1997. The election result was the next step in a slow but identifiable shift away from concentrated power and toward divided government. Power moved from the presidency into the hands of Congress. This is part of its democratic transition; an evolution of governance that continues to shape Mexico's state capacity.

The PRI was the thrust and strong-arm behind difficult reforms, but by the end of this period, its strength weakened considerably. On 2 July 2000, Partido Acción Nacional (PAN) candidate Vicente Fox was elected president of Mexico. Seventy-one years of PRI rule passed since any other party occupied the presidency, and on that day, a record 65 per cent of the electorate voted to change this.[13] Central to the argument of this chapter is that this evolution of governance – which produced the plurality of political parties that exists today in Mexico – requires a new state capacity to make credible commitments towards reform, one consensus rather than authoritarian based. This is telling of the credibility gradually eroded – the PRI's authoritarian disposition – that lent Mexico opportunity to stampede rigid reforms through successfully during the 1980s and 1990s.

In terms of the ability to implement policy, Mexico's traditional instruments to make credible commitments unravelled with the decline of the authoritarian disposition of governance. As new tools emerged to lend credibility to commitments, such as the use of 'technocrat' policy makers to create economic reform policy, the strong-arm of the PRI was still utilized to make them credible in policy implementation. However, Mexico's institutions needed to give themselves credibility as well, especially to the international community wishing to see transparency and more room for pluralism. Political reform ensued, loosening the electoral grip of the PRI and, today, a plurality of parties governs.

Mexico in the global marketplace for FDI

The credible commitments addressed in this chapter, detailed next, are analyzed as they relate to their ability to augment Mexico's global competitiveness for FDI today. But before analyzing their ability to do so, recent trends in global FDI and Mexico's performance in this capital market are necessary to assess their potential impact. Accounting for these trends is also important as Mexico's recent decrease in inward FDI flows may not accurately reflect its ability to attract FDI on its own. Other factors need to be known, such as to where was global FDI going in recent years, in what volumes and why.

Since 2001, global FDI flows declined to both developed and developing countries. In 2002, FDI flows to both fell by approximately 21 per cent (after falling 41 per cent in 2001) with yearly inflows totaling US$ 460 billion and US$ 162 billion, respectively.[14] Reasons for this include slowdowns in corporate investment as well as the global economy, plus regional factors in developing countries like declining numbers of privatization processes that traditionally attract FDI through mergers and acquisitions.[15] In this global setting, among the thirty economies most afflicted by the downturn, Mexico ranked fourth behind the USA, UK and the Netherlands in 2002 in terms of lost FDI compared to the year before.[16] Importantly, since 1999 global FDI flows into emerging markets fell, as did Mexico's, after a rapid increase during the 1990s (see Figure 6.1).[17] Speculative explanations for this range from the global economic downturn to a 'flattening out' of FDI levels after the 1990s – when many emerging markets received FDI through privatizing SOEs during structural adjustment processes.[18] Moreover, global FDI flows to emerging markets in recent years concentrated on Asian markets; FDI flows into Latin America and Mexico, especially, consequently declined.[19]

As Figure 6.1 makes clear, recent trends characterize a decline in FDI flows received by emerging markets as well as Mexico. A closer look at Mexico's recent performance shows that without the 2001 acquisition of Banamex by Citigroup subsidiary Citicorp, Mexico's decline in FDI

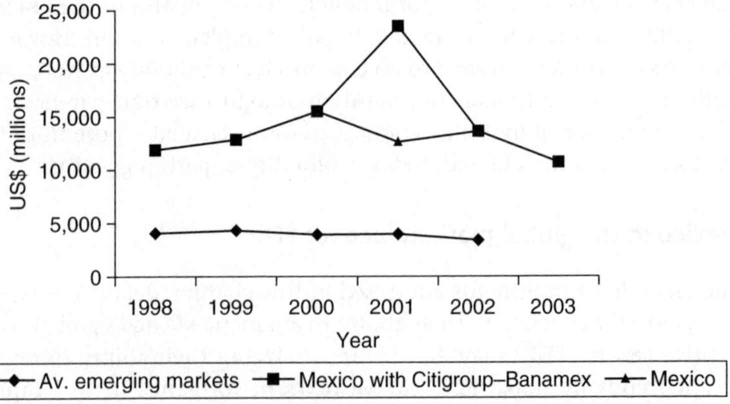

Figure 6.1 Net foreign direct investment flows: emerging markets vis-à-vis Mexico
Sources: Author's calculations based on data from International Monetary Fund (2003), UNCTAD (2002), World Economic Forum (2003), and World Markets Analysis (2003).

inflows is more or less constant. This is despite survey data that reveals Mexico maintains a relatively favourable perception as a FDI location.[20]

The timing of Mexico's underperformance is aligned with a global downturn in FDI, suggesting this could have resulted mostly from factors outside Mexico's control. However, considering Mexico's relative advantage to attract FDI because of the NAFTA and other country-specific advantages, it is useful to assess the extent to which this is true. To this end, compared to other emerging markets competing for FDI, survey data suggests significant impediments exist that hinder Mexico's competitive position to attract FDI. Moreover, these transaction costs are found to increase over the same period as Mexico's recent decline in FDI (see Figure 6.2).

Deficient infrastructure and the relatively high costs posed by labour, electricity and tax are areas especially noted for eroding incentives appealing to FDI, such as NAFTA membership.[21] To the extent this is true, and in light of the incentives for FDI captured in the NAFTA, Mexico's ability to attract FDI is weakened. Recently, the overall competitive environment for doing business in Mexico declined vis-à-vis other countries.

That high transaction costs exist and inhibit economic activity like FDI is corroborated by data from leading business executives in Mexico. Surveyed by the World Economic Forum on their perception of Mexico's

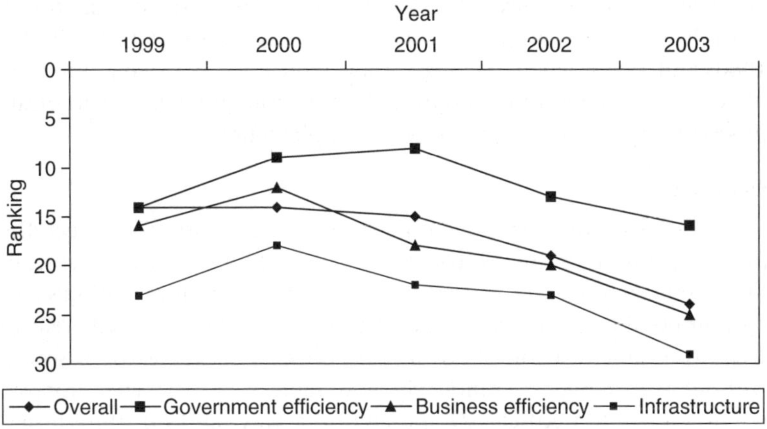

Figure 6.2 Mexico's global competitiveness, selected indicators
Source: IMD International (Institute) (2003).

business environment compared to respondents from other countries doing the same, responses yielded similarly low rankings. Out of 102 countries, Mexico's responses ranked it eighty-second in the effectiveness of its law-making body – between Angola's being more and Madagascar's being less efficient.[22] Mexico also ranked itself ninetieth out of 102 in efficiency of country tax systems and eighty-second in burden of regulations over businesses in the same survey.[23] To the extent the above survey data serve as proxy determinants for FDI, which this chapter argues is real and considerable, it suggests the potential impact credible commitments to reduce transaction costs could make on improving Mexico's ability to attract FDI is significant. In this setting and because of these trends, the need for Mexico to act to enhance its competitive position for FDI – beyond that already afforded to it by the NAFTA – is clear and urgent.

Credible commitments and the relevance of state capacity: compromise towards reform

Credibility to commitments, this chapter argues, which has the highest potential impact for the reduction of transaction costs *ceteris paribus* – increased private sector participation in the electricity sector, the easing of rigid labour regulations, and increased tax revenue – is not yet present.[24] Progress towards these reform proposals is currently characterized by political gridlock in Mexico's congress. This is in sharp contrast to the centralized nature of policy implementation in the PRI-dominated 1980s and 1990s, wherein Congress was more a 'rubber stamp' for executive policymaking. Today, political debate – and gridlock – is part of the process that lends credibility to policy implementation.

Electricity

Currently, the Mexican government lacks the finances to meet the investment needs of the electricity sector, increasing transaction costs in Mexico through rising electricity prices.[25] The Fox administration's current proposal to make a credible commitment towards electricity reform seeks to enhance the role of private participation in the electricity sector, without privatizing it completely (see Table 6.1). The Fox proposal requires amending Articles 27 and 28 of the Mexican Constitution that grants the state control of the electrical industry.[26] The intent behind allowing more room for private participation is to meet the sector's investment needs – estimated to be around US$50 billion over the next ten years due to increasing demand.[27]

Rising electricity demand has led to a corresponding increase in electricity prices and the need for a dramatic increase in investment in this critical infrastructure. Demand for electricity increased over the last decade at a rate of 5.2 per cent per year and is expected to grow by 6 per cent per year until 2010.[28] In 1997 and 2003, electricity prices for residential and industrial use rose 66 per cent and 38 per cent respectively.[29] That the Mexican government lacks the finances on its own to meet the investment needs to meet the demand creates a bottleneck for electricity generation, transmission and distribution.

The current proposal to enhance the role of the private sector intends to ease the burden on federal finances. Rising energy demands in Mexico forecast this sector's capital requirements over the next ten years to equal approximately 2.5 per cent of current GDP per year, or more than the country's health and education budgets combined.[30] In the medium to long term, these demands increase the likelihood for shortages and blackouts that ultimately undermines economic growth and investor confidence – two factors critical to attracting FDI.[31]

With high and rising electricity prices, Mexico's attractiveness as a location for FDI is weakened by the transaction costs these present. It is important to note that input costs such as electricity, used in the manufacturing sector, for example, can act as an influential FDI determinant for investors. When surveyed by the International Monetary Fund (IMF) on infrastructure-related determinants of FDI, potential emerging

Table 6.1 Credible commitments toward electricity reform

Policy agenda	Commitments	Status	Measures taken	Assessment	Impact on FDI attraction
Partial liberlization of state-owned power company (SOE)	Amendment to the Laws of Electricity Public Service – 1992	Intiated limited private sector role in CFE	Independent power production (IPP) – first plant enters service in 2000	IPPs stopgap – met short-term surge in demand fails to meet long-term	Limited ability to stem increased transaction costs associated with rising prices and demand
Reform	Electricity reform proposal introduced 2000	In congress	Proposed agency for new regulation of CFE and LFC (electricity regulator) Electricity generation to open to more private sector participation Requires amending constitution does not privatize current SOE	Political opposition frames reform as privatization; long-term demand will require increased role of private sector	Would reduce transaction costs associated with FDI by reducing input costs for manufacturers: electricity

market investors rank utility costs and institutional impediments to the access to infrastructure facilities second (behind availability of infrastructure).[32]

For a better view towards understanding how delays in reform in electricity tangibly affect Mexico's competitiveness for FDI, the argument presented here can be substantiated by data on input costs in the country's manufacturing sector. Mexican manufacturing, as described in Chapter 4, is reliant on its *maquiladora* (assembly) sector for attracting foreign investors for low-skilled manufacturing for export. Its contribution to the economy is significant. In 2002, for instance, 48 per cent of manufacturing exports were produced in the *maquiladora* sector.[33] Utility costs in electricity in recent years reflect a trend indicative of the need for increased investment in Mexico's electricity sector (see Figure 6.3).

The case of Mexico's electronics sub-sector reflects how this trend can acutely affect the manufacturing sector's prospects for FDI. In 2002, electronics received 22.4 per cent of FDI into the manufacturing sector, second only to the automotive sub-sector.[34] The numbers of electronics companies that manufacture through the *maquiladora* programme, subject to rising electricity costs, are approximately 837 out of a total of 900 companies.[35] The electronics sub-sector has suffered a decline recently in terms of jobs and FDI levels especially since 1999.[36] Recent

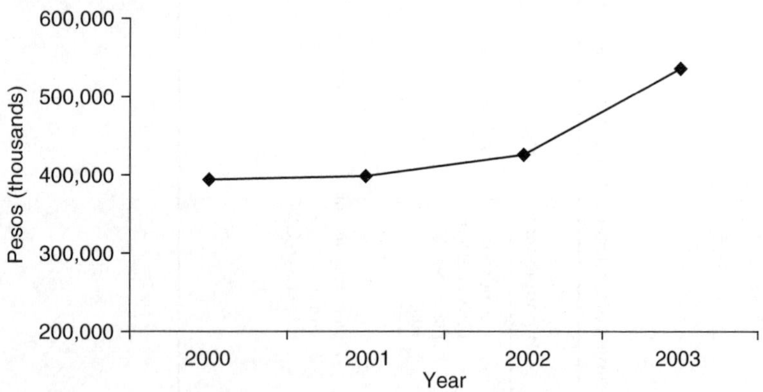

Figure 6.3 Average annual expenses of Mexico's in-bond export industry, electric energy

Source: Author's calculation based on the data from Instituto Nacional de Esatdística, Geografía e Informática (INEGI) (2004) *Estatistica de la Industria Maquiladora de Exportación*.

global declines in FDI and increased competition for low-wage manufacturing FDI make input cost differences between potential host countries more important. Thus, the data presented here reflect a cost increase that can negatively influence FDI motivation into this important sector in Mexico's economy.[37] While competitors like China offer MNEs advantages in labour costs lower than half of Mexico's, it is clear that Mexico can compete in alternative ways, such as like reducing transaction costs in input areas – for example, electricity – to remain competitive.[38] Recently, Mexico has been losing share in electronics products to such countries.[39]

Tax and labour

Global competition for low-wage manufacturing has indeed affected Mexico's ability to attract FDI.[40] Compared to countries competing with Mexico in this arena, Mexico's labour costs are significantly higher – especially than those of China's.[41] While competing on labour costs on par with China's is not an option for Mexico, as the previous example with electricity makes clear, Mexico can act in other ways that would reduce transaction costs towards the same affect.

The Fox administration currently seeks to implement part of its reform agenda to reduce overall costs posed to foreign, as well as domestic, enterprises by Mexico's labour market (see Table 6.3). Labour regulations pose significant and inflated costs to employers that discourage regular hiring practices (thus encouraging worker movement into the informal market).[42] Required benefits and labour taxes posed to employers are globally uncompetitive, for example, with numerous taxes for housing subsidy programmes, holiday bonuses and up to fifty-two paid rest days annually.[43] Current legislation proposed to address this aims to create more flexible definitions to labour activities in Mexico.[44]

Making its labour market globally competitive and attractive for FDI is closely linked to reform proposed by the Fox administration towards tax collection. Low tax revenues are due to high levels of tax evasion but also in the size of the tax base. Mexico's tax revenue as a percentage of GDP was an average of 11.1 per cent for 1998–2003, the lowest of OECD countries and one of the lowest in Latin America.[45] Publicly acknowledged by the Governor of the Bank of Mexico, Dr Guillermo Ortiz, is the need to increase Mexico's narrow tax base.[46] The Fox administration's attempt at doing this through expanding the base of Mexico's value added tax (VAT), a major contributor to tax revenues, failed before (see Table 6.2). Importantly, Mexico made a credible commitment towards reducing corporate income tax rates from 35 per cent to 32 per cent in

Table 6.2 Credible commitments toward tax reform

Policy agenda	Commitments	Status	Measures taken	Assessment	Impact on FDI attraction
Revenue enhancement	Tax reform proposal introduced 2001	Failed 2001	Proposed expansion of tax base: VAT elimination of tax exemptions	Potential for VAT to contribute to revenue enhancement: large and needed	Failure keeps transaction costs higher in areas such as electricity prices and infrastructure deficiencies
	Broaden excise tax	Enacted 2002	Additional tax on 'luxury' products	Enacted in light of 2001 VAT failure	Important contribution to revenue
	Promise	No action	Recognition of need to expand narrow tax base, likely done by commitment to eliminate VAT exemptions	Administration guess: would increase collection to 13.7%	Needed
Competitive tax law	Income tax law changes 1999–2001	Enacted income tax	Reduction of corporate rate, 2002–2005 / 35%–32%	Increases global competitiveness	Positive

Table 6.3 Credible commitments toward labour reform

Policy agenda	Commitments	Status	Measures taken	Assessment	Impact on FDI attraction
Labour flexibility	Labour law reform proposal – introduced 2002	In congress	Proposes trial/ workers (eliminates regulated fixed-term contracts) Proposes to ease rigid permanent contacts regulation	Facilitates probationary period for long-term jobs while discourages movement to the informal labour market	Reduces transaction costs posed to employers
	Promise	No action	Recognition of need to ease rigid employment protection provisions (high dismissal costs)	Real need is for creation of unemployment insurance	Reduces transaction costs posted to employers with regard to hiring and firing procedures
	Promise	No action	Recognition of need to reduce mandatory social contributions taxed on wages – ideally offset by larger tax base (VAT)	Closely linked to tax reform	Reduces 'tax wedge' higher in Mexico than elsewhere

2005. This positively influences FDI motivation by reducing the tax burden posed to foreign enterprises. However, an increase in tax revenue to offset required payroll taxes is not yet present. On balance, Mexico's income tax rates are still higher than its competition in manufacturing FDI, for instance, including China and Malaysia.[47]

Mexico's infrastructure needs, including electricity, are at a significant disadvantage in the short and medium-term because of low tax revenues. Higher tax renews would mean greater fiscal capacity to address infrastructure objectives such as financing the electricity sector's increasing need for investment. Moreover, higher tax revenues can offset required labour costs and taxes to employers and employees in Mexico. The 'tax wedge' (difference between costs paid by employers and take-home pay of employees) in Mexico is high, due to these required social contributions and other costs.[48] These costs could be offset by increased revenues, for instance, which can be accomplished by expanding the tax base.

The politics of reform: building state capacity and regaining competitiveness for FDI

Congressional opposition to the proposed commitments discussed above is largely along ideological lines.[49] As not one of the three major parties in Mexico's Congress today – the PRI, PAN or PRD – holds an absolute majority, the Fox administration must ally itself with another party (or faction of a party) to gain the votes necessary to pass its reform agenda (see Table 6.4).[50] Thus, the ability to make credible the Fox administration's commitments to reform requires inter-party cooperation and consensus.

For any reform to the country's electricity, labour or tax systems to be implemented, votes from the largest party in Congress – the PRI – are needed. Currently, the PRI is experiencing an ideological divide. In what can be seen as 'generational politics', a small, but powerful 'old guard' faction is asserting a hardline position against reforms while other, more pragmatic PRI/supporters are reform oriented.[51] Therefore, the PAN reform agenda must overcome this divide by appealing to reform oriented party members while accommodating the powerful old guard.

The Fox administration looks to the PRI for an alliance, as other parties are even less receptive to these commitments to reform. Because the left-of-centre PRD has a 'nationalist' platform against any type of reform to tax, electricity or labour, an alliance with the PRD is not a likely choice for the PAN. The PRI realizes its relative majority in Congress

Table 6.4 Political and economic position of the three major political parties in Mexico

	PRI	PAN	PRD
Role	– Largest party in congress, without absolute majority – Senate: 47% – House: 44% – Support essential for credible commitments to be made – Divided: traditionalists and reformists, but mostly latter	– Occupies executive – Senate: 37% – House: 30% – Centre-right – Biggest loser in 2003 house elections – Author of reform legislation	– Centre-left – Senate: 12% – House: 19% – Biggest winner in 2003 house elections – Strong opposition to reforms, PAN–PRD alliance unlikely
Position on reforms	– Against raising VAT but may compromise – Traditional faction: anti-reform (powerful minority) – Close labour ties makes it hostile to labour reform but gains in state governors may make compromise	– Recognizes opposition to reforms – willing to compromize with tax and in electricity, not as much with labour on party platform, founder: Cardenas	– Against 'anti-nationalist' reforms of Fox: electricity, labour and tax – Traditional left influential
Alliances and other players	– Anti-reform alliance with PRD, UNT, SME, (unions) Rejects alliance with PAN on approving electricity reform (8/03) – 20 of 31 state governorships, pro-reform influene on party	– Seeks alliances with others, mainly PRI, soon before 2006 – Precedent for attempts at compromize with PRI – Courting state governors: PRI and PRD parties, support reforms	–Alliance with PRI UNT, SME against 'privatizing' electricity – Voted with PRI on rejection of VAT increase (12/03) Close labour ties
Motives	– PRI President Modrazo eyeing presidency in 2006, wants progress on reforms – Must appease constituencies growing in importance: state governors and unions	– Alliance needed with other party ideally the PRI, for reforms – Seeks to lock-in one or more reforms before election, appease important state and municipal constituencies	– Platform seeks to appease constituencies in labour, working-class, 'anti-neoliberal' organizations

PRI = Partido Revolucionario Institucional.
PAN = Partido Acción Nacional.
PRD = Partido de la Revolución.

gives it a particular advantage in deciding whether any of Fox's reforms become credible commitments and at what pace.

Mexico's emerging democracy: other, new actors

Due to Mexico's democratic transition, states and municipalities play an increasingly important role in shaping party platforms towards these reforms. The support of state governors, for instance, especially those from states where industry is concentrated, is particularly relevant. Today, the PRI claims twenty state governors to their party out of the thirty-one Mexican states. Facing its congressional opposition, the PAN recently sought to undermine PRI's anti-reform faction by courting state governors and indirectly influencing PRI politics. As a result, the PAN currently has public support from a small but influential number of PRI and PRD governors, from states including Veracruz, Nuevo Leon, Coahuila and Hidalgo.[52]

These are industry heavy states conscious of the private investment successful electricity reform might bring.[53]

In addition to the winning over of new actors, such as like state governors, party allegiance must overcome strong opposition to reforms from organized groups, such as labour. The PRI and PRD, especially, have ties with labour, a historically important constituency to these parties. Consequently, anti-reform pressure is felt in party rank and file. Additionally, anti-reform sentiment is seen in public opinion, not only from labour but other 'anti-neo-liberal' organizations representing interests from agriculture to the poor and marginalized sectors of Mexican society.[54] Coalitions of such groups organized high-profile protests against the Fox administration's proposals in the autumn of 2003, indicative of popular unrest.[55] Their platform claims that eliminating VAT exemptions hurts the poor, labour reform harms workers' rights, and private sector involvement in the electricity sector destroys Mexico's sovereignty.

Conclusion

For Mexico, making credible commitments today is a process subject to more and better debate reflective of Mexico's democratic transition. In this new setting, political institutions must orient themselves towards consensus building among various actors in public policy making. In Mexico's recent history, the conception of instruments that lent credibility to commitments – through policy implementation – changed.

Today, instruments to bring about credible commitments are those that facilitate consensus by a plurality of parties, in contrast from earlier ones whose effectiveness rested on the dominance of one.

This chapter sought to provide a clear explanation as to why Mexico's ability to attract FDI is related to state capacity. The inability of the state to make credible commitments today, while it may be temporary, prevents the reduction of transaction costs that would favourably influence FDI attraction. It prevents the reduction of costs associated with economic activity in Mexico. By demonstrating how changes to state capacity altered its ability to make credible commitments, and its ability to influence FDI attraction, these findings support the conceptual contribution of this chapter – that the political economy of Mexico's democratic transition is directly related to the country's ability to attract FDI.

In seeking to make clear the relationship between transaction costs and FDI motivation, this chapter adopted a methodological approach, limiting the number of cases by which to illustrate this to one. That is, it did not detail the experience of other developing countries under similar circumstances. But such a study of multiple developing countries on the influence of transaction costs over FDI motivation may not effectively capture the implications the unique case of Mexico provides on its own. Mexico's proximity to the exceptionally large US consumer market, the incentives for FDI captured in the NAFTA and other aspects make the case of Mexico exceptional in assessing the impact of transaction costs on FDI.

This chapter asserts that the single-country nature of this case study contributes to our understanding of the role institutions play in attracting FDI. While this chapter did not detail other, similar cases, the conclusions reached can be generalized to other settings. Mexico's democratic transition has many political, economic and other institutional dimensions to it that make it sufficiently useful for comparison with countries such as India, for instance. India currently receives increasingly high amounts of foreign investment. This is especially true in its service sector, which in 2004 grew by 8.6 per cent Compared with the previous year, while the country's GDP in 2004 grew by 6.9 per cent.[56]

As with Mexico, India's economic environment was not always receptive to international capital. Its postcolonial industrialization strategy was largely protectionist and this repelled international capital. India made credible commitments to liberalize tariffs and barriers to capital flows only after the 1991 balance of payments crisis proved this strategy unsustainable. Importantly, the credible commitments in these reforms reflected that of a state also experiencing a democratic opening.[57]

Because democracy gave more stakeholders a say in reforms, interest groups such as bureaucrats, unions and politicians kept the pace and impact of reforms slow and incremental.[58] Their overall impact, however, in reducing costs associated with economic activity is seen today in the growing amounts of investment it receives annually.

Another country with which similarities can be drawn is Brazil, whose democratic opening occurred years ago. Today, its current president must navigate the country's notably fragile system of coalition building among political parties to make credible commitments to reforms. Economic reforms under President Fernando Henrique Cardoso (1995–2002) helped Brazil recover from a decade of high inflation and failed economic stabilization plans.[59] These garnered large support once proven effective at reducing inflation in the short term. Credible commitments toward economic reform, especially those that further liberalized trade, paved the way for the country's recent significant rise in exports. Today, through persistent compromise, President Luiz Inácio 'Lula' da Silva continues to make incremental yet significant credible commitments towards reform in fiscally important areas such as tax and Brazil's pension systems.[60]

The contribution of this chapter to studies on Mexico's recent decline in FDI goes beyond consequences of influences from new competition in emerging markets, or even beyond questioning the ability of the NAFTA to attract FDI. The conclusions reached here suggest that changes to state autonomy, and its subsequent impact on state capacity, prevents Mexico from making credible commitments that would increase its competitiveness to attract FDI by the extent that they reduce transaction costs. In accounting for Mexico's decline in FDI, here, an explanation is offered from 'within' rather than 'without', such as the popular tendency in literature today to assign responsibility to new and large FDI recipient countries like China.

Future areas of research may address how political trends in Mexico, especially before the 2006 elections, may continue influence the state's ability to make credible commitments. Democratic transitions are at times long and uncertain, and political actors are slow to familiarize themselves with new institutional environments. In light of this, Mexico's current impasse at making credible commitments towards reducing transaction costs is more symptomatic of 'growing pains' than fundamental institutional deficiencies. Thus, while seeking to answer a narrow but important inquiry into the role of state capacity on a country's ability to make credible commitments, it is clear that more questions can and should be asked to enhance or make new contributions to the findings presented here.

Notes

1. Stiglitz (1998) 85–7. The United Nations Conference on Trade and Development (UNCTAD) defines FDI as an investment 'in an economy other than that of the foreign direct investor' which 'implies that the investor exerts a significant degree of influence on the management of the enterprise resident in the other economy' (see UNCTAD 2002).
2. North (1994) 1.
3. This chapter adopts a conception of credible commitments as being commitments made by the state that are enforceable and effective.
4. The commitments Mexico made in the NAFTA can have significant implications for attracting FDI. In addition to trade related incentives such as tariff reductions and market access to the USA, dimensions of the NAFTA (such as its independent dispute resolution mechanism) reduce real and perceived country risk to foreign investors. On balance, these are meant to reduce overall transaction costs to foreign investors in Mexico compared to elsewhere.
5. See, for example, International Monetary Fund CMCG Working Group on FDI (2003), McKinsey Global Institute (2003), UNCTAD World Investment Report (2003).
6. Here, state capacity is not the same as government, or a state's autonomy to implement policy at any given time. Rather, the state's autonomy to make credible commitments, for instance, is shaped by the underlying institutionalized interests and processes – state capacity – cultivated over many years and because of the interests of many governments.
7. Dussel Peters (2000) 89, 116; Lustig (1998) 29.
8. As described by Williams (2001), 'The terms, or rules, were straightforward. State sanction provided these groups political protection, a legal monopoly to represent their constituents, and guaranteed access to decision makers; in exchange, corporatist leaders accepted limits on their members' behavior and demands.'
9. Vargas made this observation during a televised conference in Mexico City in 1999 on the prospects for democracy in Latin America.
10. For instance, enforcement of the overhauling commitments the Salinas administration took on – such as privatizing state-owned enterprises – at times evoked the stronghold capabilities of classic PRI institutional arrangement. Still resembling 'a well-calibrated authoritarian regime', force and the threat of force was used to enforce commitments especially while addressing labour issues in the privatization process (see Centeno (1994) 33).
11. On election day 1988, fearing a loss to opponent Cuauhtémoc Cárdenas, an influential PRI faction overseen by Manuel Bartlett orchestrated electioneering tactics such as burning ballots and a supposed 'crash' of the computerized counting system, reporting a Cárdenas win (see Preston and Dillon (2004) 149).
12. Levy *et al.* (2001) 89.
13. Ifill (2003).
14. UNCTAD World Investment Report, 2003.
15. UNCTAD World Investment Report, 2003.
16. Overview. UNCTAD World Investment Report, 2003. Interpreting this ranking must also consider Mexico's exceptional level of FDI in 2001 due to Citigroup's acquisition of Banamex.

17. As Figure 6.2 shows, Mexico's inward FDI flows in 2001 were unusually high due the Citigroup subsidiary Citicorp's acquisition of Mexico's Grupo Financiero Banamex – Accival Financial Group (Banamex).
18. International Monetary Fund CMCG Working Group on FDI (2003) 42.
19. Ministry of Finance Mexico (2004).
20. International Monetary Fund CMCG Working Group on FDI (2003), McKinsey Global Institute (2003), A.T. Kearney (2003), UNCTAD World Investment Report (2003).
21. International Monetary Fund CMCG Working Group on FDI (2003) 32.
22. World Economic Forum, Global Competitiveness Report (2003) 479. Survey question asked: 'How effective is your national Parliament/Congress as a law-making and oversight institution?'
23. For survey details including methodology, see World Economic Forum Global Competitiveness Report (2003) xi.
24. These commitments are highlighted in Tables 6.1, 6.2 and 6.3
25. Carreón-Rodriguez *et al*. (2003) 26.
26. Aragón (2003) 1.
27. Galloway (2001).
28. Energy Sector Management Assistance Programme, World Bank (2004) 10.
29. Consejo Mexicano de Hombres de Negocios (2003).
30. Energy Sector Management Assistance Programme, World Bank (2004) 1.
31. World Markets Analysis (2003).
32. International Monetary Fund CMCG Working Group on FDI (2003) 17.
33. Bancomext Annual Report (2002) adapted from data from Banco de México.
34. Bancomext (2003).
35. Bancomext (2003). Data adapted from Banco de México.
36. Secretaría de Economía, Dirección de General de Inversión Extranjera.
37. Dussel Peters *et al*. (eds) (2003) 252.
38. McKinsey Global Institute (2003).
39. Berges and Merrill Lynch (2003).
40. Adams (2003).
41. Average hourly wages in Mexico are 1.47 (US$) versus 0.59 (US$) in China. Source: McKinsey Global Institute (2003).
42. OECD (2004).
43. OECD (2004) 89.
44. Economist Intelligence Unit (2003) 40.
45. Author's calculation based on OECD data including 2003 projected tax revenues. See OECD (2004) 57, 215.
46. Speech by Dr Guillermo Ortiz, Governor of the Bank of Mexico, at the LXVI Banking Convention, Mérida, Yucatán, 4 April 2003.
47. Fluctuation in exchange rates also accounts for increased labour costs. Ruiz-Funes (2003) 10. The *maquiladora* sector is subject to special tax treatment, through a 'safe harbour' arrangement that taxes 34 per cent on the higher of 6.5 per cent of total assets of the *maquiladora* or 6.9 per cent of total costs. See McKinsey Global Institute (2003).
48. These include mandatory contributions towards occupational risks, housing subsidy programmes, inabilities and life insurance, various social security contributions, day care centres, annual bonuses in paid holidays and fringe

benefits such as 52 paid rest days annually. Low tax revenues are also due to high levels of tax evasion. See OECD (2004) 89.

49. Grayson (2003).
50. In the July 2003 midterm elections in the lower house (Chamber of Deputies) the PRI/PVEM (Green Party) alliance captured 45 per cent of the seats awarded, followed by PAN 30 per cent and the PRD 19 per cent. The number of senators remained the same as the 2000 election, as elections for the Senate are every six years. See Grayson (2003).
51. *Oxford Analytica* (2003).
52. *Melgar* (2003).
53. *Oxford Analytica* (2003).
54. Briefly, the strong 'anti-neoliberal' sentiment in Latin America represents groups protesting the decline in wages and living conditions, especially for the poor, since Mexico and other countries began market reforms that liberalized sectors such as trade and agriculture. See Granados Chapa (2003).
55. Granados Chapa (2003).
56. Economist Intelligence Unit (2004) 4–5.
57. Luce and Kynge (2003).
58. Economist Intelligence Unit (2003) 26.
59. Sharma (2002) 43–4.
60. Economist Intelligence Unit (2004) 8.

References

Adams, J. (2003) 'Mexico vs China', *Economic Development Journal*, 2, 36–46.

Aragón, L. (2003) 'Electricity Reform in Mexico', Conference 2003 of the British Institute of Energy Economics, September (Oxford: St John's College).

A.T. Kearney, Inc. (2003) *FDI Confidence Index*, Global Business Policy Council (Alexandria, VA: A.T. Kearney).

Bancomext (2002) *Annual Report 2002*, Retrieved 9 March 2004, from http://bancomext.com/Bancomext/publicasecciones/secciones/4186/Informe-ingles-02.pdf

Bancomext (2003) *Mexico: The Electric and Electronics Industry in Mexico* (Mexico City: Bancomext).

Berges, R. and Merrill Lynch & Co. (2003) *Mexico and the Threat from China*, Retrieved 15 March 2004, from http://www.dallasfed.org/news/research/2003/03maq_berges.pdf

Carreón-Rodriguez, V., Jiménez San Vicente, A. and Rosellón, J. (2003) *The Mexican Electricity Sector: Economic, Legal and Political Issues*, Retrieved 13 March 2004, from http://iis-db.stanford.edu/pubs/20311/mexican_dereg_3.pdf

Centeno, M. (1994) *Democracy within Reason: Technocratic Revolution in Mexico* (University Park: Pennsylvania University Press).

Consejo Mexicano de Hombres de Negocios (2003) *Análisis de la Competitividad en México: Evaluación y Determinación de areas de Oportunidad para su Mejora* (Mexico: Consejo Mexicano de Hombres de Negocios).

Crespo, J. (2004) *The Party System and Democratic Governance in Mexico*, Retrieved 15 March 2004, from http://www.csis.org/americas/pubs/ppCrespo.pdf

Dussel Peters, E. (coord.), Palacios Lara, J. and Woo Gómez, G. (2003), *La Industria Electrónica en México: Problemática, Perspectivas y Propuestas* (Jalisco, Mexico: Universidad de Guadalajara).

Dussel Peters, E. (2000) *Polarizing Mexico: The Impact of Liberalization Strategy* (Boulder: Lynne Rienner).

Economist Intelligence Unit (2003) *Country Commerce: Mexico* (New York: Economist Intelligence Unit).

Economist Intelligence Unit (2004) *Country Profile 2004: Brazil* (New York: Economist Intelligence Unit).

Economist Intelligence Unit (2004) *Country Report: India* (New York: Economist Intelligence Unit).

Energy Sector Management Assistance Programme (2004) *Energy Policies and the Mexican Economy*, Energy and Water Department (Washington, DC: World Bank Group).

Galloway, J. (2001) 'Mexico's Capital Connection', *Latin Finance*, 117, 14.

Granados Chapa, M. (2003, 25 November) 'Plaza Publica: Movilización Masiva', *El Norte*.

Grayson, G. (2003) *Beyond the Mid-term Elections: Mexico's Political Outlook 2003–2006*, Retrieved 11 March 2004, from http://csis.org/americas/mexico/0310_grayson.pdf

Ifill, Gwen (2003, 3 July) Vicente Fox Elected, *PBS Newshour*, Retrieved March 22, 2004, from http://www.pbs.org/newshour/bb/latin_america/july-dec00/mexico_election_7-03.html

IMD International (Institute) (2003) *World Competitiveness Yearbook* (Lausanne, Switzerland: IMD International (Institute)).

Instituto Nacional de Estadística Geographía e Informática (INEGI) (2004) *Estadistica de la Industria Maquiladora de Exportación* (Aguascalientes, Mexico: INEGI).

International Monetary Fund (IMF) (2003) *Foreign Direct Investment in Emerging Market Countries – Report of the Working Group of the Capital Markets Consultative Group (CMCG)*, Retrieved 28 March 2004, from http://www.imf.org/external/np/cmcg/2003/eng/091803.pdf

Levy, D., Bruhn, K. and Zebadúa, E. (2001) *Mexico: The Struggle for Democratic Development* (Berkeley and Los Angeles: University of California Press).

Luce, E. and Kynge, J. (2003, 21 September) 'The Divergent Economic Effects of Democracy', *Financial Times*.

Lustig, N. (1998) *Mexico: The Remaking of an Economy* (Washington, DC: Brookings Institution).

McKinsey Global Institute (2003) 'New Horizons: Multinational Company Investment in Developing Countries', *MGI Report*, McKinsey.

Melgar, I. (2003, 7 August) 'Privilegia Fox Relacion con los Gobernadores', *El Norte*.

Ministry of Finance, Mexico (2004) 'The Executive Submitted to Congress the Economic Program for 2004', *Secretaría de Hacienda y Crédito Público*, Retrieved 11 March 2004, from http://www.shcp.gob.mx/english/docs/epg_2004.html

North, D. (1994) 'Institutions and Credible Commitments. Economic History 9411006', Economics Working Paper Archive at WUSTL (Washington, DC: University of Washington).

Organisation for Economic Co-operation and Development (OECD) (2004) *OECD Economic Surveys: Mexico*, 2003(1) (Paris: Organisation for Economic Co-operation and Development).

Oxford Analytica (2003) *Mexico: Government Pursues Electricity Reform* (Oxford: Oxford Analytica).

Preston, J. and Dillon, S. (2004) *Opening Mexico: The Making of a Democracy* (New York: Farrar, Straus & Giroux).

Ruiz-Funes, M. (2003) 'Economic Competitiveness in Mexico: Recent Evolution, Prospects, and Repercussions for the United States', *Hemisphere Focus*, 11(11).

Secretaría de Economía. (2004) *Subsecretaria de Normatividad, Inversión Extranjera y Practicas Comerciales Internacionales, Dirección de General de Inversión Extranjera*, Retrieved February 13, 2004, from http//:www.economia.gob.mx

Sharma, V. (2002) 'Entry into Latin American BEMs: High or Low Resource Commitment Modes?', *International Journal of Commerce and Management*, 12(1), 41–67.

Stiglitz, J. (1998) 'Towards a New Paradigm for Development: Strategies, Policies and Processes', in J. Stiglitz (ed.), *Joseph Stiglitz and the World Bank: The Rebel Within* (London: Anthem Press).

United Nations Conference on Trade and Development (2002) *Sources and Definitions*, Retrieved 8 April 2004, from http://r0.unctad.org/en/subsites/dite/fdistats_files/sources_definitions.htm

United Nations Conference on Trade and Development (2003) *World Investment Report 2003 FDI Policies for Development: National and International Perspectives* (New York and Geneva: United Nations).

Williams, M. (2001) *Market Reforms in Mexico: Coalitions, Institutions, and the Politics of Policy Change* (Oxford: Rowman & Littlefield).

World Economic Forum (2003) *The Global Competitiveness Report* (Geneva: World Economic Forum).

World Markets Analysis (2003) *Mexican Government's Mid-Term Defeat Threatens Economy* (World Markets Research).

7

The Determinants of the Disappearance of Mexican Banks

Clemente Hernandez-Rodriguez

Introduction

Since the re-privatization process in the early 1990s, the number of Mexican banks has fallen by almost 50 per cent, reflecting an unprecedented number of governmental interventions,[1] (including banking bailouts) and subsequent acquisitions or mergers.

Several studies have sought to identify the characteristics that cause banks to fail. Gonzalez-Hermosillo *et al.* (1997), for instance, utilize a discrete-time duration model to study the determinants of fragility in the Mexican banking system. They employ bank specific data, banking sector variables and macroeconomic variables. Their data set covers the period 1991–95. The survival analysis presented in their paper focuses in the logistic functional form. Their results suggest that bank specific factors as well as macroeconomic conditions explain the probability of bank failure.

Hernandez and Lopez (2001) utilize a time-constant covariates proportional hazard model to study the determinants of the Mexican banking crisis.[2] They only employ financial banking indicators, using data from the period 1994–99. Their results are suggestive of the importance of their own financial indicators in explaining the banking crisis after the peso crisis in December 1994.

In this chapter, we estimate a comprehensive model relating the probability of disappearance to bank characteristics and macroeconomic conditions. We do so in a framework that permits a bank to disappear either by government intervention and subsequent acquisition by another bank, or by a merger.[3] Cox's (1972, 1975) proportional hazards models with time-varying covariates are used.[4] Although this framework is applied to the Mexican case, it can also be extended to other countries.

In the remainder of this chapter we develop a model in order to identify the determinants of bank disappearance, present the empirical results and offer the conclusions drawn from that investigation.

Duration model

A class of models that has been widely used in economics and other disciplines is the proportional hazard model. In our duration model, the lefthand side variable would measure the length of time that a bank is in business before it disappears. Following the model developed by Cox (1972), the hazard of disappearance by the *i* th bank may be written as $h_i\,(t|x_i\,(t),\beta)$, where $i = 1,\ldots,N$; $h_i\,()$, is the hazard of disappearance; $x_i\,(t)$ is a vector of time-varying covariates; β is a vector of parameters to be estimated.

We observe data for each bank *i* in the sample at distinct times $t_{i,1} < t_{i,2} < \cdots < t_{i,J_i-1}$; in addition, at time $t_{i,J_i} \geq t_{i,J_i-1}$, we observe either government intervention or acquisition, or the observation on the *i* th bank is censored at time t_{i,J_i} or in other words, the bank is still in business. In this framework, duration refers not to calendar time, but to time relative to the starting date of business for the bank *i*, so that $t_{i0} = 0$ where t_{i0} is the date of charter for the *i* th bank if the bank is a new bank, or t_{i0} is the date when the *i*th bank is newly privatized if the bank was a publicly-owned bank being re-privatized. The variables in the vector $x_i(t)$, corresponding to time $t_{i,j}$, $j = 1,\ldots, (J_i - 1)$, are assumed to reflect measurable characteristics of bank *i* over the interval $[t_{i,j},t_{i,j+1})$ for $j = 1,\ldots,(J_i - 1)$. At time t_{i,J_i}, we assume that these characteristics are represented by $x_i(t_{J_i-1})$ Hence:

$$x_i(t_{i,j} + \Delta) = x_i(t_{i,j})\; 0 \leq \Delta < t_{i,j+1}, \quad j = 1,\ldots,(J_i - 1).$$

The estimated model is time varying in the sense that covariates may vary across intervals, although they are assumed constant within intervals of time $(t_{i,j},t_{i,j+1})$.

Hazards of disappearance are estimated using an adaptation of the partial likelihood method suggested by Cox (1972, 1975). One of the issues we have to deal with in the hazards is right censoring (Han and Hausman 1990). Censoring involves removal from the sample for reasons other than disappearance. Indicator variables are defined as follows:

$$\delta_i = \begin{cases} 1 & \text{if bank } i \text{ disappears due to } \textit{acquisition} \text{ or } \textit{government} \\ & \textit{intervention} \text{ at time } t_{J_i} \\ 0 & \text{otherwise,} \end{cases}$$

to reflect right-censoring at time $t_j i$.[5] Then, the contribution by the *i*th bank to the partial likelihood is

$$L_i(\beta) = \frac{h_i(t_{J_i}|x_i(t_{J_i}), \beta)^{\delta_i}}{\sum_{j \in R_i} h_j(t_{J_i}|x_j(t_{J_i}), \beta)} \quad (7.1)$$

where $R_i + \{j|t_{J_j} \geq t_{J_i}, j = 1,\ldots,N\}$ is the risk set associated with bank i (i.e. the set of banks that did not disappear). Note that right-censored banks do not enter the numerator of any contribution to the partial likelihood, although they enter the denominator for contributions by banks that disappear due to failure and acquisition before the censoring date.

We specify the proportional hazards as

$$h_i(t|x_i(t), \beta) = \tilde{h}(t)(x_i(t)\beta) \quad (7.2)$$

where h (t) is the baseline hazard.[6] Substituting equation (7.2) into equation (7.1), taking logs, and summing across individual banks yields the partial log-likelihood for the entire sample:

$$\ln L(\beta) = \sum_{i=1}^{N} \left\{ \delta_i x_i(t_{J_i})\beta - \ln\left[\sum_{j \in R_i} (x_j(t_{J_i})\beta) \right] \right\} \quad (7.3)$$

The baseline hazard drops out when equation (7.2) is substituted into equation (7.1); the model is semi-parametric in the sense that the vector β is estimated without specifying the baseline hazard. In principle, although the baseline hazard h (t) varies only over t and not over i it is evaluated at different times t for different banks i and therefore captures individual heterogeneity among banks disappearing at different times.

The advantage of the partial likelihood estimation approach in this case lies in the fact that only part of the hazard function needs to be specified; the baseline hazard does not have to be specified, nor does the density of survivor function need to be specified. For purposes of hypothesis testing, the partial log-likelihood in equation (7.3) may be regarded as an ordinary log-likelihood concentrated with respect to the baseline hazard.

Empirical analysis

A hazard model, in the context of the disappearance of a bank, answers the question: What is the probability of a bank disappearing in the next time period conditional on being in business up to the previous time period? In this context, we have to deal with some issues such as censoring and the data structure or data organization.

Data

The sample includes data for Mexican banks that existed during the period 1990–2002. Data are collected from balance sheets and other financial records. The dataset is publicly available and can be found in the collection of bulletins (quarterly reports) of the Bank and Securities National Commission, CNBV (former CNB).[7]

We have 31 banks ($N = 31$), each of which will disappear or be censored. Let Y_i represent the duration until the disappearance occurs. Z_i is the duration until the observation is censored. Then $t_i \equiv \min\{Y_i, Z_i\}$. An indicator of censoring C_i is defined. $C_i = 0$ if observation i is censored, 1 if it is not, for $i = \{1,2\ldots,N\}$.

One of the first problems is related to bank lifetime: How do we measure the duration? Let the starting time of bank i be t_{i0} (time-in). In this chapter, the time-in will be determined by (a) the date of charter for the ith bank if the bank is a new bank or (b) the date when the ith bank is newly privatized if the bank was a publicly-owned bank reprivatized in the early 1990s. Let the ending time of bank i be t_{i,J_i} (time-out); that is, the time when bank i disappears. Mexican banks disappear mainly because government intervenes, or the bank merges, or it is acquired by another bank. The first reason is a regulatory decision by the deposit insurance agency (FOBAPROA or IPAB[8]). The second reason is an administrative decision.

This definition of bank disappearance presents some problems. Some banks could have exhibited insolvency before government intervention or, perhaps, they merged before declaring themselves insolvent. This could distort the analysis. Nevertheless, we have the following three solutions available: (i) to take into account the size of the bank; (ii) to differentiate insolvency from bank failure; or (iii) delete the smallest banks in the sample. The third solution is the one utilized in this work. So, only the banks that do not have a very small market share remain in the analysis.[9]

The sample of remaining banks is divided into (i) re-privatized banks and (ii) new banks.[10] Either the date when these banks were reprivatized or the charter date of each bank is known. The dates when banks merged with other banks, were acquired by other banks, or experienced government intervention are known. Data on banks that did not voluntarily liquidate, did not merge, were not acquired, or did not experience intervention, are recorded as censored as of December, 2002.

Table 7.1 New and foreign banks

New banks

Bank	**Time-in**	**Time-out**	**Duration (in months)**
Afirme	Jan–95	Dec–02	96
Banregio	Sep–94	Dec–02	100
Del Bajio	Jul–94	Dec–02	102
Inbursa	Sep–92	Dec–02	124
Industrial	Aug–93	Feb–98*	55
Interacciones	Oct–92	Dec–02	123
Interestatal	Jun–90	Sep–95*	28
Invex	Feb–91	Dec–02	107
Ixe	Jun–90	Dec–02	151
Mifel	Dec–93	Dec–02	109
Obrero	Jan–94	Mar–97*	39
Qaudrum	Jan–93	Aug–01*	84
Sureste	Jun–93	May–96*	36

Foreign banks

Bank	**Time-in**	**Time-out**	**Duration (in months)**
Citibank	Aug–91	Dec–02	137
BBV (Banco Bilbao Viscaya)	Dec–94	Dec–02	97
Santander	Oct–94	Dec–02	99

* Intervention by the government.

Table 7.1 shows the duration measured in months of the new banks. In addition, it includes the duration of the foreign banks that are relevant in the Mexican banking system. Five of the 13 banks have experienced government intervention, which means that 61.54 per cent of those banks remain in the hands of their original owners. Table 7.2 shows the duration, measured in months, of the reprivatized banks. Of the 18 banks, only 2 survived (11.11 per cent). Two other banks merged with foreign-owned banks (11.11 per cent), and 12 experienced government intervention.

The descriptive statistics related to both groups of banks (new and reprivatized) are the following: the mean duration for the new banks was 88.76 months; while the mean duration for the disappeared new banks was 48.40 months. The difference is 40.37 months, which is a sizable difference. On the other hand, the mean duration for reprivatized banks that disappeared was 66.5625; while for the total of reprivatized banks,

Table 7.2 Reprivatized banks

Bank	Time-in	Time-out	Duration (in months)	Acquired by	Date
Atlantico	Mar–92	Dec–97*	70	Bital	Dec–97
Banamex**	Aug–91	Jul–01 #	120	**Citibank****	Jul–01
Bancen	Jul–91	Aug–95*	38	Banorte	Sep–97
Bancomer**	Oct–91	Nov–00 #	110	**BBV****	Nov–00
Bancrecer	Aug–91	Nov–99*	100	Banorte	Dec–01
Banoro	Apr–91	Dec–96*	57	Bancrecer	Jan–97
Banorte (Mctl. Del Nte.)	Jun–92	Dec–02	127		
Banpais	Jun–91	Mar–95*	46	Banorte	Dec–97
Bital (Internacional)	Jun–92	Dec–02	127		
Confia	Aug–91	Aug–97*	73	Citibank	Oct–98
Cremi	Jun–91	Sep–94*	40	Promex	Jul–97
Inverlat (Comermex)	Feb–91	Feb–96*	49	Nova Scotia	Jul–96
Mexicano (Somex)	Mar–92	Oct–96*	56	Santander	Dec–96
Oriente	Aug–91	May–96*	58	BBV	Jul–97
Probursa (Mercantil)	Jun–91	May–95*	48	BBV	Jun–95
Promex	Apr–92	May–98*	74	Bancomer	Jul–00
Serfin	Jan–92	Jul–99*	91	Santander	May–00
Union (BCH)	Nov–91	Sep–94*	35	BBV	Jul–97

* Intervention by the government.
** These are the two largest banks in Mexico that had been acquires by the Citibank and BBv. In both cases the acquisitions involved a lot of money, and after the acquisition the old name of both banks were kept. Both banks still exist.
# Merged.

the mean duration was 73.2777. The difference is only 6.7152 months. One possible explanation for the small gap is the governmental support (capitalization) of the big institutions by buying out their loans, or perhaps the Mexican bailout was undertaken following a too-big-to-fail policy.[11]

The duration of a bank is modelled as a function of various bank characteristics, including financial ratios. This approach to evaluating the soundness of banks focuses on balance sheets and behavioural indicators. More specifically, the CAMEL-style method of analysis is followed. The CAMEL method is commonly used by regulators to assess five elements of a bank's financial condition and performance: capital adequacy, asset quality, management, earnings and liquidity.

In addition, this work analyzes the role of the following macroeconomic variables in order to capture circumstances that might have caused the financial condition of banks to vary systematically in Mexico: nominal foreign exchange rate, real foreign exchange rate, the change in the nominal foreign exchange rate, the change in the real foreign exchange rate, the ratio of foreign-currency denominated M2 to international reserves, the nominal interest rate of return on CETES, the real interest rate of return on CETES, the margin between the nominal rate of return on CETES and the short-term rate on US Treasury bills, the volatility of the nominal CETES rate, the volatility of the real CETES rate, changes in industrial production, changes in real GDP, inflation, and the level of the consumer price index (CPI).[12]

The financial indicators employed in this work are listed in Table 7.3. One of the attributes of the explanatory variables is that they are time-varying. In the literature about bank failures, the variables considered

Table 7.3 CAMEL-style explanatory variables

Variable	**CAMEL initial***	**Expected sign**
Bank capital/total assets	C	–
Total loans/bank capital	C	+
Total liabilities/bank capital	C	+
Overdue loans/total loans	A	+
Total loans/total assets	A	–
Overdue loans/total assets	A	+
Management and promotional expenses/total assets	M	+
Interest earnings/total loans	M	+
Interest expenses/traditional holdings	M	–
Interest expenses/interest earnings	E	?
ROA (returns on assets)	E	–
ROE (returns on equity)	E	–
Available funds/traditional deposits	L	–
Available funds + financial instruments/ traditional holdings	L	–
Available funds + financial instruments + prevailing credit/traditional deposits	L	?
Selling value/ book value		+
Total bank's deposits/total system's deposits		?
Percent of foreign shareholders		–

* The letters of CAMEL mean C ≡ capital adequacy, A ≡ asset quality, M ≡ management, E ≡ earnings, and L ≡ liquidity, respectively.

differ from one study to another.[13] In the present study, the model was selected based on its parsimony. Furthermore, we aimed to reduce multicolinearity in selecting the model selected.[14] The analysis is conducted in three phases. First, we use Kaplan–Meier estimates without covariates. Next, we estimate the hazard model and, finally, the structure of time-varying covariates is taken into account.

As a part of the second phase, the stepwise method is used.[15] However, the stepwise method is not sufficient because of the multicolinearity among the resulting explanatory variables. Therefore, different combinations of variables are tested, looking for the best goodness of fit and avoiding collinear variables. A ranking of the possible models (992 models) and a score using a chi-squared for each adjusted model is employed. The resulting top-ranked models have a high goodness of fit, a high statistical significance level and a reduced number of variables when compared to other models. The hazard models employed are estimated by maximizing the partial likelihood function to examine the disappearance of banks. The estimation is semi-parametric because no baseline hazard is parametrically specified.

Empirical results

Kaplan–Meier estimation

The Kaplan–Meier method is used for the product limit survival estimation for reprivatized banks and for new banks. Figure 7.1 shows a graph of the survival distribution function. Specific dates of disappearance may be inferred using Tables 7.1 and 7.2. If the survival functions are similar, then the log-negative log-survival distribution function should be parallel for each group of banks. Given that this is not the case, Figure 7.2 suggests that the survival distribution of new banks and reprivatized banks is statistically different. This is confirmed by the log-Rank and Wilcoxon tests. The equality of the two different groups of banks is rejected at a 5 per cent significance level for each test, and the Wilcoxon test rejects the null hypothesis of equality inclusive for a 10 per cent significance level.

Based on Figure 7.1, it can be seen that the survival probability of a reprivatized bank decreased little in the first months of its lifetime, and then it accelerated in the last months of its lifetime. In general, the survival function for the reprivatized banks falls more rapidly than the survival function for new banks. Hence, it is more likely for a reprivatized bank to disappear than for a new bank. These observations added to the tests of equality suggest that the covariates for the individual banks play

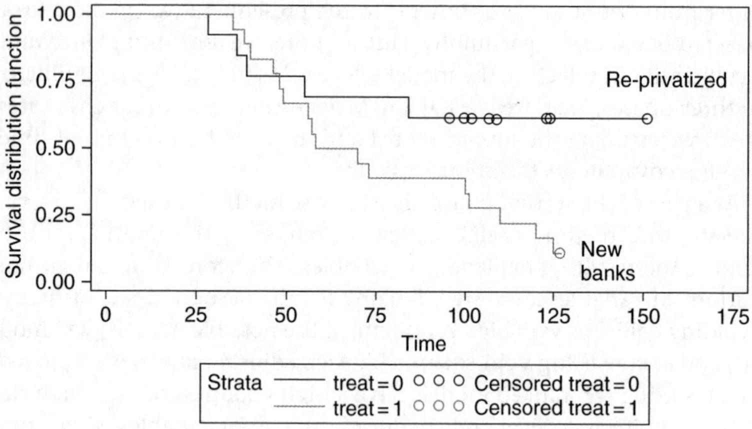

Figure 7.1 Survival distribution function

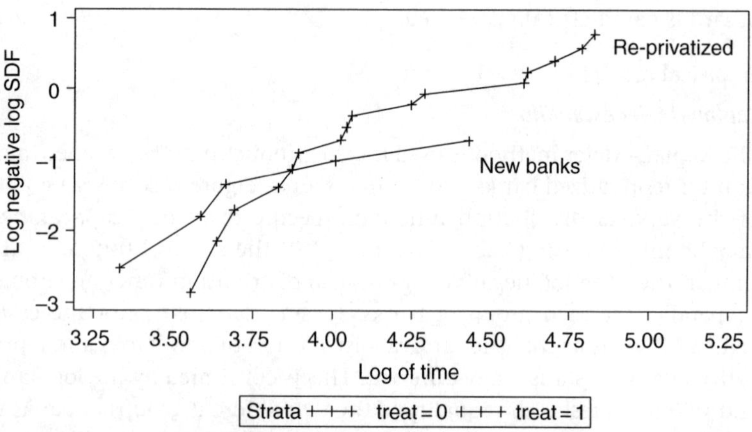

Figure 7.2 Log negative log-survival distribution function

an important role. This phenomenon seems to support the too-big-to-fail hypothesis.[16] In contrast, the new banks had a large probability of disappearance in the first months of their existence, and then in posterior months their probability of disappearance was less than that of the reprivatized banks.

The product limit survival estimates for the whole banking system (all banks) are shown in Table 7.4. Only 10 banks are in business at the end

Table 7.4 Product-limit survival estimates

Time	Survival	Failure	Survival standard error	Number of banks disappeared	Number of banks remaining
0	1.0000	0.0000	0.0000	0	31
28	0.9677	0.0323	0.0317	1	30
35	0.9355	0.0645	0.0441	2	29
36	0.9032	0.0968	0.0531	3	28
38	0.8710	0.1290	0.0602	4	27
39	0.8387	0.1613	0.0661	5	26
40	0.8065	0.1935	0.0710	6	25
46	0.7742	0.2258	0.0751	7	24
48	0.7419	0.2581	0.0786	8	23
49	0.7097	0.2903	0.0815	9	22
55	0.6774	0.3226	0.0840	10	21
56	0.6452	0.3548	0.0859	11	20
57	0.6129	0.3871	0.0875	12	19
58	0.5806	0.4194	0.0886	13	18
70	0.5484	0.4516	0.0894	14	17
73	0.5161	0.4839	0.0898	15	16
74	0.4839	0.5161	0.0898	16	15
84	0.4516	0.5484	0.0894	17	14
91	0.4194	0.5806	0.0886	18	13
96*	–	–	–	18	12
100	0.3844	0.6156	0.0879	19	11
100*	–	–	–	19	10
102*	–	–	–	19	9
107*	–	–	–	19	8
109*	–	–	–	19	7
110	0.3295	0.6705	0.0909	20	6
120	0.2746	0.7254	0.0908	21	5
123*	–	–	–	21	4
124*	–	–	–	21	3
127*	–	–	–	21	2
127*	–	–	–	21	1
151*	–	–	–	21	0

* The marked survival times are censored observations.

of the analysis (32.26 per cent of all banks in the system). From the descriptive statistics of Table 7.1 and Table 7.2, we know that the mean duration is 79.77 months for the entire sample of banks, and it is 62.23 for the disappeared banks. The difference in the mean duration is 17.53 months.

The coefficients on the explanatory variables

In the second phase of this model, we included the following explanatory variables: capital to total assets ratio; overdue loans to total loans ratio; interest earnings to total loans ratio; interest expenses to interest earnings ratio; ROE; available funds to traditional deposits ratio; and available funds, financial instruments, prevailing loans to traditional deposits ratio; change in the real foreign exchange rate; and real interest rate of return on CETES.

Table 7.5 shows the results of the hazard model for the whole sample. Moreover, we find that the explanatory power of the model is greatly

Table 7.5 All samples and test results

Total number of observations	31
Disappeared observations	21
Censored observations	10
Percentage of censored observations	32.2558

A Hypothesis testing, H_0: $\beta = 0$

Croteria	Without covariates	With covariates	Chi-squared	Degrees of Freedom	Probability
−2 log L	91.154	53.043	38.111	10	0.0001
Score	–	–	30.488	10	0.0001
Wald	–	–	17.179	10	0.0163

B Maximum likelihood estimates

Covariate	Coefficient	Standard error	Wald	Probability	Hazard rate
Bank capital/total assets	−21.41265	20.93482	1.137013	0.3625	0.000
Overdue loans/total loans	34.37130	9.90023	4.497521	0.0101	0.000
Interest earnings/total loans	14.80600	12.23304	1.369752	0.2419	0.000
Interest expenses/interest earnings	22.45060	7.71992	8.210283	0.0042	0.000
Returns on equity	−30.65056	10.44512	8.057535	0.0045	0.000
Available funds/traditional deposits	−17.71115	8.85531	9.324760	0.0023	0.000
Available funds + financial instruments + prevailing loans/ traditional deposits	−5.97026	3.28179	2.875192	0.0901	261.053

Continued

Table 7.5 continued

Covariate	Coefficient	Standard error	Wald	Probability	Hazard rate
Selling value/book value	1.11692	0.63863	3.214444	0.0730	3.142
Total bank's deposits/total system's Deposits	−18.96801	13.87110	3.126376	0.0770	0.000
Change in the real foreign exchange rate	0.12453	0.221473	0.734241	0.4680	0.424
Real interest rate of return of CETES	−0.69045	0.828765	1.162791	0.3680	1.941

Source: Results of the econometric methodology applied in this study.

increased by extending the basic model comprising only CAMEL-type financial ratios (bank-specific variables) to include macroeconomic information.

The ratio of the book value of bank equity (bank capital) to total assets is used as a measure of capital adequacy. We expect the coefficient of the bank capital to total assets ratio to be negative because the better capitalized a bank is, the greater its ability to absorb loan losses before becoming insolvent and, then, there is an inverse relation with this ratio to its probability to disappear. However, a bank with a high liabilities to capital ratio is expected to increase its probability of disappearance; that is, the coefficient on total liabilities to capital ratio is expected to be positive. If reliance on borrowed funds reflects risk taking or a weakened condition, we expect the coefficient of total loans to capital ratio to be positive because loans typically are riskier than other bank investments. These ratios have the anticipated signs, but none of these ratios are statistically significant. Therefore, only the coefficient of capital to total assets ratio is reported.[17]

The overdue loans to total loans ratio is used to assess asset quality. Loans are generally the most risky assets that banks hold. Thus, the coefficient of the variable overdue loans to total loans ratio should be positive. That is, the higher this ratio, the higher is the probability of a bank to disappear. The coefficients of the overdue loans to total loans ratio are significant at the 5 per cent level.

The interest earnings to total loans ratio is used to assess management. This variable is a proxy for management quality. The coefficient of the variable interest earnings to total loans ratio is positive. Nevertheless, the coefficient of this variable is reported even though it is not statistically significant even at a 10 per cent significance level.

The interest expenses to interest earnings ratio and returns on equity (ROE) are used to assess earnings. The coefficient of the interest expenses to interest earnings ratio is positive and statistically significant at 1 per cent. The coefficient on ROE is negative and statistically significant at 1 per cent, which means that higher returns on equity contribute to the soundness of a bank.

The available funds to traditional deposits ratio and the ratio of the summation of available funds, financial instruments, and prevailing loans to traditional deposits ratio are used to assess liquidity. The coefficients of the available funds to traditional deposits ratio are negative and statistically significant at 1 per cent. Thus, it is expected that a bank with a relatively highly-available funds to deposits ratio would, in general, be less prone to disappear, and so this coefficient should be positive. Banks whose liabilities were composed mainly of deposits had a lower probability of disappearance.

A high ratio of available funds to traditional deposits better enables a bank to accommodate unexpected deposit outflows without resorting to high priced borrowing. Deposit insurance lowers the cost of deposits, and hence the more a bank relies on deposits as a source of funds the greater the bank's probability of survival. Moreover, the coefficients of the ratio of available funds, financial instruments, and prevailing loans to traditional deposits are negative and statistically significant at a 5 per cent level. Banks with high ratios of cash and other reserves (available funds, financial instruments and prevailing loans) to deposits were relatively better protected against large or sudden deposit withdrawals, and hence had a lower probability of closure from illiquidity. Banks that rely heavily on non-deposit sources of funds might do so because they are unable to attract sufficient deposits. Alternatively, significant deposit withdrawals may force a bank to borrow against its loan portfolio or to sell assets. Conservative banks, on the other hand, are probably better able to attract deposits, and hence rely less on borrowed funds.

The last three variables of the analysis are used to evaluate different hypotheses specific to the Mexican banking system. The selling value to book value ratio assesses the hypothesis that the risk taking attitude of the bankers was explained by the high prices paid to acquire the banks when they were reprivatized. The significant positive sign for the coefficient of this variable implies that due to the high selling value the probability of a bank disappearing increases. The bank's total deposits to system's total deposits ratio is a variable to include bank size in the analysis. When this variable is significant, it implies that market share is a good explanatory variable for the probability of survival. This coefficient implies that size remains important. In this sense, the coefficient supports the too-big-to-fail hypothesis. Because it is not always statistically significant, the percentage of foreign shareholders is not recorded in the results. However, when it is statistically significant, the coefficient is negative. That is, foreign capital had a positive effect on the probability of survival of a bank.

Macroeconomic factors played a pivotal role. Up to 1997, high real interest rates imply a decrease in the likelihood of disappearance. Depreciation of the exchange rate is not statistically significant and implies an increase in the likelihood of disappearance. However, after 1998, both high real interest rates and a depreciation of the exchange rate, though not statistically significant at a 5 per cent, imply a decrease in the likelihood of disappearance.

Time-varying covariates

In the third phase of this analysis, we expect that FOBAPROA may have created moral hazard, encouraging banks to hold less capital and more risky portfolios.[18] In turn, this could provoke bank disappearance. Deposit insurance regime is not part of the covariates because the effect of deposit insurance is clouded by its possible dependence on the probability of disappearance. If moral hazard is a problem, FOBAPROA should increase risk taking, then, the higher risk banks will be predominant in the system, increasing the acquisition rate. If FOBAPROA thereby increased the probability that individual bank will disappear or be acquired, the time-varying covariate coefficients should reflect this. Using the balance sheet information available, we estimate a time-varying covariates hazards model in order to analyze the effects induced by FOBAPROA. FOBAPROA appears to have encouraged banks to diminish their asset quality, earnings and liquidity. Nevertheless, none of the coefficients is statistically significant on capital adequacy.[19] The coefficient of the interest earnings to total loans ratio is also consistent with the presence of moral hazard, although it is not statistically significant.

Time constant covariates are rejected in favour of time-varying covariates. Time-varying covariates improve the significance of the model. Moreover, we find that explanatory power of the model is greatly increased by extending the basic model comprising only CAMEL-type financial ratios (bank-specific variables) to include macroeconomic and aggregate banking sector information. We find that while the covariates add significant explanatory power to the model, the signs and statistical significance of the remaining variables are unaffected. That is, the coefficients on the bank specific variables are robust to the inclusion of macroeconomic variables. There is only a slight increase in the value of the (partial) log-likelihood. Also, the results suggest that adverse macroeconomic shocks will shorten the survival time of banks with a deteriorating financial condition. In short, the disappearance of banks in Mexico is explained by both bank specific and macroeconomic variables.

Figure 7.3 represents graphically the same coefficients of the financial ratios in the disappearance hazard. The coefficients overdue loans to total loans, and interest expenses to interest earnings ratios increased during the period in which FOBAPROA was the deposit insurance scheme, while the coefficients of bank capital to total assets, ROE and the bank's total deposits to system's total deposits ratio deteriorated in the same period. However, the available funds to traditional deposits and selling value to book value remained around the same level during the FOBAPROA period. The coefficients on the macroeconomic variables remained also around the same value. In general, we think that FOBAPROA provoked an increase in risk levels. We find that the coefficients of interest earnings to total loans ratio remained at the same level during the FOBAPROA regime and, then, they increased after the change in banking accounting. Similarly, coefficients on available funds, financial instruments and prevailing loans to traditional holdings ratio deteriorated significantly only after the change in banking accounting.

Conclusion

Using balance sheet information, we estimate a time-varying covariates hazards model in order to identify the characteristics that make individual Mexican banks more likely to disappear. In modelling the disappearance hazard, both intervened (by the government) banks and acquired (or merged) banks are treated as having disappeared at the date of governmental intervention or at the date of acquisition (or merger). The estimation is semi-parametric because no baseline hazard is specified.

In this work, we have information about two classes of banks: reprivatized banks and new banks. The estimates show that the of probability of disappearance of a reprivatized bank increased little in the first months of its lifetime, and then accelerated in the last months of its lifetime. In contrast, a new bank had a high probability of disappearance in the first months of its lifetime, and then in posterior months it had less probability of disappearance than the reprivatized banks.

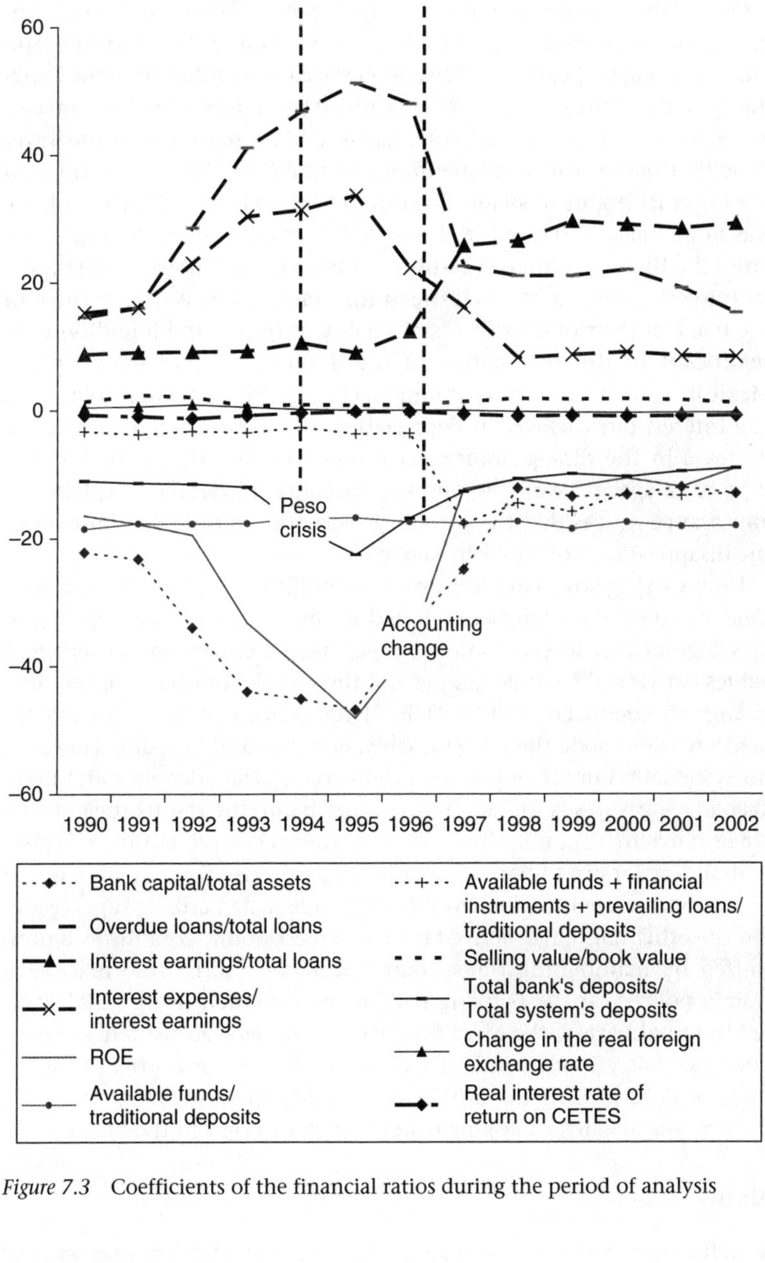

Figure 7.3 Coefficients of the financial ratios during the period of analysis

One of the findings is that the disappearance of banks in Mexico can be explained, given the statistical limitations, by a set of observable (and publicly available) variables. This implies that the evolution of the banking system in Mexico has been determined by factors other than macroeconomic factors. Hence, a bank was more likely to disappear the lower its ROE, the lower its available funds to traditional deposits ratio, and the lower its highly-available funds to traditional deposits ratio. A bank was more likely to disappear, the higher its overdue loans to total loans ratio; the higher its interest earnings to total loans ratio; and the higher its interest expenses to interest earnings ratio. However, only three of the five elements of CAMEL (asset quality, earnings and liquidity) were significant in the explanation of the disappearance of banks in the Mexican case. The macroeconomic factors played a pivotal role. High real interest rates, as well as depreciation of the exchange rate, imply a decrease in the disappearance likelihood. The fact that both CAMEL-type bank specific variables and macroeconomic variables explain disappearance means that the peso crisis was not the only determinant of the disappearance of banks in Mexico.

Time-varying covariates improve the significance of the whole model. Time constant covariates are rejected in favour of time-varying covariates. Significance levels did not change, and a comparison of coefficient values between the whole sample and the sample for each year reveals a change in coefficient values. FOBAPROA appears to have encouraged banks to deteriorate their asset quality, earnings and liquidity. However, no systematic impact of the coefficients on capital adequacy and management measures is found. On the other hand, the results suggest that adverse macroeconomic shocks will shorten the survival time of banks with a deteriorating financial condition. Bank specific risks are reduced by an appropriate legal framework and by adequate banking supervision. On the other hand, risk derived from macroeconomic conditions is minimized by maintaining transparent, predictable and stable macroeconomic policies. If the banking bailout implemented using FOBAPROA led to moral hazard, the Mexican government deposit insurance experience has policy implications. This case study of an institutional bailout offers insight for other countries considering the implementation of a bailout (specifically, a banking bailout) at some point in the future.

Notes

1. In this work, bank intervention is said to occur when a bank receives financial assistance – other than short-term liquidity support – from the government.

2. For the American case, Wheelock and Wilson (2000) utilize competing risks hazard models with time-varying covariates to identify the characteristics of individual US banks more likely to fail. They only employ bank specific information. One of their results is that the closer to insolvency a US bank is, the more likely its acquisition.
3. In modelling the disappearance hazard, banks intervened (by the government) and then acquired by another bank, or merged banks are treated as if they disappeared at the date of acquisition, the merger, or governmental intervention.
4. Originally, the estimation of a probit (or logit) model in which the likelihood to disappear was the explained variable was attempted. Similar results were obtained with parametric model (exponential and Weibull models).
5. In this context, we have censoring at the end of the observations, or right-censoring. Censoring is also typically assumed to be (conditionally) independent of both events of disappearance. This is necessary in order to get the easy conditional probability rendition of the hazard given a bank disappearance. Right-censoring does not mean that the observation has no information. An observation right-censored at t still tells us that it has a survival time of at least to t.
6. It is common practice to measure the regressors so that $h(.) = 1$ at the mean value. Then $h(t)$ has an interpretation as the hazard function for the mean individual in the sample. This baseline hazard is an unknown parameter that requires estimation (Kiefer 1988 and Greene 2000).
7. The bank specific data and banking sector data are derived from the bank-by-information contained in the *Sistema de Información Estadistica* (SIES) of the CNBV. Additional sources are the *Informe Trimestral Sobre el Comportamiento de la Economia Mexicana* published by Banco de Mexico (various issues) and FOBAPROA (1998a, 1998b).
8. FOBAPROA means Bank Fund for the Protection of Savings, and IPAB means Institute for the Protection of Bank Savings.
9. This is the reason why the following banks are not included: Anahuac, Bansi, Capital and Pronorte. The three foreign private banks are: BBV, Citibank, and Santander. They are excluded from the analysis following the suggestion of Gonzalez-Hermosillo *et al.* (1997).
10. It is important to distinguish between national and foreign banks because the initial conditions are important in the explanation of bank disappearance (Hernandez and Lopez 2001).
11. The governmental capitalization and the participation of foreign capital are measures that improve the financial indicators.
12. All these variables are attempted to be included in the analysis, following suggestions by Gonzalez-Hermosillo *et al.* (1997). Nevertheless, among all of them only the change in the real foreign exchange rate and the real interest rate of return of CETES are kept in the analysis.
13. See Lane *et al.* (1986), Cole and Gunther (1995), Gonzalez-Hermosillo *et al.* (1997), and Hernandez and Lopez (2001).
14. The use of balance sheet ratios virtually guarantees the presence of multicollinearity. In fact, inspection of the correlation matrix for the balance sheet ratios, as well as the variance-covariance matrix of parameters estimated from the hazard model indicates considerable multicollinearity. Multicollinearity

alters the significance level of the variables and may result in biased estimates.

15. The stepwise method is used in multivariate linear regression, discriminant analysis or logistic regression, and duration models to examine the explanatory power of adding or removing predictive variables in the model. A forward or backward function may be employed. In simple terms, this procedure allows to decide how many and which variables should be selected.
16. That is, a reprivatized bank, when its loans are purchased by FOBAPROA, diminishes its disappearance probability in the first months. Nevertheless, these programmes are insufficient because the authorities finally intervene in these banks, and they are subsequently acquired by other banks.
17. A similar result is obtained in Hernandez and Lopez (2001). The ratio is still not statistically significant when the Capitalization index of Banco de México is included.
18. See Hernandez-Rodriguez (2004).
19. Although no capital adequacy measure was significant, balance sheet comparisons indicated that banks that disappeared were sometimes less capitalized than banks that did not. Furthermore, the capital to asset ratio is not the only possible risk measure available, and we also test whether deposit insurance caused differences across banks financial ratios that measure asset quality, earnings, and liquidity.

References

Banco de Mexico, *Informe Trimestral sobre el Comportamiento de la Economia Mexicana, Mexico* (various issues).

Comision Nacional Bancaria y de Valores, *Sistema de Informacion Estadistica, Informes Trimestrales*, Mexico (various issues).

Cole, Rebel and Jeffrey Gunther (1995) 'Separating the Likelihood and Timing of Bank Failure', *Journal of Banking and Finance*, 19 (6), 1073–89.

Cox, David R. (1975) 'Partial Likelihood', *Biometrika*, 62 (2), 269–76.

Cox, David R. (1972) 'Regression Models and Life-Tables', *Journal of the Royal Statistical Society Series*, B 34, 187–220.

FOBAPROA (1998a) 'El Fondo Bancario de Proteccion al Ahorro y la Tradicion de Proteccion a los Ahorradores Bancarios', available online at <http://www.fobaproa.gob.mx/fobaproa/foba/sitactual/e11.htm> (October 29, 1998).

FOBAPROA (1998b) 'El Proceso de Quiebra del Sistema Bancario', available online at <http://www.fobaproa.gob.mx/fobaproa/foba/sitactual/e1.htm> (October 29, 1998).

Gonzalez-Hermosillo, B., Pazarbasioglu, C. and Billings, R. (1997) 'Determinants of Banking System Fragility: A Case Study of Mexico', IMF Staff Papers, 44 (3), 295–314.

Greene, William H. (2000) *Econometric Analysis*, 4th edn, (New Jersey: Prentice-Hall).

Han, Aaron K. and Hausman, Jerry (1990) 'Flexible Parametric Estimation of Duration and Competing Risk Models', *Journal of Applied Econometrics*, 5 (1), 1–28.

Hernandez, Fausto and Omar López, (2001) 'La Crisis Bancaria Mexicana: un Modelo de Duración y Riesgo Proporcional', *El Trimestre Económico*, 272, 551–602.

Hernandez-Rodriguez, Clemente (2004) 'FOBAPROA and Moral Hazard in the Mexican Banking System,' Memorias del XXXIV Congreso de Investigacion y Extension, Tecnologico de Monterrey, Monterrey, Mexico.

Kiefer, Nicholas M. (1988) 'Economic Duration Data and Hazard Functions', *Journal of Economic Literature*, 26 (2), 646–79.

Lane, William, Looney, Stephan and Wansley, James (1986) 'An Application of the Cox Proportional Hazards Model of Bank Failure,' *Journal of Banking and Finance*, 10 (4), 511–31.

Wheelock, David C. and Wilson, Paul W. (2000) 'Why Do Bank Disappear? The Determinants of US Bank Failures and Acquisitions', *Review of Economics and Statistics*, 82 (1), 127–38.

8

Corporate Foreign Vulnerability, Financial Policies and the Exchange Rate Regime: Evidence from Brazil

Jose Luiz Rossi, Jr

Introduction

Adverse external shocks represent a key source of risk for emerging markets. In these countries, several episodes of crises and economic downturns were triggered by external factors. One question levied by the literature and answered in this chapter is whether the choice of the exchange rate regime plays a role in reducing countries' vulnerability to these shocks.

Following a sequence of financial crises in the 1990s, a new generation of currency crises models placed corporate behaviour at the centre of the debate about the relationship between countries' external vulnerability and the choice of the exchange rate regime. In these models, a fixed exchange rate regime would increase countries' vulnerability by leading companies to disregard the exchange rate risk, biasing their borrowing towards foreign currency denominated debt and/or reducing their hedging activities.[1] In opposition, a floating exchange rate regime would help countries to mitigate their external vulnerability by inducing companies to take their exchange rate exposure seriously.

To what extent the choice of the exchange rate regime can alleviate companies' foreign vulnerability by inducing changes in corporate financial policies is still an open question empirically. As pointed out by Eichengreen and Hausmann (1999), 'gathering survey (and other) data on hedged and unhedged exposures and analyzing their determinants should be a high priority for academics.' This chapter fills this gap by taking a systematic look at the relationship between the choice of the exchange rate regime, companies' foreign vulnerability and financial policies.

The analysis employs a unique database constructed directly from companies' annual reports containing information about the currency composition of the debt and hedging activities for a sample of non-financial Brazilian companies from 1996 to 2002, a period in which Brazil adopted two different exchange rate regimes: a (quasi-) fixed and a flexible exchange rate regimes. This transition between two exchange rate regimes provides a 'natural experiment' to test whether the choice of the exchange rate regime affects corporate vulnerability to external shocks by inducing changes in financial policies.

First I analyze the relationship between the choice of the exchange rate regime and companies' foreign vulnerability proxied by their exchange rate exposure.[2] I report that, unlike their counterparts in the United States, Brazilian companies on average do not benefit from depreciations of the home currency. In fact, a 1 per cent depreciation of the Brazilian real leads to a 0.22 per cent fall in the average company's stock market returns, evidencing that fluctuations of the exchange rate are indeed problematic for emerging countries like Brazil.

The results give support to the view that the floating exchange rate regime reduces companies' external vulnerability. I show that under the fixed exchange rate regime, about 60 per cent of the companies in the sample are exposed to fluctuations of the real exchange rate and that this proportion drops to 23 per cent under the floating exchange rate regime.

Consistent with the hypothesis that there is a relationship between corporate financial policies and the choice of the exchange rate regime, I find that the floating exchange rate regime led companies to improve their prudential measures to reduce their exchange rate risk. I show that the floating exchange rate regime reduces the currency mismatches in companies' balance sheets by exerting a negative impact on companies' foreign currency borrowing and a positive effect on their hedging activities.

Following the discussion on corporate financial policies, I look at the main cross-sectional determinants of the currency composition of companies' debt and the use of currency derivatives. The results indicate that larger firms and exporters are more likely to hold foreign currency denominated debt and to keep unhedged positions, and they also reveal that the use of currency derivatives by Brazilian companies is mainly determined by their desire to reduce the exchange rate exposure of the liability side of their balance sheets.

In the next section, I describe the Brazilian experience under both exchange rate regimes and show the data that will be used throughout the text. I then define a company's exchange rate exposure as a proxy for corporate external vulnerability and I analyze whether this exposure changes across different exchange rate regimes. The subsequent section analyzes empirically the effect of the exchange rate regime on corporate financial policies and I estimate the main cross-sectional determinants of company's foreign borrowing and the use of currency derivatives. The results are then summarized and some policy implications are given.

Data and macroeconomic background

After the stabilization plan in 1994 until January 1999, Brazil adopted a 'crawling-band' exchange rate regime.[3] During this period, Brazil suffered from several speculative attacks, especially during the Asian and Russian crises. The Central Bank reacted promptly to such attacks by raising interest rates in order to maintain the regime, demonstrating clearly its commitment to the exchange rate regime even at the cost of maintaining high interest rates, increasing the public debt and causing an economic recession. Figure 8.1 displays the response of the Central Bank to these speculative attacks, and the behaviour of some macroeconomic variables from 1996 to 2002. Table 8.1 reports that this first period is characterized by a low volatility of the nominal exchange rate and by a high volatility of the nominal interest rate and domestic stock market returns (IBOVESPA).

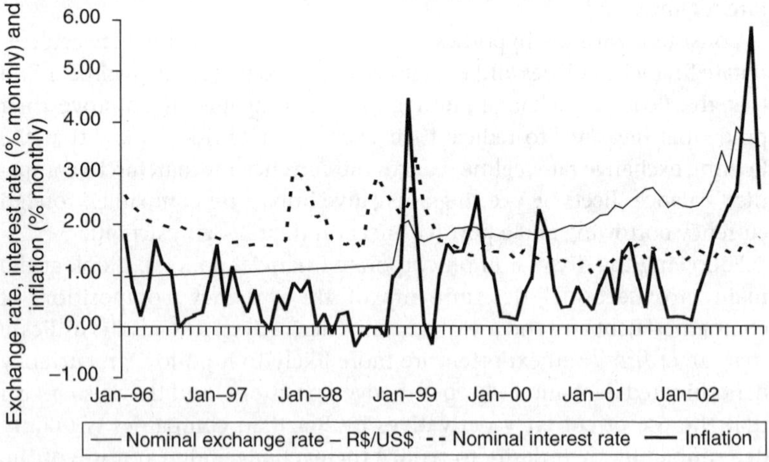

Figure 8.1 Macroeconomic performance

Table 8.1 Interest rate and exchange rate volatility

Year	Interest rate (%)	Exchange rate (%)	IBOVESPA (in reais) (%)
1996	3.11	0.08	6.04
1997	24.07	0.11	12.16
1998	24.26	0.17	16.99
1999	17.70	19.73	10.29
2000	8.23	2.00	8.89
2001	13.95	5.04	9.90
2002	11.56	11.60	10.50

Following a speculative attack in January 1999, the currency was allowed to float, and an inflation-target system was adopted. After tightening monetary and fiscal policies, Brazil succeeded in stabilizing inflation and the exchange rate, and the economy recovered quickly from the crisis. Table 8.1 shows that under the floating regime, the interest rate and stock market volatilities were much lower than in the previous period, and the exchange rate volatility increased considerably, suggesting that 'fear of floating'[4] was not a characteristic of the new regime.[5]

Data for this analysis was collected both from companies' annual reports and Economatica, a database that contains stock market and financial data for all Latin American publicly traded companies. I used a sample of Brazilian non-financial publicly traded companies from 1996 to 2002. The description of all variables used throughout the text is shown in the Appendix. The period from 1996 to 2002 was chosen not only because it is possible to compare the behaviour of the companies under different exchange rate regimes, but also because the use of derivatives was required to be reported only after 1995.[6] The sample contains information for all companies that were in the database in 1996 and stayed until 2002, a total of 165 companies. This procedure was followed in order to give a better comparison of companies' behaviour under the two different exchange rate regimes. All information was obtained from the consolidated balance sheet in case a company has subsidiaries that are also publicly traded. The final sample comprises more than 50 per cent of all publicly traded companies in Brazil and 67.9 per cent of all market capitalization.

The Sao Paulo stock exchange index (IBOVESPA) was adopted as the domestic stock market return. This index was used because the Sao Paulo stock exchange is the most important and liquid stock market in Brazil. The 30-day SELIC interest rate was used as the market interest rate. The SELIC is determined by the Central Bank and it serves as reference for all interest rates in the economy. All of these variables were deflated by the general index of prices (IGP).

Because most Brazilian trade is in American dollars and almost all foreign debt is issued in this currency, the analysis of companies' exchange rate exposure is developed by using the exchange rate real/dollar. I adopt the convention that companies with positive (negative) exposure benefit (suffer) from depreciations of the home currency. This definition will be carried throughout the text.

Data about foreign sales, the currency composition of the debt and hedging activities was collected directly from companies' annual reports. Unfortunately, Brazilian companies do not have a systematic procedure for registering information about their foreign sales. Sometimes it is reported together with a company's total gross sales, sometimes it is reported under the comments from the managers to shareholders, and sometimes it is found in the explanatory notes. In some cases, companies mention being exporters, but do not report the amount of foreign sales; in this case, I contacted the companies directly through electronic mail. I eventually discarded seven companies from my sample who mentioned being exporters but who neither reported the amount of their foreign sales nor answered my mail inquiries.

Information with respect to corporate foreign borrowing and hedging activities is available in the annual reports under the explanatory notes. The amount of foreign currency denominated debt is located under the item loans and financing, and the use of derivatives is registered under the item financial instruments.

Sample characteristics

A summary of the statistics for the main variables in this chapter can be found in Table 8.2. Table 8.2 reports that although the number of exporters is stable during the period, the ratio of foreign sales to total sales follows a different pattern. During the fixed exchange rate regime, there was a reduction in the ratio of foreign sales to total sales; this path is inverted after the currency was allowed to float, when the ratio increased steadily. This fact corroborates the idea that the traditional expenditure switching effect took place after the devaluation of the domestic currency, leading the ratio of foreign sales to total sales to rise.

Table 8.2 also displays the behaviour of corporate foreign borrowing during the period. It reports that not only the proportion of companies that hold foreign currency denominated debt but also the ratio of foreign

Table 8.2 Summary statistics

	1996	1997	1998	1999	2000	2001	2002
Number of firms	165	165	165	165	165	165	165
Exporters (%)	61.0	61.2	62.7	63.0	63.4	63.0	63.4
Foreign sales/total sales (%)	14.8	14.4	14.3	16.1	16.1	16.5	18.0
Debtors (%)	84.1	82.4	86.1	82.4	80.5	80.6	81.1
Total foreign debt/ total debt (%)	**47.9**	**49.5**	**48.1**	**50.0**	**48.5**	**47.8**	**49.4**
Exporters	57.7	59.7	56.6	59.4	58.8	57.3	59.1
Non-exporters	31.9	33.6	33.8	34.0	30.7	31.6	32.0
Tradable	51.3	52.3	50.9	53.6	51.5	50.3	53.3
Non-tradable	34.3	32.7	35.8	33.8	34.7	36.8	33.7
Foreign unhedged debt/ total debt (%)	**45.9**	**46.3**	**41.4**	**41.4**	**37.8**	**32.6**	**31.3**
Exporters	55.1	56.2	49.5	50.6	46.9	41.5	39.8
Non-exporters	30.6	30.1	27.8	25.9	22.0	17.4	16.6
Tradable	48.4	49.9	44.1	45.1	40.8	35.8	35.0
Non-tradable	28.6	26.7	29.5	25.3	24.0	17.6	14.9
Users – currency derivatives (%)	7.92	9.70	14.5	19.4	25.0	34.5	40.2
Holders of foreign assets (%)	3.63	4.84	9.64	14.5	18.3	24.2	26.9
Derivatives/total assets	0.64	0.67	1.15	1.41	1.78	3.29	4.73
Derivatives/total foreign debt	5.02	3.25	6.52	7.78	11.8	18.9	24.9
Foreign assets/total assets	0.39	0.47	0.94	1.37	1.72	2.14	2.10

debt to total debt is stable during the period. There is no indication that the ratio of foreign debt to total debt varies across the exchange rate regime or that it depends on the credibility of the monetary authority. This corroborates the 'original sin' theory that there might not be a relationship between the choice of exchange rate regime and companies' foreign currency borrowing. Table 8.2 also shows that exporters and companies in the tradable sector hold a higher proportion of foreign debt to total debt than non-exporters or non-tradable companies, but there is no evidence of differences in behaviour between sectors during the time period. Both sectors had similarb pattern, with the ratio of foreign debt to total debt being stable during the period.

The data from Table 8.2 must be scrutinized carefully, as it may be misleading to consider only the liability side of companies' balance sheets in analyzing their exposure to the exchange rate. Although the ratio of total foreign debt to total debt is stable during the period, the ratio of total foreign unhedged debt to total debt varies substantially. The ratio reaches a peak in 1997, and decreases steadily after that. These results are consistent with the implicit guarantees theory that the choice of the exchange rate regime would have an impact on companies' currency mismatches.

The data evidences that the floating exchange rate regime reduces the currency mismatches on companies' balance sheets.

The results from Table 8.2 also show that exporters hold higher levels of unhedged positions than non-exporters, and their behaviour is similar across time with both sectors trying to reduce their unhedged positions. Yet, different patterns arise when the behaviour of tradable and non-tradable sectors is analyzed. The ratio of foreign unhedged debt to total debt reaches a peak in 1997 for the non-tradable sector, and it decreases steadily afterwards. In opposition, for the non-tradable sector, the ratio of foreign unhedged debt to total debt reaches a peak in 1998 right before the currency crisis, and it reduces steadily afterwards. In 2002, this ratio is almost a half of the ratio immediately before the crisis, which is a more acute reduction than in the tradable sector. This result is consistent with the Schneider and Tornell (2003) results concerning the existence of an interaction between implicit guarantees associated with a fixed exchange rate regime and the non-tradable sector.

Finally, Table 8.2 reports that hedging activities varied considerably from 1996 to 2002. The Table shows that the number of users of derivatives and that hold foreign assets increased from 1996 to 2002. Likewise, the extent of hedging activities represented by the ratios of the amount of derivatives to total assets and the amount of derivatives to total foreign debt and the ratio of the amount of foreign assets to total assets also increased during the same time frame. This evidence contradicts Eichengreen and Hausmann (1999) who assert the possibility that an increase in the volatility of the exchange rate would lead to higher costs of hedging. They argue that one could observe less, not more hedging when exchange rates are less stable. The results are partially confirmed by the BIS triennial survey of foreign exchange and derivatives market activity in 1998 and 2001. These data show that the daily foreign exchange turnover, the sum of spot, forward and swap markets, in Brazil increased from US$ 3,418 million in 1998 to US$ 4,612 million in 2001.

Table 8.3 reports summary statistics for companies' hedging activities. Table 8.3 shows that the number of companies that use currency derivatives and those that use foreign assets increased steadily during the period from 1996 to 2002. Table 8.3 also shows that companies prefer to use currency derivatives rather than foreign assets to hedge their exposure. During the whole period, more than half of the hedgers preferred currency derivatives to foreign assets.

Table 8.4 displays the results for the choice among currency derivatives. It reports that currency swaps are the most preferred among all possible derivatives. This can be viewed as evidence that the hedging activities of

Table 8.3 Summary statistics for companies' hedging activities

	1996	1997	1998	1999	2000	2001	2002
Number of firms	165	165	165	165	165	165	165
Only foreign currency derivatives	10	12	18	22	27	35	41
Only foreign assets	3	4	10	14	16	18	19
Both	3	4	6	10	14	22	25
Total	16	20	34	46	57	75	85

Table 8.4 Choice of currency derivatives

Year/type	1996	1997	1998	1999	2000	2001	2002
Swap	8	8	17	24	27	39	49
Swap + forwards	2	3	2	4	7	10	10
Swap + options	0	0	0	0	0	0	0
Swap + options+ forward	0	0	0	0	2	3	3
Forward	3	3	3	2	4	4	3
Options	0	1	1	1	1	1	1
Forward + options	0	1	1	1	0	0	0
Total	13	16	24	32	41	57	66

Brazilian companies are linked to their attempt to reduce their foreign currency exposure, and are not for speculative purposes, since swaps are usually preferred when the sources of exposure extend for multiple periods but are predetermined. This is the case when liabilities are denominated in foreign currency. By contrast, forward contracts are preferred when the main source of exposure is related to short-term transactions that are characterized by uncertainty. This is the case of foreign revenues derived from exports.

The hedging practices reported in Table 8.4 are completely different from those found in previous studies for developed countries. Geczy *et al.* (1997) show for a sample of US companies that forward contracts, or a combination between forwards and options contracts, were the most preferred instruments. Judge (2002) finds similar results for a sample of British companies. He finds that forwards were the most frequently used instruments, followed by swaps and options. The preference for swaps is stable across periods and is therefore independent of the exchange rate regime. It might be evidence that the main concern of Brazilian hedgers was the possibility that fluctuations of the exchange rate could affect their liabilities. This fact will be tested in next section.

Corporate foreign exposure and the exchange rate regime

The international finance literature characterizes the impact on companies' cash flow as the channel through which companies would be exposed to fluctuations of the exchange rate.[7] Therefore, the determination of the relationship between fluctuations in companies' cash flow and changes in the exchange rate is the central question for a better understanding of companies' foreign exposure. Yet, as argued by Bodnar and Wong (2000), the use of cash flow variables is not easily applicable for cross-firm comparisons, since it would make the analysis extremely complex.[8]

Adler and Dumas (1984) show that assuming that a company's value is the present value of future cash flows, a company's exposure to fluctuations in the exchange rate could be determined by the elasticity of the firm value with respect to changes on the exchange rate. This approach has been extensively used in the corporate finance literature, and it is used in this paper in order to determine companies' vulnerability to fluctuations of the exchange rate and the relationship with the exchange rate regime.

Methodology

Companies' exchange rate exposure was estimated by following a two-step procedure.[9] In the first step, the market portfolio is regressed on the changes in the real exchange rate as shown by equation 8.1:

$$R_{market,t} = \gamma_0 + \gamma_1 \cdot \Delta s_t + \varepsilon_t \tag{8.1}$$

Then, the component of the market portfolio return that is orthogonal to the changes in the exchange rate is obtained by calculating

$$F_{market,t} = R_{market,t} - \hat{\gamma}_0 - \hat{\gamma}_1 \cdot \Delta s_t$$

Finally, companies' exchange rate exposure is estimated by regressing companies' excess stock market return on the orthogonal component of the market portfolio and on changes of the real exchange rate as illustrated by equation 8.2:

$$R_{j,t} = \gamma_j + \beta_{market,t} \cdot F_{market,t} + \beta_{j,exposure} \cdot \Delta s_t + \nu_{j,t} \tag{8.2}$$

Where $R_{j,t}$ is the monthly excess stock return of firm j, $F_{market,t}$ is the estimated orthogonal component of the market portfolio (IBOVESPA), and Δs_t is the percentage change in the real exchange rate over the same period.

This method was adopted as the baseline estimation because it circumvents the critiques made by Bodnar and Wong (2000), who show that if one estimates companies' exchange rate exposure by using a value-weighted portfolio return as the market portfolio return, the coefficient of the changes in the exchange rate cannot be interpreted as a 'total' exposure, but should be interpreted as the difference between the firm's total exposure elasticity and the market exposure adjusted by the firm's market beta. Therefore, if the market portfolio is exposed to the exchange rate, the distribution of the firm's exposure will be shifted. They also argue that because large firms have more weight in value weighted portfolios and these firms are more likely to be exposed to fluctuations in the exchange rate (since they usually are multinational corporations), the estimates of the firm's exposure by using a value weighted market portfolio would lead to biased results. In the Brazilian case, if larger firms hold higher levels of foreign currency denominated debt, the value weighted market portfolio would be more likely to have a negative exchange rate exposure, biasing the results towards showing more companies with positive exposure. I also report the results for the estimation of companies' exchange rate exposure by using the value weighted domestic market returns in order to verify the advantages of the orthogonalization of market returns.[10]

Results

Table 8.5 shows that some interesting results arise from the estimation of companies' exchange rate exposure from 1996 to 2002.

First, Table 8.5 reports the destabilizing potential of fluctuations of the exchange rate. On average, Brazilian companies do not benefit from a

Table 8.5 Exchange rate exposure for Brazilian companies, 1996–2002

Model	**Relative exposure**	**Absolute exposure**
Mean	−0.032	−0.22
Median	−0.10	−0.24
Maximum	2.97	2.33
Minimum	−1.48	−1.68
Negative	27	55
Positive	24	9
Number of companies	165	165

depreciation of the domestic currency. According the absolute exposure specification, a 1 per cent depreciation of the home currency leads to a 0.22 per cent fall in stock market returns. This result is consistent with the hypothesis that in relatively closed and high indebted emerging countries like Brazil, depreciations of the home currency are more likely to cause a fall in asset prices due to presence of negative balance sheet effects.[11] This result contradicts Bleakley and Cowan (2002) who found for a sample of Latin American companies that the negative balance sheet effects generated by depreciations of the home currency are completely offset by the positive expenditure-switching effects. Our results show that with respect to Brazil, this is not true. Instead, on average, the negative effect surpasses the positive effect of devaluations, leading to a fall in stock market returns.

Table 8.5 also shows that independently of the method used, about 40 per cent of the companies are exposed to fluctuations of the exchange rate. This proportion of companies exposed is higher than most studies for US companies, evidencing that fluctuations of the exchange rate, besides having negative effects, affect a large number of Brazilian companies.

Table 8.5 confirms the importance of orthogonalizing the market returns. Using the market portfolio as the control variable, the number of companies with positive and negative significant exposure is almost the same. Once the market returns are orthogonalized, the number of companies with negative exposure increases considerably. Since in Brazil larger firms dominate market portfolio, and these companies are more likely to hold debt denominated in foreign currency, the market portfolio is likely to be negatively affected by changes of the exchange rate. Indeed, the result of the estimation of the first step shows that the market portfolio is negatively exposed to changes of the exchange rate. Because market portfolio is negatively exposed to fluctuations of the exchange rate, it is expected that when controlling using the market portfolio, a higher number of companies with significant positive exposure and a lower number of companies with negative exposure show up, since these estimated exposures are relative to the market portfolio. Yet, once market portfolio is orthogonalized, there is a reduction in the number of companies with positive exposure and an increase in those with negative exposure, since now absolute exposures are estimated and not relative to the market portfolio.

The results in Table 8.5 can be interpreted as companies' average exposure over the entire period between 1996 and 2002. As argued by Dumas and Solnik (1995) and De Santis and Gerard (1998), the assumption that companies' exposure does not vary with time is too strong, especially during our period of estimation, when Brazil changed

Table 8.6 Exchange rate exposure for Brazilian companies and the exchange rate regime

	Relative exposure		**Absolute exposure**	
	Fixed	**Flexible**	**Fixed**	**Flexible**
Mean	0.009	−0.066	−0.18	−0.25
Median	−0.13	−0.041	−0.27	−0.23
Maximum	5.34	2.30	4.98	1.66
Minimum	−2.64	−2.21	−2.85	−2.32
Negative	64	13	72	31
Positive	39	14	29	7
Number of companies	165	165	165	165

its exchange rate regime from a fixed exchange rate regime to a floating one.

Table 8.6 sheds light on this subject. I divide the sample into the fixed exchange rate period from January 1996 to October 1998, and a flexible exchange rate period from April 1999 to December 2002. I discard the data from November 1998 to March 1999, since it corresponds to the period of the currency crises.

Table 8.6 reports that the floating exchange rate regime indeed helps to alleviate the problem of companies' exposure to fluctuations of the exchange rate. Under the floating exchange rate regime, 23 per cent of the companies are exposed to fluctuations in the exchange rate; however, under the fixed exchange rate regime more than 60 per cent of the companies are exposed to fluctuations of the exchange rate. Therefore, one can reject the hypothesis that the fixed exchange rate regime would give a more stable environment for business, leading companies' value to be less volatile. Indeed, the opposite is observed. Under the fixed regime, companies' value is much more sensitive to changes in the real exchange rate, leading to a more unstable environment.

Corporate financial policies and the exchange rate regime

The results so far showed that the flexible exchange rate regime is able to reduce companies' exposure to fluctuations of the exchange rate. In this section, I link the choice of the exchange rate regime with changes in corporate borrowing, hedging and currency mismatches of balance sheets. I use the following empirical specification:

$$Y_{i,t} = \alpha_i + \beta \cdot Fixed + \delta \cdot Flexible + X'_{i,t} \cdot \gamma + \varepsilon_{i,t} \quad (8.3)$$

Where $Y_{i,t}$ is one of three dependent variables: the ratio of total foreign debt to total debt, the ratio of total foreign unhedged debt to total debt (mismatch) and the ratio of α_i, total amount of currency derivatives to total assets.[12] A firm-specific effect is represented by *Fixed* is a dummy variable that assumes the value 1 during the period under the fixed exchange rate regime (1996–98). *Flexible* assumes the value 1 during the period under the flexible exchange rate regime (2000–2002).[13] $X'_{i,t}$ is a set of explanatory variables with which I try to discriminate among different theories about the determination of the currency composition of companies' debt and the use of currency derivatives besides the choice of the exchange rate regime.

This specification allows for control of not only for differences across firms that are not captured by the explanatory variables but also the effect of the change on the macroeconomic environment that took place during the period. Equation (8.3) is estimated using two different econometric specifications. Specification 1 estimates a random effect estimator.[14] In addition to this random effects specification, I also utilize a second specification in order to control for a possible endogeneity of the explanatory variables. Decisions of hedging and borrowing might be taken simultaneously by the firms; therefore, a simultaneous equation framework is estimated in order to control for this problem.[15] I use a two-stage estimation method. In the first stage, OLS regressions are estimated for the foreign debt and hedging equations, then equation (8.3) is estimated by replacing the endogenous variables with the fitted values from the first stage.

Results

The results for estimation of equation (8.3) can be found in Table 8.7, where the determinants of corporate financial policies are analyzed. The first striking result shown in Table 8.7 is that the choice of the exchange rate regime plays an important role in the determination of companies' financial policies. Confirming the hypothesis that the flexible exchange rate regime induces companies to reduce the currency mismatches in their balance sheets, Table 8.7 reports that there is a negative and statistically significant relationship between the ratio of total foreign unhedged debt to total debt and the flexible exchange rate regime. In addition, the results also indicate that the adoption of the fixed exchange rate regime led companies to disregard their exchange rate risk, since there is a positive and statistically significant relationship between the ratio of total foreign unhedged debt to total debt and the fixed exchange rate regime.

Table 8.7 Results for the determinants of corporate financial policies

	I		II		III
Variable	**Foreign debt/ total debt Coeff.**	**Derivatives/ total assets Coeff.**	**Foreign debt/ total debt Coeff.**	**Derivatives/ total assets Coeff.**	**Mismatch/ total debt Coeff.**
Fixed	0.0037(0.015)	−0.0046(0.0037)	0.004(0.16)	−0.005(0.004)	0.032(0.019)**
Flexible	−0.039(0.016)*	0.017(0.0037)*	−0.042(0.019)*	0.017(0.0046)*	−0.080(0.018)*
Size	0.064(0.008)*	0.0052(0.0015)*	0.061(0.010)*	0.003(0.003)	0.038(0.0092)*
Foreign sales/ total sales	0.22(0.07)*	−0.0008(0.011)	0.22(0.069)*	−0.012(0.005)*	0.15(0.074)*
Foreign operations	0.038(0.050)	−0.006(0.007)	0.043(0.050)	0.0002(0.0043)	0.074(0.053)
Market-to-book	0.0001(0.0008)	0.0001(0.0002)	0.0002(0.0009)	0.0001(0.0002)	−0.0002(0.0009)
Tangibility	0.061(0.058)	−0.031(0.011)*	0.075(0.061)	−0.026(0.008)*	0.21(0.064)*
Gross margin	0.11(0.056)*	−0.010(0.012)	0.11(0.057)**	−0.00048(0.0099)	0.066(0.065)
Ownership	0.034(0.041)	−0.005(0.008)	0.033(0.042)	−0.010(0.0052)*	0.032(0.046)
Foreign equity listing	0.031(0.055)	0.012(0.008)	0.030(0.054)	0.018(0.0049)*	−0.074(0.058)
Foreign assets/ total assets	–	0.028(0.040)	–	0.052(0.035)	–
Derivatives/ total assets	0.53(0.13)*	–	0.82(0.71)	–	–
Foreign debt/ total debt	–	0.025(0.006)*	–	0.030(0.006)*	–
N	1150	1150	1150	1150	1150

* Statistically significant at 5% level of significance.
** Statistically significant at 1% level of significance.

Results in Table 8.7 also shed light on the mechanism through which the choice of the exchange rate regime impacts companies' currency mismatches. Table 8.7 reports that the adoption of a flexible exchange rate regime has a negative impact on the ratio of total foreign debt to total debt and a positive impact on companies' hedging activities and opposite results, although not statistically significant, are found with respect to the relationship between the fixed exchange rate regime and corporate financial policies.

These results corroborate the implicit guarantees theory that the fixed exchange rate regime biases corporate borrowing towards foreign currency denominated debt and that the floating exchange rate regime induces companies to take measures to reduce their exchange rate risk.

Following the corporate finance literature, Table 8.7 also analyzes the main cross-sectional determinants of companies' financial policies. The results show that size represented by the logarithm of companies' total sales matters with respect to the determination of corporate financial policies. Larger firms have higher ratios of total foreign currency denominated debt to total debt and higher ratios of derivatives to total assets. In addition, they are able to keep more unhedged positions. These results confirm the market depth hypotheses that domestic financial markets are not deep enough to fulfil the financial needs of larger firms and indicate the existence of fixed costs of hedging. The fact that there is a positive relationship between size and currency mismatches might indicate that larger firms perceive a higher probability of receiving bailouts in case of a crisis, deciding then to keep more unhedged positions.

Table 8.7 also indicates that the ratio of foreign sales to total sales is a significant determinant of companies' foreign borrowing and hedging activities. There is a positive relationship between exports and foreign borrowing and, defying expectations, a negative relationship between foreign sales and hedging activities. The first result can be explained by the fact that exporters can afford to borrow more in foreign currency since they are perceived to be less likely to suffer from unexpected devaluations of the home currency, given that a proportion of their revenues is expressed in foreign currency.[16] The existence of a negative relationship between the ratios of foreign sales to total sales can be rationalized by the fact that Brazilian exporters see their foreign revenue as a 'natural' hedge to the exposure that comes from their foreign currency liabilities. Given the low probability they assign to the possibility of an appreciation of the domestic currency and the costs of hedging, they prefer not to hedge.[17] This fact is confirmed by the positive and statistically significant relationship between the ratio of foreign sales to total sales and companies' currency mismatches. Indeed, exporters expect to be protected by their foreign revenues, enabling them to keep more unhedged positions.

The presence of foreign subsidiaries does not seem to matter either to companies' borrowing or their hedging activities. The same case is true with respect to companies' growth opportunities. An interesting result arises from the significance of companies' asset tangibility. The results confirm the hypothesis that in emerging markets like Brazil where there is limited enforceability of the law, asset tangibility is not a significant determinant of companies' borrowing. Foreign lenders are aware of this limitation and they do not extend credit for companies' with a higher level of tangible assets. Yet, these companies use less currency derivatives and keep more unhedged positions. This might be an indication that these firms have a similar behaviour to exporters and because they have more collateralized assets, they can afford to keep more unhedged positions.

The results in Table 8.7 confirm the hypothesis that more profitable firms borrow more in foreign currency in order to signal their types as argued by Jeanne (2000). This evidence is provided by the positive relationship between companies' gross margin and the ratio of total foreign debt to total debt. However, Table 8.7 shows that there is no relationship between profitability and hedging activities or currency mismatches.

Table 8.7 also shows that there is a relationship, if weak, between ownership and whether companies are listed abroad and corporate financial policies. The results indicate that foreign companies make less intense use of currency derivatives, the opposite for companies listed abroad. The reason might be because foreign companies can afford to be more exposed and companies' listed abroad would like to signal to foreign investors their ability to manage foreign exposure.

The results in Table 8.7 give evidence that foreign assets are perceived by Brazilian companies as being complements to the use of foreign currency derivatives, indicated by the positive, yet not statistically significant, relationship between the use of currency derivatives and the ratio of foreign assets to total assets.

Finally, the results show that the ratio of foreign debt to total debt is a significant determinant of the extent of companies' hedging activities. There is a positive relationship between the use of currency derivatives and the ratio of foreign debt to total debt. Adding that the swap is the most used currency derivative, it is possible to conclude that Brazilian companies use currency derivatives in order to reduce the exposure of their balance sheets to fluctuations of the exchange rate.

Conclusion

This chapter studies the relationship between the choice of the exchange rate regime, companies' foreign vulnerability, and financial policies for a sample of non-financial Brazilian companies from 1996 to 2002. I find that the choice of the exchange rate regime plays an important role in the determination of companies' foreign vulnerability by inducing changes in their financial policies. The results are consistent with the hypothesis that the floating exchange rate regime reduces companies' external vulnerability by leading them to take measures against their exchange rate risk and that the fixed exchange rate regime biases corporate borrowing towards foreign currency denominated debt. I show that the floating exchange rate regime induces companies to lower the currency mismatches in their balance sheets by having a negative impact on companies' foreign borrowing and a positive effect on hedging activities, and that the opposite is true with respect to the fixed exchange rate regime.

The results of this analysis indicate that the choice of exchange rate regime is a significant determinant of countries' external vulnerability, since it plays an important role in companies' financial policies. This is a contrast to the assertions made by Eichengreen and Hausmann (1999) or Calvo and Mishkin (2003) that the choice of the exchange rate regime is of second order importance in determining countries' external vulnerability. This chapter provides evidence that the floating regime can mitigate the problem of the 'original sin'. Not only does the floating regime induce more firms to hedge, but also these companies hedge their currency exposure more, leading them to reduce the currency mismatches on their balance sheets. Such action corroborates with Goldstein and Turner (2004) who argue that there might be a relationship between currency mismatches and the choice of the exchange rate regime.

After the financial crises of the 1990s, most emerging markets bypassed similar experiences as those in Brazil by abandoning their fixed exchange rate regimes in favour of flexible ones, and, as in Brazil, this change led them to be less vulnerable to external shocks. As an example, emerging markets have gone through the recent onset of the Fed tightening cycle and survived reasonably unscathed. The rising US rates have not had the same dampening effect as in the past, when fixed exchange rate regimes prevailed.

It is important to emphasize that vulnerabilities remain and governments should carry out additional economic reforms in order to improve countries' institutions. However, as this chapter indicates, the adoption of a floating exchange rate regime by emerging markets like Brazil, indeed leads companies to be more aware of the risk of keeping unhedged positions, reducing the possibility of huge economic downturns. Thus, even if the choice of the exchange rate might not be the primary solution for the reduction of countries' external vulnerability, it is clearly an integral part of the solution toward beneficial economic reforms.

Appendix: description of variables

Derivatives – Total notational amount of currency derivatives. It includes swaps, options, forwards, and futures.

Derivatives/total assets – Total notational amount of currency derivatives divided by total assets. The amount of derivatives is reported in companies' annual reports under the item financial instruments.

Foreign equity listing – Dummy variable assumes the value of 1 if the company issues American depositary receipts.

Total foreign debt – Total foreign currency denominated debt reported by companies' reports under the item loans and financing.

Total debt – Total amount of company's debt. It is a sum in *reais* of domestic and foreign currency denominated debt.

Total foreign unhedged debt – Total foreign debt minus the notational amount of currency derivatives minus the total amount of foreign assets expressed in *reais*.

Foreign assets – The total amount of assets the company holds that earn the variation in the nominal exchange rate plus a premium during the period. These can be Treasury bonds (NTN-E), Central Bank bonds (NBC-E), assets invested in foreign banks, and cash in foreign currency.

Capital expenses – Total amount spent in the acquisition of permanent assets.

Fixed, flexible – Dummy variable that assumes the value 1 under the fixed (flexible) exchange rate regime and 0 otherwise.

Foreign sales – Sales in US$ converted to *reais* by the exchange rate at the end of the year

Total sales – Total gross sales expressed in *reais*.

Foreign operations – Dummy variable assumes the value 1 if the company has foreign production subsidiaries.

Gross margin – Total calculated EBIT divided by total sales.

Asset tangibility – Total assets minus current assets divided by total assets.

Market-to-book – Market value of equity divided by net worth.

Size – The logarithm of total gross sales in *reais* converted to US$ by the exchange rate at the end of the year.

Ownership – Dummy variable that assumes the value 1 if the firm is owned by domestic agents and 0 otherwise.

Notes

1. Since these models argue that this behaviour would arise due to the guarantees given by the government to companies, this branch of the literature is denominated the implicit guarantees hypothesis. Examples of this literature include Dooley (1997), Burnside *et al.* (1999) among others.
2. A company's exchange rate exposure is estimated as the elasticity of the firm value with respect to changes on the real exchange rate.
3. Strictly speaking, a system of bands was adopted with the top and bottom of the band being devalued at a fixed rate.
4. Calvo and Reinhardt (2000).
5. According the IMF's *de facto* classification system, after 1999, the Brazilian exchange rate regime can be classified as a free float.
6. Securities and Exchange Commission of Brazil: CVM instruction no. 235/1995.
7. Shapiro (1974), Hodder (1982), Levi (1983) and Flood and Lessard (1986).
8. See Marston (2001) for more details about the difficulties that arise from the use of cash flow variables.
9. I refer to this estimation as absolute exposure. Bris *et al.* (2002) use a similar procedure.
10. I use the term 'relative exposure' when I refer to this estimation method.
11. Similar results are found by Dominguez and Tesar (2001) for Thailand. Using aggregate data, Berganza and Herrero (2003) found that an unexpected real depreciation significantly raises a country's risk premium.
12. Similar results were found using the ratio of total amount of derivatives to total foreign debt.
13. I skip the year 1999, since both regimes coexisted during that year.
14. In order to deal with the selection bias problem, I also perform a two-stage Heckman estimation. The results were unchanged. Given the characteristics of the dependent variables, a Tobit panel estimation can also be performed, the results are also robust in the use of this specification. All results are available upon request.
15. Note that only the ratio of foreign debt to total debt and the ratio of derivatives to total assets are considered as endogenous.
16. Same result found by Aguiar (2002) and Gelos (2003) for Mexico, and Bleakley and Cowan (2002) for a panel of Latin-American companies.
17. I give anecdotal evidence by quoting a Brazilian journalist:

    > Brazilian exporters should have avoided the complaints about the appreciation of the Real if they have considered that a floating exchange rate regime does not mean a movement towards a higher devaluation of the currency. As proved in recent times, the Real can appreciate with respect to the dollar ... Exporters could have avoided the losses caused by the volatility of the exchange rate by hedging their exposures, but they didn't do it, because they expected the Real to depreciate even more, and by hedging they would limit the value of their revenues.
    >
    > Sonia Racy, *O Estado de Sao Paulo*, 8 December 2003.

References

Adler, M. and Dumas, B. (1984) 'Exposure to Currency Risk: Definition and Measurement', *Financial Management*, 13, 41–50.

Aguiar, M. (2002) 'Investment, Devaluation, and Foreign Currency Exposure: The Case of Mexico', mimeo, University of Chicago.

Allayannis, G., Weston, J., and Klapper, L. (2003) 'Capital Structure and Financial Risk: Evidence from Foreign Debt Use in East Asia', *Journal of Finance*, LVIII (6).

Amihud, Y. (1994) 'Exchange Rates and the Valuation of Equity Shares', in Y. Amihud and R.M. Levich (eds), *Exchange Rates and Corporate Performance* (New York: Irwin), 4.

Amihud, Y. (1993) *Evidence of Exchange Rate and Valuation of Equity Shares. In Recent Advances on Corporate Performance* (Homewood: Business One, Irwin).

Arteta, C. (2002) 'Exchange Rate Regimes and Financial Dollarization: Does Flexibility Reduce Bank Currency Mismatches?', mimeo, FED Research Papers.

Bartov, E. and Bodnar, G. (1994) 'Firm Valuation, Earnings Expectation, and the Exchange Rate Exposure Effect', *Journal of Finance*, 44, 1755–86.

Berganza, A. and Herrero, G. (2003) 'Balance Sheet Effects and the Country Risk Premium: An Empirical Investigation', mimeo, Bank of Spain.

Bleakley, H. and Cowan, K. (2002) 'Corporate Dollar Debt and Devaluations: Much Ado About Nothing?', mimeo, MIT.

Bodnar, G. and Wong, M. (2000) 'Estimating Exchange Rate Exposures: Some "Weighty" Issues', NBER Working Paper 7497.

Booth, L., Aivazian, V., Demirguc-Kunt, A. and Maksimovic, V. (2001) 'Capital Structure in Developing Countries', *Journal of Finance*, LVI(1).

Bris, A. and Koskinen, Y. (2002) 'Corporate Leverage and Currency Crises', *Journal of Financial Economics*, 63, 2, 275–310.

Bris, A., Koskinen, Y. and Pons, V. (2004) 'Corporate Financial Policies and Performance around Currency Crises'. *Journal of Business*, 77, 4, 749–96.

Burnside, C., Eichenbaum, M. and Rebelo, S. (1999) 'Hedging and Financial Fragility in Fixed Exchange Rate Regimes', NBER Working Paper 7143.

Caballero, R. and Krishnamurthy, A. (2000) 'Dollarization of Liabilities: Underinsurance and Domestic Financial Underdevelopment', NBER Working Paper 7792.

Calvo, G. and Mishkin, F. (2003) 'The Mirage of Exchange Rate Regimes for Emerging Market Countries', *Journal of Economic Perspectives*, 17(4), 99–118.

Calvo, G. and Reinhardt, C. (2000) 'Fear of Floating', NBER Working Paper 7993.

Campa, J. and Goldberg, L. (1995) 'Investment in Manufacturing, Exchange-rates and External Exposure', *Journal of International Economics*, 30, 297–320.

Corsetti, G., Pesenti, P. and Roubini, N. (1999) 'Paper Tigers? A Model of the Asian Crisis', *European Economic Review*, 43, 1211–36.

Corsetti, G., Pesenti, P. and Roubini, N. (1998) 'What Caused the Asian Currency and Financial Crisis?', NBER Working Papers 6833, 6834.

DeMarzo, P. and Duffie, D. (1995) 'Corporate Incentives for Hedging and Hedge Accounting', *Review of Financial Studies*, 8 (3), 743–71.

De Santis, G. and Gerard, B. (1998) 'How Big is the Premium for Currency Risk?', *Journal of Financial Economics*, 49(3), 375–412.

Dominguez, K. and Tesar, L. (2001) 'Exchange Rate Exposure', NBER Working Paper 8453.
Dooley, M. (1997) 'A Model of Crises in Emerging Markets', NBER Working Paper 6300.
Dumas, B. and Solnik, B. (1995) 'The World Price of Foreign Exchange Risk', *Journal of Finance*, 50(2), 445–79.
Eichengreen, B. and Hausmann, R. (1999) 'Exchange Rate and Financial Fragility'. NBER Working Paper 7418.
Eichengreen, B., Hausmann, R. and Panizza, U. (2003) 'Currency Mismatches, Debt Intolerance and Original Sin: Why They Are Not The Same and Why It Matters', NBER Working Paper 10036.
Flood, E. and Lessard, D. (1986) 'On the Measurement of Operating Exposure to Exchange Rates: A Conceptual Approach'. *Financial Management* (Spring), 25–37.
Froot, K., Scharfstein, D. and Stein, J. (1993) 'Risk Management: Coordinating Corporate Investment and Financing Policies', *Journal of Finance*, 48(5), 1629–58.
Geczy, C., Minton, B. and Schrand, C. (1997) 'Why Firms Use Currency Derivatives', *Journal of Finance*, 52, 4, 1323–54.
Gelos, G. (2003) 'Foreign Currency Debt Markets: Firm-level Evidence from Mexico', *Economics Letters*, 78, 323–7.
Goldstein, M. and Turner, P. (2004) *Controlling Currency Mismatches in Emerging Markets*, 1st edn, Institute for International Economics.
Harris, M. and Raviv, A. (1991) 'The Theory of Capital Structure', *Journal of Finance*, 46, 297–355.
Hodder, J. (1982) 'Exposure to Exchange Rate Movements', *Journal of International Economics*, 13, 375–86.
Jeanne, O. (2000) 'Foreign Currency Debt and the Global Financial Architecture', *European Economic Review*, 44, 153–61.
Jeanne, O. and Zettelmeyer, J. (2002) 'Original Sin, Balance Sheet Crises, and the Role of International Lending', IMF Working Paper 02/234.
Jensen, M. (1986) 'Agency Costs of Free Cash Flow, Corporate Finance and Takeovers', *American Economic Review*, 76, 323–9.
Jensen, M. and Meckling, W. (1976) 'Theory of the Firm: Managerial Behaviour, Agency Costs and Ownership Structure', *Journal of Financial Economics*, 3, 305–60.
Jorion, P. (1991) 'The Pricing of Exchange Rate Risk in the Stock Market', *Journal of Financial and Quantitative Analysis*, 26(3), 363–76.
Jorion, P. (1990) The Exchange Rate Exposure of US Multinationals', *Journal of Business*, 63, 3, 331–45.
Judge, A. (2002) 'The Determinants of Foreign Currency Hedging by UK Non-Financial Firms', mimeo, Middlesex University.
Kedia, S. and Mozumbar, A. (2002) 'Foreign Currency Denominated Debt: An Empirical Examination', mimeo, Harvard Business School.
La Porta, R., Silanes, F., Shleifer, A. and Vishny, R. (1998) 'Law and Finance', *Journal of Political Economy*, 106(6), 1113–55.
Levi, M. (1983) *International Finance* (New York: McGraw-Hill).
Maddala, G.S. (1983) *Limited-Dependent and Qualitative Variables in Econometrics* (New York: Cambridge University Press).

Marsion, R. (2001). 'The Effects of Industry Structure on Economic Exposure', *Journal of International Money and Finance*, 20, 149–64.

Martinez, L. and Werner, A. (2002) 'The Exchange Rate Regime and the Currency Composition of Corporate Debt: The Mexican Experience', *Journal of Development Economies*, 69, 315–34.

Nance, D., Smith, C. and Smithson, C. (1993) 'On the Determinants of Corporate Hedging', *Journal of Finance*, 48(1), 267–84.

Parsley, D. and Popper, H. (2002) 'Exchange Rate Pegs and Foreign Exchange Exposure in East Asia', mimeo, Vanderbilt University.

Schneider, M. and Tornell, A. (2003) 'Boom-bust Cycles and the Balance-sheet Effect', mimeo, UCLA.

Shapiro, A. (1974) 'Exchange Rate Changes, Inflation and the Value of the Multinational Corporations', *Journal of Finance*, 30, 485–502.

Smith, C. and Stulz, R. (1985) 'The Determinants of Firms' Hedging Policies', *Journal of Financial and Quantitative Analysis*, 20, 4.

Staiger, D. and Stock, J. (1997) 'Instrumental Variables Regression with Weak Instruments', *Econometrica*, 65, 557–86.

Stock, J. and Yogo, M. (2002) 'Testing for Weak Instruments in Linear IV Regression', NBER Technical Working Papers 0284, National Bureau of Economic Research.

Index